ZEN AT DAITOKU-JI

ZEN

1

Dr. JON COVELL
Abbot YAMADA SŌBIN

AT DAITOKU-JI

KODANSHA INTERNATIONAL LTD.,

Tokyo, New York and San Francisco.

脚 頭 肺 底 起 清 風

At every step the pure wind rises!

When DAITŌ KOKUSHI, the founder of DAITOKU-ji, reached profound enlightenment, he made the following verse;

Having once penetrated the cloud barrier, the living road opens out north, east, south and west.

In the evening resting, in the morning roaming, neither host nor guest.

At every step the pure wind rises.

This book, I hope, will be able to introduce to the cultural world of the West what the pure wind is, which once arose at one point in the East.

April, 1974

Nanrei S. Kobori

Photo credits: John and Barbara Upton; back cover, 54–60, 64–66, 85, 86, 97–100; Nakayasu Naoyasu; 2, 9, 28.

Note: This book follows Zen temple usage in rendering names. The Zen clergy respect the Chinese pronunciation of pre-T'ang times, when Buddhism first came to China. This is called *go-on*, a Six Dynasties' pronunciation that has disappeared from China itself and that is slightly different from *kan-on*, the common pronunciation of ideograms in Japan. Japanese names follow the Japanese order, with family name first.

Distributors:
UNITED STATES: *Harper & Row, Publishers, Inc., 10 East 53rd Street, New York, New York 10022.* CANADA: *Fitzhenry & Whiteside Limited, 150 Lesmill Road, Don Mills, Ontario.* CENTRAL AND SOUTH AMERICA: *Feffer & Simons Inc., 31 Union Square, New York, New York 10003.* BRITISH COMMONWEALTH (*excluding Canada and the Far East*): *TABS, 51 Weymouth Street, London W1N 3LE.* EUROPE: *Boxerbooks Inc., Limmatstrasse 111, 8031 Zurich.* AUSTRALIA AND NEW ZEALAND: *Paul Flesch & Co. Pty. Ltd., 259 Collins Street, Melbourne 3000.* THAILAND: *Central Department Store Ltd., 306 Silom Road, Bangkok.* HONG KONG AND SINGAPORE: *Books for Asia Ltd., 30 Tat Chee Avenue, Kowloon; 65 Crescent Road, Singapore 15.* THE FAR EAST: *Japan Publications Trading Company, P.O. Box 5030, Tokyo International, Tokyo.*

Published by Kodansha International Ltd., 2–12–21 Otowa, Bunkyo-ku, Tokyo 112 and Kodansha International/USA, Ltd., 10 East 53rd Street, New York, New York 10022 and 44 Montgomery Street, San Francisco, California 94104. Copyright in Japan 1974 by Kodansha International Ltd. All rights reserved. Printed in Japan.

LCC 74-77956
ISBN 0-87011-227-9
JBC 1070-784425-2361

First edition, 1974

CONTENTS

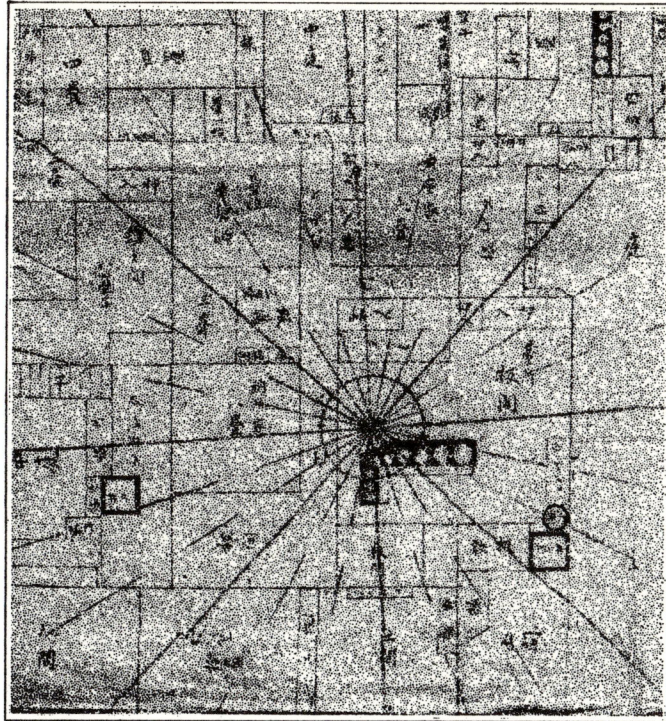

I

KYOTO
AND DAITOKU-JI

We must treasure Daitoku-ji as a pearl in Japan's cultural history. Even though small, we must not lose it.

Kobori Nanrei (1918–)
Abbot of Ryōkō-in

For over a thousand years one sloping valley, three by three and a half miles, has been the spiritual home of the Japanese to the extent that even the syllables of its name evoke a special response in the heart of anyone born and brought up in Japan. No other site in the Far East has proved to possess such lasting powers of cultural survival. Otherwise world-weary travelers are refreshed by its pervading serenity and charmed by its ancient ways.

The allure of its present-day reality is no less fabulous than the legends of bygone days. In experiencing Kyoto, the moisture-laden air serves as a prism, suffusing many tones of light over the city's gardens and the curving silhouettes of its temple roofs. Not only in out-of-the-way corners but even along the main thoroughfares lies evidence of a timeless beauty that refuses to succumb to modernity. In any other large Japanese city to discover this traditional past is now either extremely difficult or frankly impossible, yet Kyoto, though it houses over a million and a half people, in its lifestyle still retains the inbred habits of its elegant past. As a governmental entity, Kyoto has allied herself in sister cityhood with Italy's Florence, Germany's Cologne, France's Paris and America's Boston, all guardians of cultural heritages. One guidebook in English says with finality: "Kyoto is the single most important place in all Japan, the center, the best and largest part of everything you see and do in this country."

Whereas many cities experience their growth for one period only, a visitor to Kyoto can virtually choose his historical milieu, since it has been Japan's cultural capital from the eighth until the present century. A short walk becomes an enchanting kaleidoscope in time, although it must be admitted that each year the twentieth century comes to occupy more and more of Kyoto's energy and atmosphere. Still, each year forty million Japanese transform themselves into tourists and visit Kyoto to recharge their cultural batteries, to experience their national roots.

For the elderly Japanese in particular, Kyoto occupies a special niche because for so long it remained the home of the imperial family. This living descendant of the Sun Goddess, plus the aristocracy attendant upon him, gradually gave the culture of this capital city a degree of refinement that was not possible elsewhere. Modes of behavior and canons of artistic taste were formulated here that became the basis of Japanese social and economic life for the succeeding centuries. Even a Westernized Japanese must admit that Kyoto holds the essence of Japan's spirit because it still retains the treasures of more than a millennium of history, while the only other early capital, Nara, remained a center for only seventy years. The site of Tokyo, now one of the planet's largest cities with its eleven million inhabitants, remained largely an uninhabitable mud swamp for eight centuries after Kyoto first sheltered the emperor. Thus, in many senses, Kyoto's history stands as the history of Japan. Most Kyotoites today dread the idea of visiting crowded, bustling, modern Tokyo; they return home with relief. Most Tokyo residents, on the other hand, find Kyoto slightly unbelievable—a montage of charming fantasies. Is it merely a dream from long ago?

It was Emperor Kammu (reg. 782–805) who chose the site for Kyoto. He was one of the strongest and wisest of Japan's line of 126 emperors, yet, like his contemporaries, he believed wholeheartedly in ghosts, a factor that contributed to Kyoto's becoming the capital in A.D. 794. A dozen years before, when Kammu ascended the throne, he realized that the old capital of Nara was completely dominated by degenerate Buddhist clergy and that they, rather than he, would rule unless he moved his court quickly. Originally Kammu had chosen another valley called Nagaoka, about ten miles to the southeast of modern

Kyoto, but its water supply did not prove adequate. Then his most trusted Minister of State, Fujiwara Tanetsugu, who served as Commissioner of Imperial Buildings, was assassinated by the emperor's younger brother, Sawara, a jealous and ambitious man. Sawara was exiled to Awaji Island and died soon after, perhaps the victim of foul play. After these two political deaths, Emperor Kammu became ill; later the crown prince also sickened, and soothsayers blamed Sawara's avenging spirit. Many prayers were chanted to appease his ghost, and Sawara was even promoted to the rank of posthumous emperor to placate him.

At this tense moment in Kammu's life, a member of the wealthy Hata family stepped forward to offer his huge estate, the land of the lower two-thirds of the valley floor now known as Kyoto, as a better site for a new capital. Presumably its soil was not plagued by ghosts. Another reason in its favor was that the Kamo clan, which owned the northern reaches of this valley, were Shintoists, and so would be a counterforce to the influence of the Buddhist clergy. By moving his imperial palace to Kyoto, Emperor Kammu influenced the destiny of Japan for the next eleven centuries. An imperial edict issued in 793 directed that work commence at this new site.

It is interesting to note that the Hata family were friends of the murdered Fujiwara Tanetsugu. They were descendants of a Korean family which had emigrated to Japan several centuries before, and had been richly rewarded for introducing their knowledge of mulberry tree cultivation and the silk weaving craft to Japan. After Hata's offer of land was accepted, the family subsequently received promotion at court in gratitude, and the silk industry has flourished in Kyoto's valley from the eighth century until the present day.

Of course, there was also much Confucian ceremony and Taoist magic ritual to justify the choice of the site. Geomancers discovered that the new site fulfilled the Confucian requirements of "three surrounding hills and two rivers," and was auspiciously protected by "the Azure Dragon on the east, the White Tiger on the west, the Dark Warrior on the north, and the Red Bird on the south." (Kyoto actually has five rivers running through it from north to south.) The grid of the city's streets was laid out according to the principles of *yang* and *yin*, as was the T'ang-dynasty capital of China, Ch'ang-an. Kyoto's rectangular area was simply a slightly smaller-scale version of the Chinese capital, which was the world's largest and most splendid city to date. As on the mainland, the emperor ordered a peasant corvee to do the physical labor. Over a third of a million men worked feverishly on his new site, setting up a palisade of bamboo posts with a moat around the edge, roughly three and a half miles from north to south and three miles from east to west. The Imperial Palace, like the Ch'ang-an palace and the Forbidden City of Peking, was given Kyoto's most honorable section to the north, an enclosure about a mile square. (Today the Imperial Palace in Kyoto stands somewhat to the east of its original site because the western side proved too damp.) In the beginning, the present Sembon Avenue exactly bisected the new city and was two hundred feet wide. Today the willow-bordered canal that runs down the center of the eight-lane Horikawa Avenue is the major reminder of the plan of Emperor Kammu's eighth-century city.

Because Kammu was a Confucian scholar and wished to dilute Buddhist influence in his new city, a university was built just south of the palace enclosure and here Confucian learning was taught to young nobles, along with Chinese. Commoners were allocated the southern sector of the city, about forty thousand lots of fifty by a hundred feet. Even today, the southern part of Kyoto remains the commercial heart, while the best residences stand along its northern edges.

A faint idea of Emperor Kammu's palace may be obtained from the present reconstruction made in 1854. His eighth-century palace was also constructed of cedar pillars painted with red lead to weatherproof them, and the architecture followed the Chinese model. In accordance with continental taste, blue-green ceramic tiles roofed its halls. The most gorgeous single building was the Hall of State, 170 feet in length and constructed with fifty-two stately pillars. In the center of this hall was a raised platform or throne area, covered by a canopy surmounted by the imperial insignia, golden phoenixes.

Just south of this imperial enclosure was a pleasure garden with a lake for boating. It was named "Divine Spring Garden" and covered a total of thirty-three acres. Around the borders of its large lake were willow, cherry and maple trees. Today this ancient garden has been built upon by real estate developers until only a small pond on a quiet street remains.

Emperor Kammu's dream city had no ghosts, but his residence proved especially vulnerable to fires. In the ninety-eight years between 960 and 1058, the Imperial Palace was burned down fifteen times! But so important had the palace become as a national symbol that it was rebuilt each time, though on an increasingly smaller scale because succeeding emperors came to reign but not to rule. The real power was held by the Fujiwara ministers for several centuries and then passed to the military governors in Kamakura.

The present nineteenth-century reconstruction of the Imperial Palace still dominates the layout of Kyoto city. Fifty years ago the present reigning emperor was enthroned within its Hall of State, but many things have changed since then. Today the imperial family lives in a postwar palace where the decor of many of its fifty rooms is Western in style,

though, of course, not the four-and-a-half-mat tea-room. But the Japanese cherish tradition, so even if the major part of the next coronation ceremony takes place in Tokyo, which has been the political capital since 1868, the new emperor will probably have an investiture at Ise Shrine, the spiritual source of the throne, and in Kyoto's Imperial Palace, which may be regarded as its cultural source.

The Kyoto of the ninth and tenth centuries, however, has now almost totally disappeared. A trip into the foothills surrounding the city reveals one structure dating from that time, at Sangen-in. Emperor Kammu's "Capital of Peace and Tranquillity" suffered from many fires and was, for ten years from 1467 to 1477, quite literally a battlefield, with two hundred thousand soldiers engaged in a war of attrition that produced no clear victor and left ninety percent of Kyoto in ruins. Very little is left in Kyoto that predates this Ōnin War of 1467–77, during which the Imperial Palace, the imperial Zen temple of Daitoku-ji, and all other major structures were burned to the ground.

On March 22, 1474, the flamboyant priest Ikkyū, elderly son of the hundredth emperor, was asked by the reigning emperor to become Daitoku-ji's forty-seventh chief abbot and to rebuild this important Zen temple for the spiritual peace of the capital. Warfare had done tremendous damage, but just at that time the armies were stalemated. And so even before the Imperial Palace was rebuilt or the Silver Pavilion (Ginkaku-ji) constructed by the war-weary shogun Ashikaga Yoshimasa, the octogenarian priest Ikkyū began rallying his powerful friends and started the reconstruction of the imperial Zen compound called Daitoku-ji, meaning "The Temple of Great Virtue." When Ikkyū finished his task of rebuilding, about five hundred years ago, Daitoku-ji stood near the center of Kyoto, at the northernmost reaches of its north-south bisecting street.

If the visitor to present-day Kyoto has a little time, he should inspect Nijō Castle and Katsura Villa, both of which reflect seventeenth-century splendor. But these sites today are empty architectural shells, museums that are open from nine in the morning to four-thirty in the afternoon, and thus they are only ghosts of their former living meaning. Yet inside the foot-thick adobe walls of Daitoku-ji's compound, the atmosphere is strikingly different. Of course relics are preserved that reflect all the centuries from the fifteenth down to the present, but, in addition, there are still people living there, even though nowadays they might appear to be following medieval ideals as patterns of behavior.

Of the thousand Shinto shrines and over six hundred Buddhist temples in Kyoto, Daitoku-ji is easily the most rewarding to visit. Not only does it possess a host of paintings and ceramics from China and Korea that Zen priests held in esteem, but it also reflects Japanese cultural history for the past seven centuries. Since it is Zen that has directly inspired abstract gardens, tea gardens, the tea ceremony itself and all its attendant paraphernalia, and has exerted a profound influence on almost every other Japanese art, Daitoku-ji can be considered the fountainhead of Japanese Zen aesthetics.

For six centuries, however, the public was barred from entering its compound, and until World War II the gates were closed at sunset and only opened again at dawn. Today the outer gates are never locked, and one can walk its paths before daybreak and watch the mists of morning settle on the silver sea of rooftiles; one can stand in wonder by full moonlight as one pine tree rivals another in silhouette patterns; one can listen to the sound of bells, sonorous in the still darkness of dawn, and observe the silent striding figures of the abbots, resplendent in embroidered robes, their wooden clogs tapping on the cobbled paths as they converge on the Bud-

dha Hall from all directions. These men have spent the prime of their youth following a routine leading to the "great death," when they may discard the "unreal" world and reach the ecstatic experience of *satori*. Because this routine is ordered according to a tyrannical regularity, whether daily, monthly or annually, it might seem that life within this framework is restricted and lacking in any individuality. However, this conformity is a result of their agreement on certain principles of living, and beyond this there is great scope for individualism. Each abbot leads a life that is to him full of purposeful action: Zen has no time for laziness, Zen has no time for boredom.

Even though the emperor has left Kyoto now, his imperial Zen temple carries on as if his presence were expected tomorrow. All is in readiness; three times a month the abbots assemble in the Buddha Hall at daybreak to chant for the welfare of the present emperor and, in a larger sense, for the whole nation and for every sentient being. Scarcely thirty-five acres in size today, and not much more than a hundred acres at the time of its greatest extent, why has this Temple of Great Virtue moved to the pulsebeat of so many memorable events, been the favorite haunt of so many great men, sheltered so much of the most valued art of China, Korea and Japan?

There is no simple answer, and so one must approach the Zen compound of Daitoku-ji from every aspect, observing the rituals that are its life pattern, examining the architecture that shelters it, the paintings that decorate its walls, the gardens that frame its teahouses, and the men who set its standards today. Only through experiencing Daitoku-ji from so many angles can its importance be grasped and the secret of its long-lasting influence unraveled.

Let us, then, make our first approach to Daitoku-ji on foot. Although most taxis and tour buses deposit visitors at the temple's East Gate, it is more pleasant to enter through the South Gate and walk up the long pathway with subtemples on either side. In this way the Mountain Gate (Sammon), a two-storied, top-heavy structure, appears gradually through the intervening pine trees.

At the time Zen established its first temples in China in the eighth century, it was influenced by the popular T'ien-t'ai (Japanese: Tendai) sect which emphasized the cosmic diagram of the universe, the mandala. (Originally from India, the mandala was adapted in China to the strong feeling of the Chinese for the four directions of the compass, plus a fifth direction, the center. Also incorporated in the fifth was Indian Buddhism's stress on the Sacred Mountain called Mount Sumeru.) With this in mind while strolling along the cobblestone paths of the temple compound, there comes a sudden realization that one is walking amid a giant mandala. The Sacred Mountain is symbolically represented by the highest point in the gardens, the roof ridge of the Doctrine Hall, which is over sixty feet high. The Mountain Gate now takes on new meaning; it becomes the gate to the Sacred Mountain and one realizes why Zen temples are always referred to as "mountains," even when, as Daitoku-ji, they lie in a plain.

In ancient India, the traveler was meant to circumambulate the holy mountain with his right side toward the center, moving in a clockwise direction like the sun. Today the east side of Daitoku-ji's cobblestone path is only a service path, and since the abbots themselves only use the walkway north of the Sacred Mountain (the Doctrine Hall) one day a year, this rite of circumambulation, so important in Buddhist India, is almost forgotten. However, the service path is always open and allows a more leisurely study of the architectural forms.

A wooden plaque high on the Mountain Gate reads "Golden-haired," a reference to the golden-maned lion statue that sat as guardian in front of early Buddhist temples. If the gate is envisioned as a huge lion sitting on his haunches and protecting the temple, the awkward, squat structure becomes more understandable architecturally—it functions as a symbol of protection.

Up its ladderlike stairs is one large room, with a Buddha and the sixteen arhats (early disciples of Buddha in India), and with a dragon painted by Tōhaku on the wooden panels of the ceiling. The statues sit with their backs to the north, the honored direction, supported by a sculptured mountain range, the foothills of the Himalayas. In a niche on the west stands a life-size wooden effigy of Rikyū, the tea master who made Daitoku-ji so famous. An earlier version of the same statue almost caused the dictator Hideyoshi to burn the whole compound down, thus making it a rather ironic twist that the statue should be placed within this building, which symbolically protects the whole temple. However, since it was Rikyū who purchased the thirteenth-century arhat statues that are in the same room as his effigy, who has a better right to be there?

This Mountain Gate (Pl. 2) is so significant in Japan's history that the government recently spent over one hundred million yen renovating it. For five years it was curtained off while expert carpenters took the entire building apart and replaced all the termite-eaten wood. Today it is painted a cinnabar red, whose brightness is only slightly muted by the greenness of the young pine trees nearby. Unfortunately, few people are given permission to mount the stairs and enjoy the excellent view of Kyoto from its second-story balcony.

It is only when the visitor is abreast of the Mountain Gate that he notices the Imperial Messenger Gate (Chokushi-mon), since it is only one story high. It originally served as the southeast gate for the Kyoto Imperial Palace, a gift to the emperor from Hideyoshi in 1597, but around 1640 Empress Meishō gave it to Daitoku-ji. She was the first woman ruler in Japan for eight centuries, succeeding to the throne at the age of seven, when Emperor Go-Mizunoo abdicated to show his anger toward the Tokugawa shogun who was harassing Daitoku-ji. Since Meishō's accession was due in part to Daitoku-ji, she made the temple many gifts, including this historic gateway. It is the most restrained of all Momoyama-period gates and its cypress-bark roof has a beautiful curve.

Once past the Imperial Messenger Gate and the Mountain Gate, following the main south to north path, the visitor will arrive at the weathered brown mass that is the Buddha Hall. This building, with its gray-blue roof forming an endless sea of small waves, is used for most of the communal rituals, almost all of which occur at dawn, and thus the casual visitor sees only a shuttered and barred building, which is raised on a stone platform about sixty feet wide and four feet high. The bell-shaped windows with their curved scallops are faithful copies of those of the Zen temples built in China during the Southern Sung dynasty. Inside the Buddha Hall, raised on a tall altar, sits the twenty-foot-high statue of Śākyamuni, the Historical Buddha, with his back to the north, smiling and brightly gilded. This is the only gift which the Tokugawa shogunate bestowed on Daitoku-ji, for most of the time the ruling family tried to control the temple and keep it from growing more powerful, perhaps mindful that the emperor who had recognized Daitoku-ji had, for three brief years, regained political as well as ceremonial power.

If the visitor walks the paths of Daitoku-ji at dawn on the first and fifteenth of each month, he cannot miss the boom of a giant bell from the two-storied belltower, northwest of the Buddha Hall. It rings once a minute at five forty-five and very soon young priests from the Sōdō, dressed in black and accompanied by abbots in ceremonial capes, will appear, walking hurriedly along the paths from north and

south and paying no attention to anyone as they proceed to the Shutō, or Dawn Ceremony. The twenty-three abbots, twelve monks from the Sōdō Training Hall, and three or four monks from the subtemples enter the Buddha Hall through the north door, slip into their boatlike Chinese felt slippers and take their places in line along the west wall of the hall (Pl. 55).

It is worth remembering, however, that it has been less than a hundred years since the public has been allowed to walk inside the compound of Daitoku-ji. The Meiji Restoration removed all support from Buddhist temples, and the subtemples in Daitoku-ji were forced to sell off some of their land and even some of the buildings on the edge of the temple compound. Today the outer gates are not permitted to be shut and all visitors can walk to the Buddha Hall and watch the Dawn Ceremony from the three-foot-high wooden grill in the south door.

These services by tradition have no audience but serve as a sort of ritual cement within Daitoku-ji, making the individualism of Zen-enlightened men slightly more homogeneous. Like the architecture of the hall in which it is held, in form this ceremony dates back to Sung China. Through the chanting, the offerings of food, the burning of incense before the major statues, and the kinetic responses of kneeling and walking in line in sun-oriented compressed circumambulation, the abbots link themselves to their heritage in India and China and Japan itself. These men have learned the ritual and never question the reasons behind it. They perform it almost as a reflex action, perhaps unconsciously influenced by its mystical geometry, for without thinking they know that north, the direction in which they prostrate themselves, is the honored direction.

The Buddha Hall has six bays with fifty-foot pillars of zelkova (keyaki), a wood strong enough to bear the colossal weight of the tile roof and not

23

March 2001
S	M	T	W	T	F	S
				1	2	3
4	5	6	7	8	9	10
11	12	13	14	15	16	**17**
18	**19**	20	21	22	23	24
25	26	27	28	29	30	31

®AT·A·GLANCE

Friday, March 23

24

Saturday
March
2001

March 2001

S	M	T	W	T	F	S
				1	2	3
4	5	6	7	8	9	10
11	12	13	14	15	16	17
18	19	20	21	22	23	24
25	26	27	28	29	30	31

April 2001

S	M	T	W	T	F	S
1	2	3	4	5	6	7
8	9	10	11	12	13	14
15	16	17	18	19	20	21
22	23	24	25	26	27	28
29	30					

Saturday, March 24

weaken after five centuries. The pillars are painted cinnabar red, a color that from India to Japan is held to be most auspicious. The floor of square-cut pewter-colored tile is just as it was in the Zen temples of Sung-dynasty China that the first Daitoku-ji buildings tried to emulate. Whenever it is time for the ceremonial leader to kneel, a boy appears with a mat and places it before him, thus preventing the elaborate robes, which may cost as much as a thousand dollars, from touching the tile floor.

On this tile floor are marked white lines to help the abbots walk in the mandalalike movements of the ceremony with half-closed eyes, for at dawn the Buddha Hall is dim. Occasionally the outside world intrudes when a dog barks or an old woman paddles across to the half-open south portal and tosses a coin in the wooden offering box before she bows with hands clasped in the Indian gesture called *gasshō*. The abbots, engrossed, pay no attention.

The first of the five chants of the ceremony is in honor of the reigning emperor and the whole country. It is slow and dirgelike, but its very slowness implies great homage. Each successive chant becomes more rapid and is led by an abbot who is appointed as ceremonial leader, a post which rotates once a month among the "higher clergy," which means those entitled to wear the purple silk robe. Formerly the robe was a personal gift from the reigning emperor to the new chief abbot of Daitoku-ji, but today the present chief abbot of the temple lives in Kyushu, and any subtemple abbot may pay for an instalment ceremony and thus be entitled to wear the purple robe and serve once every two years as ceremonial leader. All the other abbots wear outer robes of gold, blue, green and red silks with embroidered capes in contrasting colors—all, that is, except for one abbot, who still follows the Ikkyū tradition of wearing black as a sign of humility and of contempt for ostentation and ceremoniousness. Each abbot carries a fan, a four-

foot-long rosary, made up of a hundred and eight beads, draped over his left forearm, and a ceramic box containing powdered incense inside his left sleeve. The rosary is purely ornamental and never used during the ceremony, but a pinch of incense is burned before each of the wooden effigies of the great patriarchs of Chinese Zen.

The most difficult tasks in the two-hour ceremony fall to the young priest who echoes the abbots' communal chanting and to the ceremonial leader who performs some complicated footwork. This includes slipping out of his broad Chinese shoes, taking out his silk prayer rectangle (*zagu*) that is folded over his left sleeve, gripping one corner of it with his toes, anchoring it over the mat that has been spread out before him, and prostrating his body three times while lying on the silk. He raises his upturned palms slowly above his bowed head in the worshipful gesture of "Raising the Buddha above all Things" and of supporting the Buddhist canon with his prostrate body.

At each of the other three smaller altars there is an incense burner, candlesticks, teabowls, and offerings of plants. In front of the gilt Buddha is a long table that bears offerings of salt, representing products of the sea, rice, representing products of the land, and also vegetables in season that have been washed and tied into bunches with special red and white cord and arranged on a black lacquer tray. A small, gold paper stand on the left holds some spongecake, while to the right there is a mound of tangerines. Two candlesticks with four-foot-high stands and two six-foot-high gilt lotuses in bronze vases flank the whole arrangement before the Buddha.

During the winter months, clouds of vapor emerge from the mouths of the chanting abbots during the ceremony in the dim, unheated hall, when the only concession to the cold is to start the chanting thirty minutes later. This may well be because it is still too dark to see and it seems unfitting to use artificial light for a religious pageant in which ninth-century-style robes are worn and which proceeds in the manner prescribed twelve centuries ago, when Zen had its first independent temples.

After this initial Shutō ceremony in the cold, half-dark Buddha Hall, whose exterior and interior reflect the Chinese love of verticality and spaciousness, the abbots proceed to the Headquarters Temple for the second chanting of sutras. Whereas the first ceremony in the Buddha Hall pays honor to the emperor, together with Japanese nature gods, to the Chinese founder of Rinzai Zen, to Bodhidharma, the traditional founder of Zen, and to Fu-an, the Chinese care-taker god of buildings, the second ceremony in the Headquarters Temple is exclusively in honor of Japanese personages.

As the abbots enter the low-ceilinged, *tatami*-matted hall, they take their prayer silks out, spread them out and prostrate themselves three times. In the meantime the ceremonial leader and his assistant enter the Holy Room that is dedicated to Daitoku-ji's founder, Daitō Kokushi. Incense is lit before his life-size wooden effigy. The assisting abbot pours hot water from a copper ewer into a *temmoku* teabowl; the ceremonial tea offering is stirred and then gently placed in front of the founder's effigy. Incense is then offered before the spirit tablets of the two fourteenth-century emperors, Hanazono and Go-Daigo, who were responsible for the recognition of Daitoku-ji as an imperial temple. Hanazono was so sincere a student of Zen that on October 22, 1335, he became a Zen priest and had his hair cut off by the founder, Daitō Kokushi. (This hair is still enshrined in a pagoda-shaped box on the east of his effigy, which, of course, is on the north side of the Holy Room.)

Three chants in Dharani are intoned to honor Daitō and all those who have been benefactors in the past, including the noble family of Konoe and the dictators Nobunaga and Hideyoshi. Although the origins of Zen in China sprang from the common people, in Japan the religion has remained with the educated elite. Indeed, until the Meiji Restoration in 1868, the only reliable methods of education were in the schools established by Zen abbots.

The most ironical ceremony of all in Daitoku-ji's calendar is the reading of the Sutra of Perfect Wisdom (*Prajñāpāramitā*), which occurs four times a year in addition to January when it is performed five times, as though to start the New Year off well-fortified with wisdom. The abbots sit before the ten volumes of the sutra and act out a symbolic reading of it, each one barking out phrases at random from the first volume, followed by the second, and so on until all ten volumes have been "read." The irony lies in the fact that Zen is associated with scorn of the written word, for its transmission is essentially word-less and thus does not depend on any religious tran-scriptions.

The ceremonies described above are available to any early riser who visits Daitoku-ji. Later in the day, eight of the twenty-three subtemples are open to the public, and, for a small fee, their historic treasures can be viewed. But in order to penetrate deeper into the essence of Zen and into Japanese cultural history, the "closed" temples, those to which the public is not freely admitted, must also be seen. In them lie count-less aesthetic vistas; quiet gardens, sheltered spots, walls that bear priceless paintings, and storehouses that contain some of Japan's greatest ceramic and calligraphic wealth. The lifestyle in the closed temples is also different, for Zen is an individually oriented religion and thus each abbot has a different person-ality, which affects the atmosphere of his temple. Although the public knows little of the lifestyle with-in the closed temples, the aesthetics and the master-pieces that Daitoku-ji has inspired are renowned throughout the world.

2

THE HISTORY

If your ears see
And your eyes hear,
You'll cherish no doubts.
How naturally the rain drips from the eaves!

Daitō Kokushi (1282–1337)
Founder of Daitoku-ji

1. Daitoku-ji as it appears in modern Kyoto, ▷
six hundred and fifty years after Daitō chose
this site.

2. The Mountain Gate (Sammon), seen from the Buddha Hall, with two *kōzō* doing morning *samu*. The juniper in the foreground was planted by Hideyoshi in 1587.

3. The Doctrine Hall (Hattō), rebuilt in 1636 and used only once a year, on the anniversary of the death of the founder, Daitō.

4. The Buddha Hall (Butsuden), rebuilt in
1665, where the Dawn Ceremony takes place.

5. The Founder's Hall of Ryōkō-in, where
many Westerners now do *zazen*.

6. A *chinzō* (official portrait) of Daitō (1282–1337), painted in 1334 and attributed to Tosa Yukimitsu, with Daitō's own calligraphy above.

7. Emperor Go-Daigo (1288–1339) on his dais, with protecting Buddhist lion-dogs, painted between 1333 and 1336 by an unknown artist. Seated in front of him is his closest adviser, Fujiwara Fujifusa.

Before Zen Buddhism became established in Japan or found any powerful patrons, it had already been introduced into the country more than a dozen times. Buddhism itself was imported around A.D. 552 and the imperial court took advantage of its potential for ritual pomp to consolidate its position. Since the first forms of Zen were extremely simple and lacked this aspect, they encountered difficulty in gathering any strong support from the ruling classes.

Indeed, early Zen (Ch'an, as it was called in China) was without the usual trappings of a religion. While probably not historically true, the story of Bodhidharma reflects this simple beginning. Unable to speak or read Chinese, this foreigner may well have sat facing a rock wall for nine years as the legend says. What he brought to China was the Indian yogic posture of meditation, which the Chinese temples, with their great sophistication and accumulated wealth, had tended to forget was basic to Buddhism. Bodhidharma attracted only one disciple, Hui K'o, who is said to have been a Taoist until his thirty-third year. This is significant because it was Taoism, together with the discipline of yogic meditation, that constituted the Ch'an, or Zen, of eighth- and ninth-century China. Anecdotes of the early Chinese masters, up through the time of Rinzai, show an intuitive recognition of the naturalistic philosophy that can only be termed Taoism, but which was stripped of the effete qualities that had accumulated for almost a millennium around the simple doctrines of Lao-tzu and Chuang-tzu, traditional "fathers" of Taoism in China.

By the time that Zen first took firm root in Japan in the twelfth century, the military had replaced the imperial court as the major wielder of power, and they looked to a religion that emphasized discipline and that was not supported by the aristocracy. By this time also, the Zen that was imported was a more sophisticated version of the doctrine, one that was patronized by the Sung emperors and had devel-

oped all the regulations necessary for the successful organization of thousands of monks living together in vast monasteries.

Japanese history accords Eisai (1141–1215) and Dōgen (1200–53) the title of "fathers of Japanese Zen." Dōgen found Kyoto rather inhospitable; older, more established sects burned his temple, so he went off into the mountains and founded what is now called Sōtō Zen. Simpler than its rival, Rinzai Zen, since Dōgen taught that sitting itself was enlightenment, the country folk could understand it and consequently it attracted far more popular support than Rinzai, which prescribed a long and harsh period of training with kōan, or religious riddles; furthermore, Sōtō was much less hostile to women followers. Today Sōtō has about three times the membership of Rinzai. However, the discipline of the latter has resulted in a profound and lasting influence on the art and culture of Japan, whereas not a single garden, teahouse, or fusuma (sliding paper door) painting of major importance is connected with a Sōtō Zen temple.

Of the twenty-three "streams" of Rinzai Zen that have existed in Japan, Eisai founded the earliest at Kennin-ji in Kyoto in 1202, though because of the political strength of the Tendai Buddhist sect at the time, he was forced to incorporate some Tendai magic ritual into his Zen. Meanwhile, the military rulers at Kamakura were importing Chinese Zen masters and sending their own students to China, but all of these early streams died out when the power center shifted to Kyoto. Kyoto's first totally Zen temple was Nanzen-ji, founded in 1300 by a disciple of Mujun, and it stressed literary accomplishment in the Sung style. For a couple of centuries, patronized by the Ashikaga shogun, it flourished and headed the list of the Gozan (Five Mountains), the ranking of the five most important Zen temples. Eventually the Ashikaga fell from power and this temple declined, together with others supported by the Ashikaga faction, like Shōkoku-ji in Kyoto.

The stream of Rinzai Zen that has survived to the present day was imported to Japan by Daiō in 1267 and is traced back to Kidō, who was the last of its Sung-dynasty abbots. It is a stream that was based more on self-discipline than on literary achievements, and thus, as we have seen, it did not flourish at first in Japan, but the resultant poverty forced it to develop inward strength. Daitō, the founder of Daitoku-ji, was of this school and it was his disciples, Tettō and Kanzan, who upheld this rigorous discipline at Daitoku-ji and Myōshin-ji respectively. Daitoku-ji entered a period of great creativity and wealth in the sixteenth century, but in the seventeenth century it and all the other branches of Zen experienced a great decline. It was not until Hakuin (1685–1768) that the Daitō stream of Zen returned to its earlier earnestness during the eighteenth century. This was fortunate because otherwise it might not have been strong enough to survive the black period of Buddhism, which occurred from Emperor Meiji's accession in 1868 until his Shinto-biased advisers reversed their policy of destroying Buddhism in Japan around 1910. It was during these years that many temples disappeared and most Daitoku-ji subtemples had to sell sections of their architecture or painted wall panels to survive economically. Only in recent years have temples become tourist meccas as a rapidly modernizing Japan realizes how much of its cultural heritage is linked with Buddhism, especially Rinzai Zen Buddhism, and with Daitoku-ji more than any other compound in the entire country.

The Founder and Two Emperors

The belief that stress is conducive to great achievement is inherent in Japanese Zen Buddhism, and certainly Daitoku-ji's foundation occurred in a period of Japanese history that was particularly troubled. After a hundred years of stability, the Hōjō regents who wielded political authority had become corrupt and weakened. Imperial authority, due to the practice of abdication that meant that there were several ex-emperors living at one time, was fragmented and the succession was subject to intense intrigue and bitter rivalry.

In 1318, on the abdication of his cousin Hanazono, Emperor Go-Daigo succeeded to the throne, and the prevailing atmosphere of instability and unrest may well have encouraged him to try to wrest power from the Hōjō regents and to rule in fact as well as in name. His attempt was to fail and result in the division of the imperial family into the Northern and Southern branches and cause almost a century of confusion and struggle for power.

It was these two emperors, however, who bestowed imperial patronage on Daitoku-ji as "an imperial temple for the recitation of litanies," and who were responsible for the rapid emergence of the temple to the fore of the political scene in Kyoto. Both emperors were close to the founding priest, Myōchō, now known by his posthumous Buddhist name of Daitō Kokushi (Kokushi meaning "Teacher of the Country"), though Go-Daigo's recognition of the temple may well have been motivated by the Sung China practice of expecting a temple's loyalty in return, a considerable reinforcement of his power base.

Daitō Kokushi (1282–1337) led a life which exemplifies the Zen ideal—studying, satori (enlightenment), a withdrawal period, and a return to the world in maturity. He had been in the priesthood since the age of eleven, first at a Tendai temple and then at a Zen temple in Kamakura. On hearing of the famous Daiō (1235–1309), who had spent nine years in China learning Zen at its source, Daitō Kokushi went to study with him. This Zen leader had founded Sōfuku-ji at Dazaifu, the northern Kyushu governmental headquarters, and he formed a link between Japan and China when Sung power was disintegrating under Mongol pressures. Daiō had received his Zen from the last Sung master, Hsü-t'ang Chih-yü (1185–1269), known as Kidō in Japan, and he had also learned Chinese. He served as a translator and adviser to the military government of the Hōjō regents while he was living at Sōfuku-ji at Dazaifu (now Fukuoka) in Kyushu. After both Mongol invasions of Japan had been turned back, Emperor Go-Uda invited the now elderly priest to come to the capital of Kyoto to become chief abbot of Manju-ji, and it was here that the young Daitō Kokushi met him.

In 1308, the Hōjō regents invited Daiō to become chief abbot of Kenchō-ji in Kamakura, Japan's oldest Zen temple which headed the list of the Gozan, the five principal temples of the Zen sect, and Daitō accompanied him there. Ten days after arriving, Daitō Kokushi experienced *satori*, occasioned by the sound of a key falling upon a wooden table. The next day, as was customary, he presented a poem of four lines with seven Chinese characters in each to his teacher to show the depth of his enlightenment. (This custom of a literary aftermath to *satori* had become a standard practice during Sung times, and is in direct contradiction to Zen being "beyond words." It reflects the importance of literary men in the Zen movement of Sung times and of fourteenth-century Japan.)

On receiving his poem, Daiō said, "I approve. Both in visible and invisible aspects you are one with the truth. Your attainment surpasses mine; the Zen sect will prosper under your guidance. But you must experience twenty more years of maturing before you let people know of my approval." He gave Daitō Kokushi a robe and an *inka* (a certificate of enlightenment), both of which are displayed at Daitoku-ji's annual Mushiboshi (the day when art objects are aired to prevent insect damage) in mid-October.

Daitō Kokushi returned to Kyoto, but when his master died in Kamakura the following year, he hurried back to participate in the forty-nine-day mourning period so important in Buddhism. As soon as this was over he went back to Kyoto and stayed at Ungo-an, a small Tendai Buddhist hermitage, where he lived by begging at the Gōjō Bridge in the morning and doing *zazen* meditation in the evening. This pattern of life continued for at least six years, but the legend that he did this for twenty years is groundless.

Daitō Kokushi was gradually to become drawn into the political contest that was shaping up in Kyoto. In 1314, six years after his *satori*, Hanazono, who was then emperor, recorded in his *Diary of Hanazono* the following passage:

> When it became night, the minister Hino Toshimitsu visited me, accompanied by a monk. He lives like a hermit, hidden away from the public, but he is reputed to have completed his Dharma training [achieved *satori*] and is already well known, so he was invited.
> Our conversation lasted throughout the night. His understanding of Zen life really goes beyond the ordinary. It is wonderful. This sort of man can be described as a dragon among men. He is to be revered and believed as well.

In 1314, Daitō moved to a small building, probably provided by the Akamatsu family since they were related to his mother. He called the site "The Hermitage of Great Virtue," or Daitoku-an. At this time he had already attracted his first disciple, whom he named Tettō. In 1316, Emperor Hanazono recorded another meeting. In such imperial audiences, the emperor normally sat on a higher dais than the visitor, but Daitō suggested that they should do away with this formality and that they sit on the same level, since all sentient beings are Buddhas. Daitō said, "It is inconceivable that the Buddha-heart and the Imperial-heart should compete with each other," a statement that might be viewed prophetically, considering that for the next six hundred-odd years the temple Daitō was to be the imperial temple.

By 1324, Daitō's popularity among court circles had made other Buddhist sects jealous. On January 21 of that year, a religious debate was held at the urging of the Tendai Buddhists from Mount Hiei and the Shingon monks of Tō-ji on Kyoto's southern flank. According to the *Diary of Hanazono*, two priests represented the Zen side, the young Daitō Kokushi of Daitoku-an and the elderly Tsūō Kyōen, chief abbot of Nanzen-ji, and opposing them were about a hundred monks. The Tendai scholars were headed by Genne, supported by Shingon priests from Tō-ji and representatives of the ten larger temples of Nara. The judge of the contest was Emperor Go-Daigo, who had succeeded to the throne after Hanazono in 1318, assisted by the ex-Emperor Hanazono and attended by other members of the imperial court.

Genne asked Daitō, "What is the essence of Zen that goes beyond words?" Daitō's answer was, "Everyone knows that a meteor rushes across the sky, yet they cannot explain it in words." Genne fell silent.

Koshō, the chief abbot of Onjō-ji, a Tendai temple at Mii-dera by Lake Biwa, then stepped forward, carrying an octagonal tray of ritual treasures. "What is that?" asked Daitō. Abbot Koshō replied, "This box contains the universe." In Tendai philosophy all is one and one is all, so the box was all. Daitō took the short stick he used in teaching and with a quick gesture smashed the box. "What happens when the universe is crushed?"

Emperor Go-Daigo decided the contest in favor of Zen and presented a wooden palanquin from the imperial storehouse for the two Zen priests to ride back to their temple in. This still hangs from the ceiling rafters of Daitoku-ji's Headquarters Temple. In the subtemple of Shinju-an there is an original horizontal scroll illustrating this contest and the presentation of the palanquin. After this episode, Genne of Enryaku-ji became a disciple of Daitō and with his own money erected a *hōjō* (abbot's hall).

Though a Tendai monk had been Daitō's adversary in this contest, the Tendai sect itself had become so powerful since its foundation in the ninth century that even the Zen temples of Kyoto at this time were syncretic, practicing Tendai rituals as well as Zen meditation. Daitō himself, like all early Zen leaders in Japan, including Eisai (1141–1215) and Dōgen (1200–53)—the founders of the Rinzai and Sōtō sects respectively—began his religious life as a Tendai monk.

Daitō had broken completely away from Tendai and thus the 1324 contest was especially important for Zen and for Daitoku-ji, because it induced the Kyoto court, headed by Hanazono and Go-Daigo, to prefer Zen over Tendai, and recognition of Daitoku-ji by the two emperors came the next year, in 1325.

With imperial recognition, Daitoku-ji needed more splendid buildings, so structures were given by families loyal to the court, and on the anniversary of the enlightenment of the Historical Buddha, December 8, in 1326, an official dedication was held. In 1327 Daitō welcomed as librarian a middle-aged monk named Kanzan who had first studied at Kenchō-ji in Kamakura but had become dissatisfied. Legend says that after he heard of Daitō's "pure Zen," he walked so single-mindedly along the Tōkaidō road that he did not even turn and glance at the beauty of Mount Fuji, in view on his right for an entire day. Kanzan's "awakening" occurred the following year.

Daitō was taken sick in 1329, perhaps with a rheumatic illness since thereafter he appears to have been lame. Soon after, he sent Kanzan, his most intuitively able follower, to a Gifu farming area to become a cowherd, with instructions to deepen his enlightenment for twenty years. This move may also have been to protect Kanzan in case the political trouble in Kyoto should worsen. His oldest disciple, Tettō, he retained at Daitoku-ji, and he was eventually to take over the administration of the compound.

Meanwhile, on the island of Kyushu, the powerful Ōtomo generals invited Daitō to Sōfuku-ji, the temple of his former teacher, Daiō. Daitō, who had recovered from his illness, wanted to go for a prolonged stay, but Emperor Go-Daigo was in great trouble and did not wish him to leave. Finally it was decided that Daitō might be absent for ninety days.

While he was away, the political situation grew worse. Go-Daigo's life was in danger, so Daitō returned immediately. It is recorded that a follower of the emperor asked Daitō what should be done, to which the abbot replied, "Matters have gone so far that only fighting will settle things." But Go-Daigo lacked the military forces to risk a battle, so he fled. The Hōjō regents sentenced him to exile on the island of Oki between Japan and Korea; forces of the Hōjō occupied the capital and set up a new puppet emperor, even though Go-Daigo had refused to abdicate and had taken the imperial regalia (a sword, jewelry and a mirror, all of ancient Shinto lineage) with him in flight.

It was about a year and a half later that Go-Daigo escaped from Oki Island, hidden under seaweed in a fishing boat. Daitoku-ji's residents must have rejoiced to learn of Go-Daigo's escape and his subsequent rallying of forces opposed to the Hōjō. Finally the Hōjō sent a new contingent of troops to Kyoto under General Ashikaga Takauji. Takauji, however, allied himself with the emperor and went to escort him back in triumph to the palace.

Go-Daigo returned in June, 1333, and immediately began to implement his dream of restoring absolute power to the emperor's hands. He took back all rice lands and placed them under imperial jurisdiction, although Daitoku-ji was confirmed in its rice land-holdings and was even given additional ones. In fact, at this time its total area was increased to about one hundred and fifty acres.

Go-Daigo had previously made his eldest son, Morinaga, chief abbot of Enryaku-ji, Kyoto's Tendai Buddhist center, to disqualify him from any important secular position. When trouble started, Morinaga cast aside his priestly robes and became a military commander, and, apparently, a successful one. Perhaps jealous of his own son (records are somewhat contradictory), after his return to the capital and to power, Go-Daigo sent him a letter, saying:

> Since peace has again been restored, you should immediately cut your hair, don your priestly robes, and return to your duties at Enryaku-ji.

The prince, knowing his father's weakness for ancient history, replied:

> There are many instances in the histories of both Japan and China when, during times that demanded wise council and military leadership, men who have taken Buddhist vows have returned to lay life and sovereigns who have abdicated have returned to the throne. . . . Which course on my part would be better for the country—to live in obscurity on Mount Hiei guarding but one temple, or as a great general to pacify the country to its furthest extent?

The prince asked for the title of shogun and a direct commission from the throne to attack Ashikaga Takauji, whom he mistrusted. The emperor gave him the title in order to get him to return to Kyoto, but kept him inactive. Since he had refused to go back to the Tendai center, Prince Morinaga's attention turned to Daitoku-ji. It is recorded in the temple's history that he gave landholdings to the new temple and that on New Year's Day, 1334, he gave a banquet for its monks. Within the year the emperor allowed him to be arrested for plotting against General Ashikaga Takauji, which he was probably doing with Go-Daigo's tacit approval. In any case he was transported to Kamakura and eventually killed. Thus the imperial restoration lost one of its most intelligent supporters and the young temple of Daitoku-ji missed a powerful friend.

Emperor Go-Daigo's esteem of Daitoku-ji is attested to by a letter, brushed in his own hand and dated August 24, 1333, which is still exhibited every mid-October at Mushiboshi:

> Daitoku-ji, among all Zen temples, is now placed at the very top. Many priests are living there in safety and spending long and peaceful lives praying there. This is appropriate because the Imperial Order rules within Daitoku-ji.
> No one from outside can succeed to its abbotship. The reason for this is that Daitoku-ji is not a private temple [but an imperial one], so a clear, unsullied stream of succession is important.
> Thus, because I respect its Dharma stream, I write this letter and bestow it upon the temple so that it may be kept on forever, until the Dragon Flower Time [when all beings will be saved by Maitreya Buddha].

In October of the same year, Go-Daigo gave public evidence of this esteem by placing Daitoku-ji, along with Nanzen-ji, at the head of the list of the Gozan, the five leading temples of Zen. This practice had been begun by the Sung emperors, and the Hōjō regents had adopted it, naturally favoring the temples where they lived, in Kamakura. After Go-Daigo lost power, Daitoku-ji subsequently slipped down on the list, and when it found itself at the bottom in the fourteenth century, Abbot Yōsō asked for it to be withdrawn from consideration.

The period around the end of 1333 marks one of the peaks in Daitoku-ji's development. However, Daitō was again unwell. His official portrait (chinzō) was painted the next year, and this painting (Pl. 6) is still preserved in the Headquarters Temple and is displayed every year at Mushiboshi. In the painting his robes, staff, slippers, chair and footstool are all Chinese and attest to his having received Zen from the mainland through his teacher, Daiō. The custom of having these official portraits was established in Sung-dynasty China and then seems to have been adopted in Japan.

According to temple tradition, this portrait was painted by Tosa Yukimitsu, the prominent Yamato-e artist in Kyoto at that time. His facial expression is severe, especially because of the pucker on his forehead, but the plump cheeks and rosy lips humanize the expression. There is a dignified classical quality in the ample figure, framed by the Chinese chair. The footstool is near the bottom edge of the silk rectangle so that there is little vacant space on any side, and this crowding propels the whole figure toward the viewer and gives the impression of immediacy rather than a sense of withdrawal.

Since the fourteenth century the painting has been used as a religious icon during the ceremony on the anniversary of his death on November 22 (Kaisanki). Daitō really died a month later, but December being very cold, the pragmatic Zen priests celebrate in November.

Every participant is familiar with the prose that is brushed on the silk above the portrait. Full of Zen references and difficult to translate, the founder's calligraphy suggests:

[A pose of] Springing into instant action [to bring Enlightenment].
The eyes flashing anger, the tongue beyond the logic of speech.
From ancient times, such a face frightens people.
But upon this bit of silk, whose spirit really exists?
The real Transcendental Wisdom (*Prajñā*) goes beyond the realm of subject and object.
In the vastness of the sky shines the radiance of one moon!

This suggests that the artist has represented him in a *sanzen* aspect, in which the master tries to frighten the disciple out of his logical or intellectual concepts through one-to-one personal confrontation within the *sanzen* room. The portrait, then, is to serve as a confrontation to each man of Zen who views it. It is not to be viewed as a work of art, but as a religious device.

Presumably it was in the same year, 1334, at the peak of Go-Daigo's power, that he brushed in a eulogy in praise of Daitoku-ji's founder which reads:

Holding a bamboo staff in his hand,
With a glance swifter than lightning,
Even when the hammer [of the blacksmith or the Zen leader] is not swung.
He has finished training Buddhas and patriarchs,
He has trained a multitude of monks,
But there remains no trace of him.
Though he was the teacher of two emperors,
There is no pride revealed in his face.
The dignified spirit emanating from his body

makes him unapproachable.
Who can see the enlightenment sparkling from his eyes?

There is a wooden plaque that reads "Radiance from the Eyes" (*Reikō*) hanging above the curtain of the Holy Room in the Headquarters Temple where the founder is worshiped three times a month. Zen greatly admires the lightning glance of an awakened mind.

Another important piece of calligraphy that is also displayed on Mushiboshi day is the "Final Instructions" (*Yuikai*) of the founder. The first half was written in 1327, only two years after the official recognition of the temple and seems to have been an attempt to bolster the severity of the discipline. The last part was added in 1336, shortly before his death, and seems even more stern. These words are so well known that they are chanted as part of the religious service of most Rinzai Zen temples today, even in Rinzai Zen temples in the U.S.A. A free translation follows:

All you people! You enter this monastery to study Zen, not just for clothes and food. If you have shoulders, you won't be without clothes. If you have a mouth, you won't go without eating. Always direct yourself, twenty-four hours a day, to the place beyond knowing. Study hard, reach it, master it, and leave. Time is like an arrow, so be careful; don't occupy your mind with miscellaneous things. You must realize this! You must realize this!

The addition in 1336 reads:

After this old monk's pilgrimage, some of you may have rich temples, with large halls and volumes of sutras decorated with gold and silver, and many noisy, enthusiastic followers. Or you may read sutras and recite prayers, do *zazen* for long periods without lying down, eat only breakfast and work day and night. Although you do all these things, if you don't set your minds on the marvelous, untransmitted way of Buddha and the Patriarchs, you immediately deny cause and effect, and the true teaching falls to the ground. Then all of you are a bunch of devils, and although this old monk may have left this world for a long time, you are not allowed to call yourself my descendants. But if there is one person who seriously studies his own affairs, even if he lives out in the fields in a straw hut, cooking his meals of vegetable roots over a grass fire in a broken pot, he is the one who will recognize my tradition and be grateful for what he has received. Do you wish to be careless? Work hard! Work hard!

In September of 1336, Daitō's illness became worse and it is recorded that Emperor Go-Daigo, despite the chaotic state of his life, took the time to send him flowers (Go-Daigo's rule was to end in December). In March, 1337, the founder summoned his eldest disciple, Tettō, and put him in charge of the temple. Ex-Emperor Hanazono sent a letter approving this action, because at this time Daitoku-ji's fortunes were uncertain: many things associated with Go-Daigo were being destroyed by the victorious general, Ashikaga Takauji, and Go-Daigo could do nothing from his retreat in the Yoshino mountains. Since further support from Go-Daigo would only hurt Daitoku-ji, Hanazono sent another letter to the temple in an attempt to bolster its position. There was danger that Daitoku-ji's lands might be appropriated by the conqueror, and to some extent this did occur. The text of Hanazono's letter is:

Among Zen temples, Daitoku-ji most closely

follows the true transmission of the Sixth Patriarch. It is in Daruma's awesome tradition and is truly a model for all Zen temples. Among Zen temples, Daitoku-ji will exist into the infinite future, and its abbot's chair will be passed down to future generations through Daitō's line of succession. Men from other schools must never occupy this position. This is just not my personal opinion. The Daitoku-ji school must remain distinct, no matter what happens. These adamant instructions for future succession must never be changed.

> The twenty-sixth day of
> the eighth month, 1338

In the spring of 1338, Tettō was installed as the first chief abbot (the founder not being counted in the numbering system). Daitō had not lived through the winter. On December 22, 1337, realizing that it was his last day on earth, Daitō sat in *zazen* and addressed his leg, which was lame. "I have followed you for a long time, but now you should obey me." He then adopted the double-lotus position. As he forced his crippled leg into place, he broke the bone and the blood gushed out over his robes. (These blood-stained robes of its founder are displayed by Daitoku-ji at its Mushiboshi in October.) Thus Daitō had the satisfaction of meeting death in a perfect *zazen* position. His last words epitomize his life:

Having cut off Buddhas and patriarchs,
Always keeping razor-sharp the ultimate sword
  [Zen training],
When life's wheel turns,
The Infinite Void gnashes its teeth.

Institution versus Individual

When Daitō Kokushi died, the temple he had begun, which Emperor Go-Daigo had elevated to such an influential position during his short reign, quickly lost its power. Shōkoku-ji, the temple supported by the Ashikaga shogun, became the most important religious center, and, indeed, it was only by becoming inconspicuous that Daitoku-ji managed to survive at all. This situation continued until the middle of the fifteenth century when Yōsō, the twenty-sixth chief abbot of Daitoku-ji, began to interest the merchants of Sakai in the temple. Sakai was the site of an important Shinto shrine called Sumiyoshi, and thus it was inclined to support the imperial rather than the shogunate cause.

Throughout Daitoku-ji's history, the weight of tradition has tended to crush individualism and only occasionally has creativity managed to flourish there. This constant conflict was dramatized in the fifteenth century in the relationship of two of its priests, Yōsō (1376–1459) and Ikkyū (1394–1481). Yōsō lived at Daitoku-ji for several decades, serving as its highest official, and he appears to have been a stable, conservative man who devoted himself to his institution and who was honored by it in return. Ikkyū, on the other hand, roamed all over the Kansai area in central Honshu, only visiting Daitoku-ji infrequently and then just for important ceremonies. He accused his Zen "brother," Yōsō, of superficiality in his Zen and even of dishonesty. In his poetry he dared equate sex with the transcendental wisdom of Mañjuśrī (the patron bodhisattva of Zen training halls), and even suggested that the sexual experience gives a wisdom not found within monastic walls. These attitudes were strikingly heretical at the time and indicate Ikkyū's rebellious and at least superficially contradictory character.

Thus these two men appear to have been diametri-

cally opposed in their lifestyles and personalities, and yet they studied with the same master, Kasō, who gave them both *inka*, certificates testifying to their enlightenment. Strangely enough it was these two priests who in turn were to be responsible for getting Daitoku-ji constructed again the two times it was ravaged by fire: Yōsō rebuilt it in 1453 and Ikkyū after its total destruction in 1467.

Today Yōsō is almost unknown except among the monks of Daitoku-ji. These count him as their spiritual forebear and it is in his spirit of orthodoxy that the temple's chief abbots have been selected. In contrast, Ikkyū's name is familiar to virtually every Japanese adult and his influence is felt in almost all branches of Japanese arts. He affected the development of Nō drama, started the tea ceremony on its crazy climb to fame, and greatly stimulated ink painting, particularly of the Soga school so that it might be termed the Ikkyū school.

In Ikkyū's memorial temple, Shinju-an, to the right of the central niche which contains his wooden effigy, there is a spirit tablet of his father, Emperor Go-Komatsu, the hundredth emperor of Japan in whose reign the opposing Northern and Southern branches of the imperial family were brought together in 1392. After a schism of almost sixty years the Northern branch had emerged the stronger and thus, since Ikkyū's mother was of the Southern court, the empress was able to have her dismissed from the palace. So it came about that Ikkyū Sōjun, the unrecognized son of Go-Komatsu, was born on New Year's day, 1394, in an ordinary house rather than the imperial palace. This circumstance of his life may well have influenced Ikkyū psychologically and contributed to his rebelliousness.

Yōsō and Ikkyū became Zen "brothers" when both were disciples of Kasō, the head of a temple at Lake Biwa who was noted for the severity of his discipline. In Zen, normal family connections are abandoned, and so monks studying under the same master become religious brothers, a tie supposedly more binding than any blood relationship. After Kasō's death in 1428, Yōsō moved immediately to Daitoku-ji and served it so well that within three years he was elected its chief abbot. Meanwhile, Ikkyū adopted the life of a wanderer, traveling where his fancy took him, clad only in one dark robe, with a straw raincoat to protect him from the weather and straw sandals on his feet. Eventually, in his *Crazy Cloud Collection* poems he was to admit that he spent ten years frequenting fish stalls, *sake* shops and brothels and that sometimes he prefers them to a mountain hermitage.

In Zen, the ultimate experience is the "return to the phenomenal world," "the return to the marketplace," and this comes after *satori*. This return is an essential characteristic of Rinzai Zen, but it is a feature that was little understood in the rigidity of fifteenth-century Japan. In his early education, Ikkyū had been steeped in the history and literature of China and this led him to a clearer understanding of this complete liberation which Rinzai represented. Placed in a Zen temple at the tender age of five, he was already studying the Vimalakirti Sutra by the age of eleven and had begun composing Chinese-style poetry. His early brilliance and love of poetry was a trait that continued throughout his life, and it is said that he composed a minimum of one poem a day in the classical style of T'ang China.

When Ikkyū became a disciple of Kasō, he was obliged to render obedience to his master as long as he was alive, but after his death, while Yōsō was becoming established at Daitoku-ji, Ikkyū was free to adopt a life of wandering. In this he seems to have reverted to the influence of his first master, Kenō, who was an unconventional priest and who refused to give *inka* as acknowledgments of enlightenment, a heretical idea in Rinzai Zen and one that Ikkyū followed all his life, insisting that his disciples be strong without the support of a piece of paper.

Without understanding this "return to the phenomenal world," Ikkyū's whole attitude and criticism of Yōsō and other conventional monks cannot be grasped. The Zen life may be divided into various stages through which a man progresses. By practicing *zazen* meditation and hard physical work (*samu*), he attempts to conquer his ego. In Rinzai Zen, to help the normal and logical mind escape from its habit of separating physical things from other things in the phenomenal world, *kōan* are used. These *kōan* were evolved in China to combat the inflexibility of Confucian thinking, but they are as effective in Japan, which also has a Confucian background, or in the West, with its dependence on Aristotelian logic. Rinzai Zen has its own logic in its four categories of "to be," "not to be," "to be and not to be," and "neither to be nor not to be." With such means as *kōan* Zen Buddhism came to specialize in techniques to help a man reach a continuum of consciousness which is indivisible into "things" because it is an ever-existing completeness. This state cannot be described in words, so *mu*, negation, is used to convey it.

Zen Buddhism has no monopoly on people who reach this state in which the relative world and the Absolute interpenetrate, but what makes Zen unique is that after dwelling in the Absolute or reaching this state, its followers are urged not to rest there. Rather the monk should return and live in the phenomenal world again. Since, however, he is enlightened, his actions in the phenomenal world, performed from the Absolute world, become a manifestation of the Absolute. If he rakes a garden, this is a sacrament; if he cleans a toilet, this, too, is a holy act. Once he slips back to distinguishing "things" and "categories," the whole process is lost, and must be begun again.

Ikkyū believed that Yōsō had slipped back into the world of categories, or lost his Buddha-nature, engrossed as he was in the rituals and routines of an important temple. The Spartan life they had shared as disciples under Kasō had been forgotten by Yōsō as he gave talks on Zen for money. Ikkyū felt that his vagabond life, sleeping in improvised shelters, was closer to the great Zen leaders of the T'ang dynasty. Ceremonial prostration, burning incense, "selling Zen" were not the way.

In 1439 Yōsō erected a sub-temple at Daitoku-ji in memory of Kasō, and put up a signboard reading "Daiyū-an," which means "Hermitage of Great Works." Ikkyū criticized the name, and suggested that another inscription be placed there instead. This should read:

> The temple [Daitoku-ji] seems wealthy, but the
>   Five Mountains [Gozan] are declining.
> Its abbots are false masters; there exist no real
>   masters.
> How nice to take a rod and just go fishing.
> Nowadays everything drifts toward degenera-
>   tion.

The next year Ikkyū was invited to be abbot of Nyoi-an, a subtemple of Daitoku-ji. The thirteenth anniversary of Kasō's death was imminent. Yōsō had invited wealthy patrons from Sakai to be present, undoubtedly with hopes of substantial donations from them. Ikkyū protested all the commotion over these guests, and contrasted it with his simple way of living.

> Everyday things in this cottage [Nyoi-an]—
> A wooden ladle and a bamboo basket hang on
>   the east wall.
> Even these things are not necessities [to one who
>   has]
> Spent years traveling the world with only a
>   straw raincoat and hat.

He decided to leave Nyoi-an, and wrote another poem to Yōsō, again in protest, suggesting that there were other, better places than Daitoku-ji. His composition reads:

> After ten days here, my mind is spinning—
> My emotions are at white heat.
> If you wish to find me in the future,
> I'll be in a fish shop, a *sake* shop, or a brothel.

Putting on his straw sandals, his farmer-type raincoat and his straw hat, Ikkyū left the temple, which he labeled a "walled cage" in another poem. Yōsō was to live in this "cage" or another near Sakai until his death in 1459.

Only once in their turbulent rivalry did Yōsō and Ikkyū agree on anything. That was in the year 1444, when the Hosokawa, constables of Kyoto, were so strong they forced the emperor to appoint Nippō, a Myōshin-ji man, as chief abbot of Daitoku-ji. Yōsō and Ikkyū and all other Daitoku-ji priests were unanimous in their opposition, but for seventy years almost half the chief abbots were "interlopers" from Myōshin-ji!

In the autumn of 1447, when Ikkyū was fifty-three, some scandal occurred at Daitoku-ji which resulted in one of the monks committing suicide. Probably caused by the Hosokawa, other monks began talking and scandalmongering, and about half a dozen were imprisoned by the Hosokawa police.

Ikkyū could not bear this disgrace, which seemed to reflect not only on the imperial temple but on all Japanese Rinzai Zen. He walked straw-sandaled until he reached the mountains north of Osaka, a retreat he had used before, known as Izuriha. He arrived on the ninth day of the ninth month, one of the three major festivals in old China. For the occasion Ikkyū composed nine Chinese poems. Legend has it that he had resolved to starve himself to death to protest the situation. He does not expressly state in these poems that he will commit suicide, but he indicates that the Daitoku-ji disturbances make life not worth living.

When Ikkyū arrived at Izuriha, a dramatic storm was raging in the distance. The priest felt a parallel between this turbulence and Daitoku-ji's troubles. His first poem in free translation (most of his poems have at least two levels of meaning and some three) is:

> Daitoku-ji has reached its autumn [it was a hundred years old]; the sky holds a storm.
> Since evening, rain and wind have increased and there is no quiet.
> If people speak evil against others,
> The barrier of Ummon is their reward.

(This is the barrier which must be smashed to understand Zen fully—the barrier of categories between "good" and "evil," and so on.)

Ikkyū is despondent. The world, which to the enlightened man appears clean and pure in its natural state, now seems turned into a hell by the gossiping, contentious monks at Daitoku-ji. He writes that words have wounded him more than a real battle could. One poem states that now he feels as though his forehead has been cut by a sword and the blood is gushing out. This is the mood in which he writes his nine poems of despair. One poem reads:

> I am ashamed to be still among the living,
> Practicing Zen, studying the Way, but heavy problems have arisen.
> The Truth that Buddha preached has totally disappeared.
> Instead the King of Demons grows a hundred feet tall.

Perhaps Ikkyū stopped in the midst of his compositions, as Chinese poets did, to drink a little wine, and this relaxes him a bit. He writes another poem, which begins with an obscure reference to Abbot Kidō of Sung China, and then proceeds:

> My body hesitates [about suicide]; I walk about.
> Resting a bit calms my heart-rending situation.
> At the same time, [there exist] troubles and pleasures, cold and heat,
> Only yellow leaves [are without emotion], ninth of the ninth [month].

Still the storm rages in the mountains. He writes:

> Outside the wind blows pines and cedars in confusion amidst clouds.
> Everywhere people are distraught and confused.
> I cannot understand how human life moves on.
> One cup of cheap *sake*—and I am drunk.

Eventually, according to the biography by his oldest disciple Bokusai, called *Ikkyū Nempu*, Emperor Go-Hanazono sent a messenger to dissuade him from starving himself to death.

These nine poems that he composed in the midst of his despair reveal Ikkyū as a man of strong emotions. The composure of *zazen* is missing and yet he was never tempted to conceal this. He did not write at white heat and then destroy the poems, nor keep his poems secret from his disciples. There exist at least four hand-written versions by disciples at the present time, although some of Ikkyū's disciples were not as "free" as he was and wished to preserve a more conventional reputation for their master by eliminating poems that were too strongly emotional or that mentioned *sake* shops and sexual experiences with women.

Ikkyū is said to have contemplated suicide three times, always because he felt that he could not master the situation which he faced. Events at Daitoku-ji had deteriorated, and he felt helpless. The occasion at Izuriha was the third and last time suicide is associated with his life. Thereafter he decided to live out his allotted span, paradoxical though it might seem.

Fate had in store an even crueler blow when most of Daitoku-ji caught fire in 1453. It may have been accidental, or it may have been arson, a repercussion of the Hosokawa enmity. Yōsō had retired, but he was called back to become chief abbot again. Now the responsibility of rebuilding the temple fell upon his shoulders and he was worldly enough to enlist the help of rich merchants from Sakai. In appreciation of his quick rebuilding of the three canonical buildings of Daitoku-ji, the emperor gave Yōsō the title of *Zenji,* or "Zen Master." This was the first time it had been bestowed on a living master.

This unusual honor really aroused Ikkyū's wrath. His teacher Kasō had not been so recognized, and here his bitterest enemy was being singled out simply because of a financial matter. In fact, Ikkyū's poem accuses Yōsō of giving a large sum of money to the imperial house in order to receive such an honor. It reads:

Congratulatory Poem on Receiving the Honorary Title of Zenji
> You wear the purple robe [of the chief abbot of
>   Daitoku-ji] and now bear an honorary title, so
>   the exchequer must be rich.
> This honorary title must have cost you a pretty
>   penny!
> The temple appears to be very busy—but what
>   an old charlatan you are!
> Just looking at you, it is clear that your
>   lineage is from P'u Chou [a Chinese province
>   famous for thieves].

Ikkyū felt that his rival Yōsō was "selling Zen" at Daitoku-ji by talking and preaching to those who really could not understand it, simply because they were rich. Furthermore, he accused Yōsō of selling

certificates of enlightenment to swell the coffers of the temple or his private wealth. Rinzai Zen had sunk to a low point and enlightenment was "sold," particularly by those temples associated with the shogunate. Zen temples also made money in *sake*-brewing and through usury. In the mid-fifteenth century one Zen temple, Shōkoku-ji, furnished all the advisers to the shogunate's government and received most of the bribes. The imperially-sanctioned temple of Daitoku-ji was only on the fringe of this corruption, but Ikkyū felt he could not criticize it enough. One of his poems calls those Zen monks who had given poetry-writing priority over Zen as "intimates of the demons." Since he put his Zen first and used his poetry as his vehicle of criticism, he was not comparable to men of the Literary School of the Five Mountains (*Gozan Bungaku*), who made the turning of a fine phrase their primary goal.

Despite Ikkyū's unceasing attack on him, Yōsō, Daitoku-ji's twenty-sixth chief abbot, never replied so much as a line to Ikkyū's barbs and slanders. He continued to be a loyal member of the institution, unquestioning of its "Zen." Yōsō had known no other life but that of a Zen priest from the age of seven, when he was taken by his parents to Tōfuku-ji. He was born in 1376, near present-day Himeji. At first Yōsō served as a boy monk at Kennin-ji, but later he moved to the shores of Lake Biwa to study under Kasō. Yōsō was his senior disciple and eighteen years older when Ikkyū arrived at the age of twenty-one. Sometimes older disciples are harsh on younger ones, and a thirty-nine-year-old disciple is a rarity in any case, and should have been head of his own temple. If conflict occurred between them, it would help account for the later bitterness. Yōsō appears to have been the quiet, obedient type, who did what was expected of him. His portrait, painted in 1452 by Bunsei, is the saddest among all Daitoku-ji's *chinzō* (Pl. 37); it suggests a man who knew no joy, but rather experienced something deeper than sadness, a quiet submission to conditions, without hope of relief. The lines about his mouth give a sagging expression to the face, suggesting that Yōsō's burdens were heavy indeed. Ikkyū termed him a "poisonous snake," as he himself drifted further and further from the expected pattern of a monk's life.

At this time Rennyo, the leader of Jōdo Shinshū, was insisting that the priests of this sect marry, and he himself is said to have fathered over thirty children. Rennyo often stayed in the same area as Ikkyū, and it is true that at one time Ikkyū became so angry over Zen that he became a convert to Jōdo Shinshū in 1462. Both leaders were striving to lessen the distance between priests and ordinary people. If Ikkyū's precepts had been followed, Zen would have become more democratic. Instead it was to become more elitist in the sixteenth century.

Ikkyū became, increasingly, a free individual and felt that institutionalized monasteries were a farce. Ikkyū admitted through his poetry to enjoying "wine, women and song." His "song" was his poetry, and he used it to castigate those who pretended to be chaste and virtuous yet secretly indulged in all the "vices" he enjoyed openly and without shame. He was living his Buddha-nature, his Zen, while they, in wearing colorful robes, in holding traditional ceremonies, in chanting sutras, were merely pretending to be pious. Ikkyū felt that arguments about points of dogma were a waste of time. The mind should be free of pedantic debate. Ikkyū was a total iconoclast, and even went so far as to denounce incense, a daily necessity for every Buddhist sect and ceremony. His poem reads:

I hate incense
Who can tell if a master is really enlightened?
Some talk forever of Zen and how to attain it.
Piety, in itself, is something to be despised.

In the dimness [of the hall], my nose wrinkles at the incense before the Buddha.

Ikkyū seems to have come to feel that he was a reincarnation of the Sung-dynasty Zen master Hsü-t'ang (Kidō in Japanese), and had his portrait painted as such. Kidō was a poet, a wanderer, and not a dogmatist.

Since Rinzai Zen meant complete liberation to Ikkyū, he might have felt that he was its only true heir in fifteenth-century Japan. The monasteries of this period, such as Shōkoku-ji, were walled enclosures, decorated by their own priest-painter inhabitants. They were "a world within a world," but Ikkyū resented the pretensions of the Five Mountains, which thought they monopolized the best of Zen. He felt Zen belonged to anyone.

Because of the fires and destruction of the Ōnin War, most records have been lost, but enough remains to show that Ikkyū, in his rebellion, gave birth to his own "artistic group." While wandering over the countryside of Japan, he inspired other men; some became great painters and Nō actors. He started Shukō on his way to making the tea ceremony and gardens instruments to bring the Zen Void into a secular setting. The spread of Zen attitudes among the samurai (Soga Jasoku) and the merchant class (Ōwa Sōrin), and a reconciliation between society and art was to be accomplished through the tea ceremony. Ikkyū's own ink paintings are unpretentious and seemingly artless, always with the ink-flinging technique. His calligraphy (Pls. 101–2) is ranked among history's greatest because of its fire and its freedom.

Ikkyū's Zen was the most complete in the entire history of Zen in Japan. He associated with Japanese from every class. Ikkyū, representing the demand of an individual for full expression, in his poetry expresses *ninjō*, or humaneness, as opposed to *giri*, which binds the individual to his community. In Ikkyū's case, his "community" was Daitoku-ji, and he was in constant conflict with its value systems. He saw the gap existing between the ideals of Zen and the actuality of its daily practice. Alienated as a Zen priest, alienated as an artist-aesthete, he challenged the social conventions of his time.

While in his seventies at Shūon-an during the Ōnin War, Ikkyū experienced the great love affair of his life. The woman was forty, and a temple attendant at Shūon-an. She played the *koto* (zither) and sang, while Ikkyū was master of the seven-holed bamboo pipe, or *shakuhachi*. More than a dozen erotically tender poems are addressed to Lady Shin and preserved among his writings.

Meanwhile Yōsō had died. Ikkyū in his writings describes how Yōsō died painfully from leprosy, a death reserved for those who falsify the Buddhist truth. Probably this is an exaggerated fantasy of Ikkyū's, reflecting that he felt his rival deserved a painful death. Ikkyū was never half-hearted in his feelings.

Practically everything in Kyoto was burned with the Ōnin War: the Imperial Palace, the Ashikaga family's "Flowery Palace," and the Hosokawa's Zen temple of Ryōan-ji. The Golden Pavilion remained, but Daitoku-ji was completely razed. Ikkyū saved the calligraphy of the founder, Daitō Kokushi, and various monks took other important relics of Daitoku-ji's first century and fled to the country.

After the fire, for at least seven years Daitoku-ji was deserted. It lay a charred ruin to the north of Kyoto, surrounded by untilled fields, with no bells tolling for litanies. The emperor appointed various disciples of Yōsō to the post of chief abbot, but they lacked the strength to resuscitate a ruin. The monastery of Daitoku-ji and its line of chief abbots descending from Daitō Kokushi existed in name only. The imperial family itself had reached its hardest period economically and could not furnish any support.

Only a miracle could save Daitoku-ji.

The miracle, of course, was Ikkyū. This individual did for the institution what it could not accomplish for itself. The wanderer was now over eighty, and not in the best of health. His beloved Lady Shin had died, and it seemed as though even his extraordinary strength had waned. He could no longer roam the countryside, but had to be borne in a *kago*.

In his eighty-first year Ikkyū was requested to take the post of chief abbot of Daitoku-ji and restore the institution. On February 22, 1474, Ikkyū, who had heretofore criticized those who wore colorful robes, spent one day in an inaugural ceremony, wearing the purple robe that the hundred and third emperor, Go-Tsuchimikado, had bestowed upon him because of his position. But he still felt chagrin at the whole affair and wrote:

> The one remaining light of Daitō's school has
> been destroyed.
> How to explain the heart's singing, the eternity
> of all?
> The priest who for fifty years wore only a straw
> raincoat and hat,
> Shamefully, is a purple-robed monk.

A painting showing Ikkyū wearing this special robe is reproduced here (Pl. 38), though the artist made him look younger than his eighty years. In another *chinzō* in ink (Pl. 39), painted just after his death, Ikkyū's face reveals the effects of the worries attendant on reconstructing an entire compound.

Success seemed doubtful at first. Ikkyū was repeatedly ill in his eighties. He ordered his own tomb built at Shūon-an, the site of his most significant romance. In his six remaining years of life, Ikkyū restored all the major buildings of Daitoku-ji; he even rebuilt its three subtemples, Tokuzen-ji, Nyoi-an—where he had been abbot for a few days long before—and

Daiyū-an, the hermitage of his despised rival, Yōsō.

No help came from the destitute imperial family or its nobility. Even Ashikaga Yoshimasa, who was dreaming of a Zen villa-retreat in the Higashiyama hills, could not erect his hermitage until about 1480, and only then with Hosokawa's help.

Ikkyū's previous wanderings and the friends that he had made now proved useful. He had associated with merchants, the lowest class in Japan's hierarchy, because of their wider outlook on life gained from traveling. One, in particular, was now his best friend, Ōwa Sōrin. This man had dared to cross often to China at a time when the voyage was extremely hazardous. The free port of Sakai had remained relatively untouched by the Ōnin War, and this was where Ōwa Sōrin lived. It is recorded that Ōwa donated the masts from his ocean-going vessels to support the high roof of the Doctrine Hall, which Ikkyū felt must be rebuilt first. Another Sakai merchant named Awaji gave Ikkyū the money to rebuild the living quarters (kuri) of the Daitoku-ji Headquarters Temple.

But this huge undertaking took more than money in these desperate days of the 1470's when the capital city of Japan had shrunk to a tenth of its former size and raw materials, such as wood, were almost unobtainable. In the countryside, private armies and brigands controlled the roads; each local baron set up his customs barrier. Among Ikkyū's four older disciples was a nephew of the Asakura daimyo. Their feudal strength lay far to the north, in mountain hinterlands where seventy-foot-high zelkova trees grew. The Asakura, who admired Ikkyū, ordered their retainers to fell the majestic trees on their mountain property and trim them to thirty-foot logs. These were floated to the capital city, via sea, river and canal barge. Sometimes Ikkyū stayed at Daitoku-ji and directed activities. When there, he lived in a small detached house on the site of the present-day Shinju-an.

Ōwa Sōrin and Ikkyū talked of a memorial temple to be built there, to be known as the "Pearl Hermitage," after a Sung-dynasty poem which implies that true jewels are not material things, but one's mental outlook. Even snow, falling through a leaky roof, can make a hermitage seem pearl-strewn. The Pearl Hermitage (Shinju-an) was to be built ten years later.

Much of the time the octogenarian priest was now traveling in a kago. His baggage was zeal and determination. He, who had always hated money, now sought money for the enterprise. Ikkyū, the individual, was rebuilding an institution which he had criticized all his life. Ikkyū Sōjun, who believed that the real Zen temple lay inside the enlightened individual, was now building a series of wooden structures. And inside these, false teachers might soon chant litanies and burn incense, and "talk Zen" and sell inka.

Why was the self-styled "Blind Donkey," the self-styled "Crazy Cloud," rescuing the institution? Hate and love are really close emotions, rather than opposites, since both are equally strong. Ikkyū hated Daitoku-ji, and fled from its ceremonies. He castigated its traditional leadership. Yet, in another sense, Zen was Ikkyū's only love. His Zen center of Daitoku-ji was in deep trouble. Lady Shin lay dead, so he could not help her, but he could, perhaps, still help the monastery of Daitoku-ji. He was born the son of an emperor, and the imperially-sanctioned temple was destroyed; another emperor had asked him to restore it.

Daitoku-ji's gratitude is embodied in one memorial temple, Shinju-an, and this was the gift of Ōwa Sōrin. Ikkyū's self-portraits are all somewhat different, but several of them look out at the world with a quizzical expression, a note of irony in the glance. They seem to say, "Life is a joke, a transient joke. Why not rescue the institution, so it can perpetuate its stupid conventions? 'Crazy Cloud' had nothing better to do after he was eighty."

Fame in a Troubled Period

Daitoku-ji did not expand much in its first two centuries because Emperor Go-Daigo, its initial patron, lost in the fourteenth-century dispute over the imperial succession. The victors, the Ashikaga shoguns, favored other Zen temples in Kyoto. However, just before its two hundredth and fiftieth anniversary, the temple once more rose to national prominence when it became a sort of tea finishing school for Japan's two most colorful dictators in turn, Nobunaga and Hideyoshi. Concurrently the temple developed into the country's most prestigious location for a funeral or gravesite. And Sen no Rikyū gave Daitoku-ji an unparalleled sanctity in the world of the tea ceremony, a position that it still retains.

Unfortunately the tea ceremony soon became embroiled in power politics, and overnight Daitoku-ji, which had risen to great fame from 1570 to 1590, was suddenly threatened with total destruction over the wooden statue of a tea master! Hideyoshi ordered the compound burned to the ground, the same Hideyoshi who had built three subtemples here and richly endowed the temple with rice lands, and who had also made use of its influence in his startling rise to power. All these events were part of a strange drama that involved bowls of powdered tea, sticks of incense, and *seppuku* swords, within the tree-shaded quiet of the Temple of Great Virtue.

Little more than a century before, around 1475, Ikkyū had inspired Shukō to mix Zen principles with tea etiquette and thereby uplift the somewhat degenerate Ashikaga shogunate under Yoshimasa. It happened that Zen tea succeeded to a greater extent than Ikkyū could have foreseen and Daitoku-ji's monastic Zen became famous for its cultural by-products. Ikkyū had been on friendly terms with several Sakai merchants, and this bond—between Daitoku-ji and Sakai—was one that continued to affect the tea cere-

mony for a long time. In fact it became the custom for rich Sakai merchants to become tea masters and to learn their Zen through Daitoku-ji abbots.

When Oda Nobunaga (1534–82) and Toyotomi Hideyoshi (1536–98) rose to power, both wanted friendly connections with Sakai and with tea ceremony experts. Although Nobunaga began life obscurely, with a small fief acquired by murdering his older and younger brothers, cunning and courage enabled him to unite a number of unsettled provinces nearby and give them stability. His goal was to unify the entire country, and he had brought about half of Japan under his rule when one of his companions, Akechi Mitsuhide, turned traitor.

In 1566 Nobunaga appeared to be the new strong man and Emperor Ōgimachi sent a message asking him to travel to the capital and calm the city. Since 1550 Kyoto's actual ruler had not been the Ashikaga shogun but a warlord named Miyoshi Chōkei. This general had been murdered in 1566 and his son erected Jukō-in at Daitoku-ji for the peace of his soul. Nobunaga hesitated for two years before going to Kyoto, unsure of his strength. Then he came and established his headquarters at Tōfuku-ji, a Zen temple on the city's southern outskirts. He did not trust the people at Daitoku-ji, for they had been associated with Miyoshi. Nobunaga defeated Miyoshi's son, installed a boy in the shogun's position, and became *de facto* shogun himself.

Nobunaga's military successes were in large part due to his use of guns and gunpowder, which the Portuguese had brought to Kyushu. The first merchant to bring guns from Tanegashima near Kyushu and sell them to Nobunaga, was, interestingly enough, an ancestor of the present Daitoku-ji abbot of Nyoi-an, Tachibana Daiki. To help pay for his new flintlocks, the ancient temple of Horyū-ji was assessed 1,000 *kan* and the even more prosperous Osaka temple of Ishiyama Hongan-ji the sum of 5,000 *kan*.

Both temples paid quickly to avoid being attacked by Nobunaga, for he was known to be ruthless. Since he was buying his guns from Sakai, Nobunaga imposed on the port city a war tax of 20,000 *kan*. The city was less vulnerable to attack and some leaders wanted to resist, but the tea masters advised caution and acted as intermediaries from October 1568, until the sum (the equivalent of six million dollars today) was finally paid in the first month of the next year.

Since Nobunaga was a devotee of tea, the Sakai tea masters were generally favorable to his cause. On April 1, 1570, Imai Sōkyū recorded in his diary that he had entertained Nobunaga at a tea ceremony, using and later presenting to the general the tea caddy named "Matsushima" (Pine Island), and that Rikyū had served as tea master. Meanwhile Nobunaga continued to place his orders for muskets at Sakai and this involved him yet more deeply with Sakai merchants and tea men. It was Imai Sōkyū who introduced him to the abbots of Daitoku-ji who were interested in tea.

By 1569 Nobunaga had become more closely associated with the imperial family. Two days after repairing the Shogun Yoshiaki's palace, Nobunaga ordered the workmen to begin reconstructing the Imperial Palace for Emperor Ōgimachi. It was finished the following year, at which time the general visited Kyoto and stayed at the home of Nakarai, a tea devotee who was also the emperor's physician of Chinese medicine. The emperor had given six rooms of the former palace to Nakarai for his use, but Nakarai felt that he was not worthy to have rooms that still held "an imperial perfume," and as a devout Buddhist he bestowed them on Shinju-an, the only subtemple at Daitoku-ji directly connected with the imperial family, since it honored Ikkyū, the son of the hundredth emperor. These rooms are still at Shinju-an and are called by Nakarai's Buddhist name, Tsūsen-in, meaning "Pathway of the Immortals."

The Nakarai were, for centuries, buried in the graveyard at Shinju-an.

In this same year of 1570, Nobunaga did something that was unprecedented. He was allowed to enter the Imperial Repository at Nara (perhaps the emperor feared he would break in otherwise) and remove part of a famous incense stick for use in his tea ceremonies, the first time this had happened since the establishment of the Shōsō-in in 756. The incense, the most valuable of all fragrant woods, had been brought from India, and had been used in the eighth century but not since then, and the giving of it to Nobunaga may well have been in return for the rebuilding of the palace. Nobunaga is said to have taken out a fan and placed small pieces of the famed incense stick upon it, inviting the assembled group to share it. On this occasion two Sakai tea masters were present, Imai Sōkyū and Sen no Rikyū. Through them, Nobunaga had become increasingly acquainted with the leading abbots of Daitoku-ji. The start of the connection between Nobunaga and Daitoku-ji must have been around 1568.

Nobunaga had already employed the ceremony as an instrument of state by giving tea utensils instead of rice lands as rewards for merit on the battlefield. By 1572 Nobunaga was using Rikyū as his tea master, so for a decade Rikyū was with this despot in many of his more intimate and informal moments. Weary from battle, generals took up the tea ceremony for relaxation and thus became susceptible to the influence of their tea masters, particularly in matters of aesthetics.

Nobunaga was perhaps the most completely irreligious ruler in Japanese history. Neither the natural nor the supernatural awed him. To him, religions were a curiosity, ultimately meaningless except for their possible political advantages. Rikyū had studied Zen under Abbot Shōrei in his youth and then under Kokei, who also came from Sakai and became chief abbot of Daitoku-ji in 1573. By this time a group consisting of Chief Abbot Kokei, Nobunaga, the two tea masters Rikyū and Sōkyū, and Akechi Mitsuhide, a relative of Nobunaga and a general in his army, often gathered at Daitoku-ji. Nobunaga never became religious, but some Zen culture must have rubbed off on him by association. He began to dress less eccentrically and became less violent in nature, although in 1573 (fourth day of the fourth month), when some sections of Upper Kyoto refused to pay him a war tax, he ordered them burned. Their real crime was supporting the Shogun Yoshiaki, whom Nobunaga now considered his enemy. A few days earlier Nobunaga had destroyed several other districts of the capital, from Shimogamo to Saga. It is quite likely that the Daitoku-ji abbots wooed him over bowls of tea so he would not burn their compound.

One of Nobunaga's constant worries was the power of the Buddhist clergy. Daitoku-ji was not armed, but the Tendai sect was, and so he destroyed the latter's temples on Mount Hiei by encircling them with troops and burning all the buildings—and the priests within them. This was about the time that Nobunaga corresponded with Christian missionaries and signed himself "Satan Nobunaga." Despite his antireligious attitudes, Nobunaga was able to enjoy the tea ceremony within the walled compound of Daitoku-ji. It strikes an ironical note that one of his Daitoku-ji tea guests was to cause Nobunaga's suicide and another guest would preach at his funeral ceremony. The atheist Nobunaga would be buried within Daitoku-ji and the ashes of the tea master Rikyū would be deposited a few hundred yards to the east.

During Daitoku-ji's two hundred and fiftieth anniversary in 1575–76, a great celebration was held and Nobunaga honored the temple by giving it more rice lands. In addition, when he cancelled his debts by means of the *tokusei* edict, those to Daitoku-ji were not included, so its capital funds did not suffer. No-

bunaga had by this time deposed the puppet shogun and was absolute dictator.

Nobunaga decided that the tea ceremony should be a pleasure restricted to the elite, rather than a purely religious ritual, and so he issued an order that his subordinate generals could not hold a *cha-no-yu* party unless he gave them permission. The simple ceremony had become the ultimate privilege of the most powerful people in Japan. Of course Zen priests and ordinary tea enthusiasts could hold private tea ceremonies, but generals dared not do so without his permission. Once permission was granted, they could continue to serve tea unless Nobunaga revoked the privilege. It was almost poetic justice that Nobunaga met his death after attending a night tea ceremony in a Kyoto Buddhist temple. He was surrounded by a superior force under his old tea companion, Akechi Mitsuhide, and committed ritual suicide to avoid falling into the general's hands.

Within a week Mitsuhide had sent emissaries to Daitoku-ji and the Five Mountain Temples of Zen, and given them a present of a hundred silver coins each to win their favor, while the imperial court had received even more money. Within eleven days, however, Hideyoshi, who was off in the west on a campaign against the Mōri generals, had heard the news of Nobunaga's death, made a truce with them, and hurried back. It is interesting that Nobunaga, knowing that the campaign would be a difficult one, had loaned Hideyoshi his personal tea master, Rikyū, to help him relax between battles. Hideyoshi hastened back to Kyoto where he defeated Mitsuhide and became the new man of power. Japan was to have no shogun for some decades because Hideyoshi was too lowborn to be given this rank, though other imposing titles were thought up for him.

As has been seen, Mitsuhide, like all the leading military men, had been a tea devotee, and this is underlined by the legend that on seeing from his Sakamoto Castle lookout that he would lose the battle of Yamasaki, he lowered sixty of his choicest tea utensils to the ground, after wrapping them carefully in silk brocade coverlets, before setting fire to the castle and fleeing (he was killed nearby). Among the articles said to be saved in this way were celadon and *temmoku* teabowls, the pottery incense burner "Chidori," the famous tea caddy "Nara-shiba," and paintings suitable for the tea ceremony. Akechi surrendered them to Hideyoshi saying, "These treasures, in truth, belong to the world."

Nobunaga's death in 1582 left a vacuum in the power hierarchy in Japan that was eventually filled by Hideyoshi. It was fortunate for Daitoku-ji that he was a man who loved tea, knew and respected its chief abbot, Kokei, and admired Rikyū. Hideyoshi was the cleverest of Nobunaga's generals, but he was not a blood relative, an important disadvantage in a country that places great stress on lineage. He was of the peasant class, while Nobunaga had twelve sons! The eldest had been killed by assassins at Nijō Castle, but the second and third sons were eager to succeed. A conference was held at Kiyoshi, a town near Kyoto, but the two sons began quarreling. Hideyoshi went into the next room and, scooping up into his arms the eldest son's baby boy, he announced, "Here is the successor, and I will be his protector." Even after this, however, the succession was not beyond dispute. A hundred days after his death, Nobunaga's sister held a memorial service at Myōshin-ji in his honor. Hideyoshi, not to be outdone by a blood relative, arranged through Chief Abbot Kokei to have a memorial funeral service for Nobunaga at Daitoku-ji. This was held on the fifteenth day of the tenth month of 1582; Nobunaga's sons were not invited. Hideyoshi now gave Daitoku-ji ten thousand *koku* (a *koku* represents five bushels of rice a year) of rice land for Sōken-in, a subtemple to be built there in Nobunaga's honor. The painter Tōhaku, the most talented

independent artist in Japan, was asked to decorate the walls of Nobunaga's memorial chapel with birds and flowers, monkeys, which were his speciality, and landscape paintings. He was a friend of Rikyū and his appointment as artist may well have been on Rikyū's recommendation. Hideyoshi, for the decoration of his subsequent palaces and his mother's temple at Daitoku-ji used the Kanō family, particularly Eitoku, who had worked for his predecessor, Nobunaga.

As Hideyoshi's seizure of power progressed smoothly, he regarded Daitoku-ji with increasing gratitude for its support. Through association with its Zen circle, he must have felt an aura of culture, even though he was born a peasant. He decided to build a mortuary temple for his mother, who was still living though elderly, and the site was naturally Daitoku-ji. The first building did not satisfy him, so he gave this to the Mōri generals who had signed a truce with him (this is now the religious hall of Daitoku-ji's subtemple of Ōbai-in). Hideyoshi ordered a much larger main hall, or *hondō*, for his mother's memorial services, and commissioned Kanō Eitoku to decorate its walls with landscapes, bamboo, pines, and chrysanthemums in the bright and colorful Momoyama "grand manner." Kanō Eitoku had developed this colorful style in 1566 at the Daitoku-ji subtemple of Jukō-in, and had subsequently used it to decorate the walls of Nobunaga's castle at Azuchi in the 1570's. Now, in the 1580's, Hideyoshi wanted it used for his mother's mortuary temple, to be named Tenzui-ji, meaning "Temple of Heavenly Happiness." This was the largest of all subsidiary temples to be built at Daitoku-ji and was probably somewhat in the manner of Nijō Castle's living quarters, only not so garish. Unfortunately, when the Japanese government cut off all support of Buddhism around 1868, it could not be maintained, and Chief Abbot Bokuju sold its mural decorations and even its architecture. Today it is impossible to trace what became of these or if they still exist. Hideyoshi's younger brother also realized that Daitoku-ji was the most prestigious site for a mortuary temple, and built one there for himself, though it was sold at about the same time.

In the decade of the 1580's, Daitoku-ji's compound was busy with workmen as never before or since. In 1585 Hideyoshi held a large tea party, or *chakai*, at Daitoku-ji, and put Rikyū in charge of it. One can assume that the higher clergy at Daitoku-ji, who had managed to prevent Nobunaga from burning their temple, now cooperated fully with Hideyoshi, for his hand held a golden wand—and safety. Surely he would never burn the compound that included his mother's mortuary temple and also his predecessor's grave and temple, the temple that had supported his succession by holding the memorial service for Nobunaga within its grounds.

With the money donated by Hideyoshi, who was now the absolute ruler of Japan, a ceremonial breakfast and chanting were offered daily to Nobunaga's wooden effigy in the central niche of his mortuary temple. In this way did the antireligious general, who feared no one, secular or sacred, have his memory preserved at a Zen temple. Nobunaga's grave, his chair of state, and other mementos are still kept at Sōken-in whose recent building stands adjacent to Jukō-in, where Rikyū's ashes are buried, and where chants each morning are intoned to Miyoshi, the general who ruled Kyoto for ten years before Nobunaga came to power.

If Nobunaga had enjoyed Daitoku-ji occasionally, Hideyoshi now cultivated it assiduously. Not only did he hold the *chakai* there, but he also conceived a highly ambitious plan around 1587. He decided to build a huge temple, to outshine anything in Kyoto, and put Kokei in charge as its chief abbot. The new temple was to be just south of the present Daitoku-ji, located on top of Funaoka Hill, and it would honor Nobunaga (and, incidentally, its sponsor Hideyoshi).

Since there was an important lake, Rokubei-no-ike, in the way, Hideyoshi proposed building a bridge across it, so the two temples could become "twin Zen centers." This might be interpreted as part of Hideyoshi's move toward a political unification of Japan using the imperial temple of Daitoku-ji as a pivot. Hideyoshi had first accepted a low court rank from the emperor and seemed to respect the imperial family more than previous military rulers.

The reigning emperor, Ōgimachi, was pleased with this idea of expanding Daitoku-ji, the imperial prayer temple of his ancestors. Hideyoshi, who had been studying with Rikyū, served tea to Emperor Ōgimachi as a sign of his cultural competence, and received an even higher court rank, until he became "Great Prince" (Taikō) and finally "Regent" (Kampaku).

Just at this point in the 1580's, when Daitoku-ji seemed about to become the largest Zen temple in Japan through the twin Zen temple idea, a setback occurred, probably resulting from intertemple political bickering. The abbot of the subtemple of Sangen-in became jealous of Abbot Kokei. He, Abbot Shun'oku, cultivated Hideyoshi's right-hand man, Ishida Mitsunari, or it may have been the other way around. In any case, Ishida had served Hideyoshi since he was thirteen and had risen to become his most trusted general by the late 1580's. Apparently Ishida Mitsunari was very jealous of Abbot Kokei, who was now slandered and forced to go into exile on Kyushu Island, three hundred miles to the west of the capital city.

Daitoku-ji was now in the middle of political intrigue. At this time Hideyoshi had two major wives among the many women in his household. The older wife, Kita Mandokoro, was serious, religious, and at his death became a Zen nun, the custom for childless wives of important men. His much younger and prettier wife, although not yet twenty, was already politically active. This girl, Yodogimi, did not favor too much influence from Rikyū or his Zen friends. Her partisan was Ishida Mitsunari, who had brought about Abbot Kokei's banishment and stopped the building of the twin Zen centers. Subsequently Yodogimi bore Hideyoshi a son, his first offspring, though legend suggests that Ishida Mitsunari may have been the father.

Another interesting legend exists that Rikyū gave Abbot Kokei a farewell tea ceremony before his departure, using Hideyoshi's new "Palace of Assembled Pleasures" as its setting. This would have been a defiant gesture toward the dictator, who was off on a campaign. Rikyū probably reasoned that Kokei had done no wrong except to get in the middle of a political squabble. He admired Abbot Kokei rather than Abbot Shun'oku, and in about a year and a half was able to persuade Hideyoshi to recall Abbot Kokei. But the plan for the twin Zen centers had been abandoned by then. Hideyoshi gave the main Daitoku-ji temple an additional one thousand five hundred *koku* of rice land, enough to feed one thousand five hundred monks three meals a day for one year. Although records were not kept, it can be assumed that Daitoku-ji's population was probably three hundred and its area was about a hundred acres. At this time the abbots of its subsidiary temples were either from the families of court nobles, wealthy Sakai merchants associated with tea, or sons of samurai with good connections at court. It was the most prosperous Zen compound in Japan, thanks to Hideyoshi and to tea.

Its art collection was also expanding rapidly. About this time Daitoku-ji received a handsome present of art from Hideyoshi, a hundred hanging silk scrolls depicting "Five Hundred Venerable Disciples," painted in 1178 by two Southern Sung dynasty artists for a temple just south of the seaport of Ning-p'o, China. Hideyoshi had originally intended these ancient religious paintings for a "Great Buddha Temple" he

was then erecting, but he asked Rikyū, his tea master and art expert, what he should do with the scrolls. Rikyū suggested Daitoku-ji as the most logical recipient and the safest place in Japan. The "Great Buddha Temple" in fact was later destroyed in an earthquake, but because of Rikyū the scrolls are still extant and exhibited (five per year) each mid-October at Mushiboshi.

Rikyū was approaching old age, and began to think about his own grave site. He gave the subtemple of Jukō-in a rice field producing seven *koku* of rice a year, and a stone lantern to be used as his grave marker. Rikyū's income as Hideyoshi's tea master was three thousand *koku* a year, so he could not bequeath such large areas of rice land as the military. He gave Daitoku-ji, however, something far more precious—an artistic and aesthetic legacy.

Hideyoshi and Rikyū were still employer and employee, but a rift had begun to appear. Hideyoshi felt that he was the arbiter of Japanese taste, and he used tea ceremonies as though they were one form of military strategy. Rikyū, on the contrary, was something of a purist. In his long life he had witnessed the most incredible events, from Nobunaga's taking of the incense stick from the Shōsō-in Repository to Hideyoshi's tea extravaganzas. In his old age he was increasingly preoccupied with medieval Zen's stress on austerity. Rikyū, nearing seventy years of age, was a medieval man serving tea to Hideyoshi, who typified Japan's surging renaissance.

Since he was a layman and not a priest, Rikyū had built his house just outside Daitoku-ji's South Gate and for many decades he had been passing the half-finished Mountain Gate of the temple. The poet Sōchō had built the first story in the 1520's and a temporary roof had been put on. Rikyū, nearing the end of his life and seeing no progress being made on it, offered to pay for the completion of the second story. He asked his friend, the artist Tōhaku, to paint a huge dragon and flying angels on the ceiling boards. (Pl. 50). As for the central sculptural images, Rikyū searched out sixteen *rakan* sculptures of the Kamakura period, from the very temple where Daitō Kokushi had reached *satori* in 1308.

Kokei, who had returned from exile late in 1589, was very pleased. Since the tea master had been largely responsible for his pardon, Kokei felt particularly grateful to him. It is customary in a Zen building for a statue of the financial donor to be erected in a prominent position, and undoubtedly it was Kokei who directed that a life-sized wooden statue of Rikyū be carved and placed on the second floor of the Mountain Gate, as a gesture of gratitude to the tea master. The statue showed Rikyū in priestly garb, wearing wooden clogs.

Hideyoshi returned from a campaign and heard about this image, perhaps from Ishida Mitsunari, his right-hand man and the enemy of Kokei. Hideyoshi flew into a rage, saying that he and imperial visitors to Daitoku-ji would be on a lower level than this statue when they passed through the gate. He ordered the total destruction of the vast religious compound, and dispatched four generals to carry out his orders. These were Maeda Gen'i, Hosokawa Sansai, Maeda Toshiie and Tokugawa Ieyasu.

Kokei was then currently in charge of Sōken-in, Nobunaga's mortuary temple. He heard of the threat, and went forth in full priestly regalia to meet the generals. In his own calligraphy he recorded the ultimatum he gave them: "If you burn Daitoku-ji, I commit *seppuku* [ritual suicide]." The document is still preserved in Kōtō-in subtemple. None of these four generals wanted to carry out this destruction. Hosokawa Sansai already had plans to build a subtemple (Kōtō-in) here and make Daitoku-ji his final resting place. Sansai was Rikyū's personal tea student, albeit one of the greatest of military leaders. Furthermore, none of the four generals wanted to be held responsible for Abbot Kokei's suicide. He had taught Zen to both Rikyū and Hideyoshi. And suppose the dictator changed his mind tomorrow and blamed *them* for hasty action?

A compromise was reached. The statue of Rikyū was removed; the head was taken off and posted on the bridge to Hideyoshi's "Palace of Assembled Pleasures." The rest of the wooden effigy was thrown in the Kamo River. Daitoku-ji was spared.

No statue of Hideyoshi exists today in the Temple of Great Virtue, but another standing image of Rikyū, clothed in black priestly robes but this time in sandals, was given to the temple in the early twentieth century and is now on the second floor of the Mountain Gate, as originally planned by Kokei.

The Mountain Gate affair seems to have left scars that never healed on the strained relationship between Hideyoshi and Rikyū. Hideyoshi had a "golden tearoom" built, one that was collapsible so that it could be exhibited around the country to impress the populace. Apparently Rikyū had completely lost the aesthetic battle for a restrained type of tea ceremony. Perhaps Hideyoshi was also becoming jealous of his tea masters, for he ordered the Sakai tea master Yamanoue Sōji to be executed after having his ears and nose cut off. It is also said that he desired Rikyū's daughter, and was refused; she committed suicide on January 18, 1591. Four days later Hideyoshi's younger brother, Hidenaga, who was a devoted disciple of Rikyū, died. In February, 1591, Rikyū was put under house arrest in Sakai and ordered to commit ritual suicide. No specific charges are recorded. He was allowed to choose his time and locale. Historians still argue the exact cause, but the roots lay deep and the causes were many. Hideyoshi was not an easy man to live close to and Rikyū had tried to temper his moods and elevate his taste for a decade. Hideyoshi had the wealth of the whole country at his disposal; Rikyū was sure of his own aesthetic taste.

Hideyoshi's mother and his older wife, Kita Mandokoro, both offered to ask the ruler for Rikyū's pardon. Furthermore, Hosokawa Sansai visited him during his house arrest and volunteered his good offices. But Rikyū refused all offers. As a Zen Buddhist he believed that life was a continuum of moments of awareness, and the tea ceremony was a means of intensifying that awareness. Death, too, is only a moment, and part of that continuum. If, as Hideyoshi's tea master, he was unable to stem the drift of frivolity toward tea, then in his last moments he could set an example of the potentiality of awareness in the *wabi* tea ceremony.

On February 28, Rikyū served his last tea ceremony. He gave away various utensils to friends and disciples and then made a last bowl of tea for his guests. His two death poems, one in Chinese and one in Japanese, show an acceptance of death with calmness, almost relief.

The Chinese poem is:

> Over seventy years of life,
> What trouble and concern.
> Welcome, sword of eternity,
> Which slays all Buddhas, all Bodhidharmas.

The Japanese poem reads:

> The sword which has been
> Close at hand for so long,
> Now I toss into the sky.

The sword's movement in *seppuku* is across and upward. On the lid of the tea caddy he had just used, he wrote, "That which I always dreamed of is here: to go beyond this bothersome life into true Reality."

The tearoom, Kan-in (Pl. 10), located in the Jukō-in subtemple of Daitoku-ji, is said to be the room where Rikyū committed *seppuku*. A memorial tea service occurs here on the twenty-eighth of each month, with the fifteenth-generation descendants rotating the honor of being tea master, since three separate schools of tea have arisen from Rikyū. He has become unofficially canonized as a tea saint, not only of Daitoku-ji but of all Japan. Almost every educated Japanese knows where Rikyū is buried, whereas only a few historians are aware of where Hideyoshi's grave is. Who won the aesthetic battle that raged between them? As Abbot Tachibana Daiki has said, "His suicide was the smartest thing Rikyū ever did."

Confrontation with the Shogunate

The present-day abbots of Daitoku-ji place their founder, Daitō, in a special category for religious veneration, but the people of Japan long ago awarded the most fame to Ikkyū, and after him to Takuan. Thus, of the approximately five hundred abbots installed since 1338 when Daitō died, the forty-seventh, Ikkyū, and the one hundred and fifty-third, Takuan, stand out in popular memory, perhaps because of the flamboyant strength of their characters. It is not surprising then that they are alike in many ways. Both exemplify the freedom that comes with the *satori* experience; both exhibited an independence unrepressed by the rigidities of Japan's social system or the institutional weight of a vast monastery such as Daitoku-ji.

Takuan Sōhō (1573–1645) was the offspring of a poor samurai farmer while Ikkyū was an emperor's son, yet Zen brought them both to much the same outlook. Takuan was born the very year that Nobunaga overthrew the Ashikaga shogunate, and at the age of nine entered a Jōdo sect temple. At thirteen he moved to a Zen temple nearby, Sukyō-ji, and when twenty-one, in 1594, he arrived at Daitoku-ji to become Shun'oku's disciple. He lived at Sangen-in at a period when that temple was deeply involved in politics and so he must have soon learned how extensive intrigue and treachery were in Japanese affairs. For example, in 1599, Ishida Mitsunari, who had forced Hideyoshi to abandon the "twin Daitoku-ji" idea and sent Kokei into exile, invited Shun'oku and his disciple Takuan to his Sawayama Castle on the east side of Lake Biwa; yet only a year later Ishida was to die on the battlefield of Sekigahara.

In his life, Ikkyū, though he was born of the highest class of society, tended to associate with the ordinary people; Takuan, on the contrary, was to associate with the rich and powerful of the land, shoguns and emperors, the figures at the center of the political stage. Nevertheless he maintained his independence, even to the extent of being sent into exile for his views. Of his seventy-odd years, Takuan spent three in exile and eventually forced the shogunate to retreat from its position.

Like Ikkyū, Takuan gave religious instruction and taught ink painting, the precursor of what Hakuin and Sengai were to achieve. Like Ikkyū also, Takuan gave lessons in Zen to the Komparu line of Nō actors. Both men also wrote biographies of Daitoku-ji's founder and appear to have respected his Spartan spirit.

Although Emperor Go-Mizunoo became Takuan's pupil in Zen and tea ceremony, Takuan was not a professional tea master, though during his lifetime tea and Zen were extremely close, since Rikyū's descendants had not yet come to dominate the tea ceremony scene. Takuan's Zen master, Shun'oku, had taught Zen to the famous tea master Oribe, Rikyū's successor. When Takuan became Daitoku-ji's chief abbot, he simultaneously became abbot of the subtemple of Daisen-in, headquarters of the Northern branch of Daitoku-ji subtemples. This was the group of subsidiary temples that promoted the tea ceremony, as opposed to the Southern branch, under Ryōgen-in, which was not involved with tea.

Takuan became the chief abbot of the Daitoku-ji compound at thirty-six, an unprecedentedly youthful age. Ikkyū had become chief abbot at eighty, the oldest in its records. Both men, however, show great similarity in their tastes and determination; both hated the formalism for which Daitoku-ji stood. Takuan expressed his disgust dramatically by resigning the post of chief abbot abruptly. Some records state that he only occupied the position for three days; others allow six days. In either case, he declared that he "could not live like a bird in a gilded cage." His concept of freedom, like Ikkyū's, demanded a wanderer's life, and Ikkyū's example may well have been an inspiration to him. At one point toward the end of his life, Takuan stayed two years at the Shūon-an temple outside Nara, where Ikkyū's grave is located. Perhaps Takuan liked its quiet; even today it is very isolated.

As a man and a priest Takuan was extremely popular and had a number of Zen temples built, though he refused many invitations from daimyo to settle in their provinces. In one instance the mighty Hosokawa of Kyushu built a Zen temple for Takuan, and when he refused to go there as founding abbot, a wooden effigy of him as founder was still put on the altar, so greatly was he respected. Another instance of his favor with the most powerful people in the land was his invitation by the scion of the Konoe family, Nobutada, the emperor's chief minister, to be his *rōshi*, or spiritual adviser, and to give him *sanzen* teaching, leading to enlightenment.

Despite all this, Takuan took the idea of humbleness very seriously. Sometimes he signed his calligraphy or paintings, "Done by the blind monk, who is nameless as grass." This was in keeping with Zen egolessness. A piece of calligraphy hanging in his room read:

> Why does one eat? Merely to satisfy hunger. If one is not hungry, there is no need to eat. People have the bad habit of saying they cannot eat food unless it is tasty. The Buddha himself said, "Take food as though it were medicine." What need is there for relishes?

Takuan's versatility matched Ikkyū's. He wrote many treatises, covering such subjects as Zen philosophy, swordsmanship, classical poetry and tea. In addition to his writings, Takuan won fame as a calligrapher, a potter and a swordsman. He instructed the most noted swordsman of his time, Miyamoto Musashi, in both ink play and swordsmanship. Furthermore, Takuan taught Zen fencing, or *kendō*, to the fencing teacher of the Tokugawa shogun, Iemitsu. Although Ikkyū and Takuan resented the institutionalism that Daitoku-ji represented to the point where they were forced to flee from it, when an emergency occurred each priest fought for Daitoku-ji's survival in his own way. Ikkyū gave the last measure of his life's energy to rebuild the compound after fire had totally wiped it out; Takuan fought to retain its allegiance to the emperor alone, and suffered exile as a result.

The cause of this protest lay in the tradition that began with the monastery's foundation in the early fourteenth century. Daitoku-ji's chief abbot had always received his commission directly from the reigning emperor because this was an imperially sanctioned compound. However, in 1628, the Tokugawa shogun placed this appointment under his control. Three Daitoku-ji abbots, Takuan, Gyokushitsu, and Kōgetsu, traveled to Tokyo to protest directly to the shogun about this usurpation of the emperor's prerogative. The shogun's answer was to exile Takuan to the northeast, Gyokushitsu to another distant province, and to send Kōgetsu back to Daitoku-ji. Emperor Go-Mizunoo then played his strongest card: he abdicated and turned the throne over to his seven-year-old daughter, perhaps to show that the throne was now without substance. The last woman to reign was almost a thousand years before!

Takuan made use of his three years of exile; he composed Nō plays and wrote poems in the manner of Ikkyū's *Kyōun-shū* (*Crazy Cloud Collection*). A daimyo built a special Zen hermitage for Takuan, which he named "Spring Rain Retreat" in reference to the bad political weather.

Upon the death of the second Tokugawa shogun, the successor, Iemitsu, invited both of the Daitoku-ji abbots to return from exile. According to legend, the shogun asked his fencing master, Yagyū, the secret of his superb swordsmanship and Yagyū said that it was due to practicing Zen under Takuan. True or not, Takuan and Shogun Iemitsu became well acquainted in 1635, while Takuan was staying with his disciple.

Iemitsu came to have tremendous respect for Takuan. He invited him to his castle often and even went to the extreme of erecting a large Zen temple in the Shinagawa district of Tokyo for him. This temple was Tōkai-ji, "Temple of All Japan," and was Tokyo's major Zen center. Takuan was invited to become its founding abbot and Kobori Enshū to design its garden. Takuan did spend much time there in his old age, but he never completely gave up traveling, for he attended many celebrations and dedicated many new Zen temples in various parts of the country. Such was his favor that Go-Mizunoo called him in audience to bestow upon him the title of "Teacher of the Country," or Kokushi, which previously had always been a posthumous honor. Takuan, however, refused, and suggested that this title be granted to Tettō, Daitoku-ji's first chief abbot; the emperor agreed. The quarrel between the shogunate and Daitoku-ji was officially patched up in 1641, when the imperial family regained the power to appoint Daitoku-ji's chief abbot.

One of the greatest fears of Takuan was that Buddhism would become the monopoly of the shogun, for the Tokugawa used the Buddhist temples of Japan to consolidate their own feudalism. Every family was compulsorily registered in a nearby temple, so that the Buddhist priests became census-takers and funeral directors. This was fatal to the spiritual development of Buddhism in general and to Zen in particular, until Hakuin tried to reverse the process in the eighteenth century. Daitoku-ji, however, because of its special position as an imperial temple was not assigned any parishioners. (Even today many of the townsmen who live only a block or two away have never been permitted inside the closed subtemples.)

During Takuan's last years he painted a great deal, with loose, free brushwork, avoiding sophisticated techniques. His calligraphy was also informal, and his ceramic teabowls do not fit into any strict category but are masterpieces nevertheless. There are several records of the Tokugawa shogun, accompanied by Kobori Enshū, his official tea master, going to Tōkai-ji to participate in a cha-no-yu, with Takuan as host.

The subtemple of Jukō-in owns a chinzō of Takuan as chief abbot of Daitoku-ji, but it shows simple steps made of Japanese wood rather than the elaborate Chinese-style footstool that every other abbot used. Above his portrait is a poem in his own hand, which, while not a death poem, suggests Takuan's direct attitude toward life's transience:

> Spring has passed;
> Autumn has come.
> The flowers have fallen;
> The birds cry.

Takuan, like Ikkyū before him, had refused to give inka, the written acknowledgment of satori, to any of his disciples, and on his deathbed in November, 1645, he would not follow convention and write a death poem. It is said that at length he drew with his finger the single ideograph yume, which means "dream," implying that life is only a shadow of reality. Previously he had written a set of "Final Instructions," or Yuikai, which it is interesting to compare with those of Daitō Kokushi on pages 31–32. Takuan's can be translated as follows:

> Bury my body in the mountain behind the
>   temple.
> Do not cover it over with soil; go away
>   [without a funeral ceremony].
> Do not chant sutras; do not construct an altar.
> Do not receive any obituary gifts.
> Do not prepare clothes or meals for the priests.

[All the above were customary for the Buddhist
      funeral of an important person]
Do not ask [the emperor] for a posthumous title.
Do not erect a tombstone, or even make a
      wooden mortuary tablet [ihai].
Do not write my biography.

But eighteenth-century Zen was so encrusted with
tradition that all the things Takuan requested not be
done were done. The only wish of his that was accorded was that the emperor not be asked for a title,
since, while alive, Takuan had refused the highest
title in Zen, that of "Teacher of the Country."

The tone of these "Final Instructions" recalls Ikkyū's
attitude, vividly expressed in poems attributed to him.
One is a dōka, a sort of moral poem that is easy to
understand, and can be translated thus:

Before I was born,
I never existed.
So when I die,
There's nothing either.

Another poem attributed to Ikkyū is:

From washing bowl [as a baby]
To washing bowl [as a corpse]
[Life is just] So much rigmarole!

The bullet train of the 1970's shoots out of Tokyo
Station and within less than three minutes passes
about fifteen feet from a very strange, upright stone,
part of the cemetery of the Zen temple of Tōkai-ji,
now bisected by the new railway line. This single
stone marker is unengraved, but it is shaped in the
form of a pickle, a tribute to Takuan as well as to
Zen humor. For almost daily the average Japanese
eats a pickle that Takuan devised when he decided to
find a way to utilize each autumn's more than adequate crop of daikon, or giant radish. Like Ikkyū,
who added nattō (fermented beans) to the meager diet
of a Zen monastery, Takuan added a pickle to perk
up the rice, and its name, takuan (after his Buddhist
pseudonym) has become part of the Japanese language.
If, in spite of his wishes, Takuan had to have a tombstone, perhaps this is the most appropriate.

3

THE TEA CEREMONY

On entering a tearoom, one should be free from differentiation between oneself and others. One should be reverent, sincere, pure in heart and quiet.

Murata Shukō (1422–1502)

What is cha-no-yu *but boiling water, making it and drinking it with Buddha-mind?*

Sen no Rikyū (1521–91)

A Tradition of Six Centuries

In the emptiness of the tearoom lie infinite possibilities. Buddhism believes that its doctrines should be expounded in accordance with the capacity of each individual to understand, and thus there are many levels of Buddhist revelation, from simple to sophisticated. These are termed "skillful means," or *upaya* in Sanskrit and *hōben* in Japanese. The metaphysical level of Buddhist enlightenment is brought down to the realm of the concrete or particular through the Zen tea ceremony—that is, when it has no commercial implications. This religious type of tea ceremony is here called Zen tea to distinguish it from the more common tea ceremony used as a means of social intercourse. In the late fifteenth century, under Ikkyū's inspiration, the drinking of tea became a means of teaching Zen on an experiential level, without words, but in an aesthetic realm where silence can be more freighted with meaning.

In architecture, Japanese Zen adopted the Sung Chinese vertical-axial style, yet it also incorporated the native Japanese low-slung style; in a similar way, the Rinzai temple of Daitoku-ji adopted the formal Sung temple style of drinking tea in *temmoku* tea-bowls before an image of Bodhidharma, the founder of Zen, and then adapted it to suit a more intimate ceremony. The exact nature of the Chinese tea ceremony is unknown, except that it was a religious ritual, performed in silence and with great formality.

In Japan the legendary origins of the tea ceremony go back to Daiō in the thirteenth century (teacher of Daitō, the founder of Daitoku-ji). He spent five years studying Zen in China and brought back a lacquer stand (*daisu*) for serving tea. Presumably, in his time and that of Daitō, tea was drunk from imported *temmoku* bowls in front of a statue or painting of Bodhidharma in the formal Chinese manner. Seeds for the tea bushes are said to have been brought from China by Eisai, the founder of Japanese Rinzai Zen, and as the plants flourished and tea became more plentiful, tea drinking was adopted as an elegant pastime by the upper classes.

Even as late as 1450, drinking tea was still only an aristocratic game, wagers being made on one's ability to guess the provenance of the tea leaves, with wine, women and communal bathing as the finale. Yet by 1490 a completely different atmosphere was associated with it: it had become a profoundly moving religious or aesthetic experience performed in the silence of a dimly lit tearoom. This change came about through Ikkyū and his pupil Shukō, and the patronage of Shogun Yoshimasa. During the centuries since, the tea ceremony has drifted down to the level of ordinary people in accordance with their depth of Zen understanding. It is for this reason that the major present-day schools of tea look to Daitoku-ji as their mecca. This Temple of Great Virtue became the Zen center of a movement that made the tea ceremony aesthetically fashionable, if not always spiritual. Today the tea ceremony is flourishing in all gradations, from misappropriation by social climbers to, ideally, an ontological experience moving the individual to the bedrock of his being.

Three times a month, at their dawn chanting ceremonies, the abbots, in rotation, offer a cup of whipped powdered tea before the wooden statue of their founder, Daitō Kokushi, in the candle-lit shrine at Daitoku-ji's Headquarters Temple. In a sense, this sacred room, which no layman is allowed to enter, becomes a tearoom at that time.

The highpoint of the entire year at Daitoku-ji is November 22, Founder's Day. Then there is a two-hour-long, rigidly formal ceremony in the Doctrine Hall, which is otherwise not used. About three hundred dignitaries attend, including abbots from all the branch temples. The climactic moment occurs when the Grand Master of one of Japan's three leading tea schools whips a bowl of powdered tea, and this teabowl is presented by a young monk before the altar and effigy of Daitō Kokushi (Pl. 58). The hands that whip this bowl of tea are secular; the hands that carry it to the statue belong to a future abbot. Thus both the secular and the religious worlds acknowledge the importance of *cha-no-yu*, so ordinary, yet so miraculous.

Zen means, in essence, total experience, and total awareness summarizes *cha-no-yu* neatly. Preparing and drinking a cup of powdered tea can be a religious act in secular clothing. For Zen recognizes ordinary actions to be equally important as acts normally designated "spiritual." According to Zen, mopping floors or cleaning toilets can be as religious a sacrament as chanting sutras or practicing *zazen*. Drinking tea, a mundane action, can represent the spiritual dimension made concrete in the everyday world.

The ritual of the tea ceremony was developed in the mid-fifteenth century when Zen's early habits stressing simplicity had been lost through an excess of wealth and power. The Ashikaga shogun's mortuary Zen temple of Shōkoku-ji was particularly corrupt. Less rich, Daitoku-ji was also less vulnerable to corruption, but, even so, Ikkyū in his poetic writings lamented that Zen needed to be brought back to its core of simple living. He evolved the tea ceremony as a means for emphasizing this aspect.

Ideas germinate in freedom and solitude, and Ikkyū enjoyed both during the Ōnin War, when he stayed at Shūon-an, near Nara. Here he taught a former Nara priest, Murata Shukō, so much about Zen aesthetics that a few years later Shukō became the first official tea master to a Japanese ruler, serving the Shogun Yoshimasa at his retirement temple villa, the Silver Pavilion.

Zen tea was born in Shukō's mind with Ikkyū serving as catalyst. From training under Ikkyū, Shukō learned Zen's preference for action over words, its

respect for the negative, or Void—the emptiness that holds potential for action. He combined these qualities with Zen quiet and forms of Japanese etiquette already in existence; stress was placed on awareness of the potential of the tactile, auditory and visual senses.

To follow the artistic evolution of *cha-no-yu*, the understanding of one word is absolutely essential: *wabi*. Today the term implies the highest possible praise for an object from a follower of *cha-no-yu*, yet this word is so imbued with Zen wordlessness that it is difficult to define. Attempts to render it into English, such as "rustic simplicity," "refined poverty," or "naturalness tinged with restraint," are inadequate.

The term *wabi* represented an ideal, but over the centuries the word assumed different nuances for various tea masters. The aesthetic concept of *wabi* itself changed, and tracing its evolution reveals the history of the tea ceremony. In the middle and late fifteenth century Ikkyū was the leading exponent of *wabi* aesthetics. Even his paintings never depend on color but rather on black alone, and they are far more eloquent in their voids than in their forms. *Wabi* lies in this, in the rejection of everything pretentious and gaudy; it consists instead of seeking the simplest expressions, those that are closest to nature.

The idea of understatement is implicit in late fifteenth-century *wabi*. Ikkyū, besides giving the idea of *wabi* simplicity to Shukō for the tea ceremony, taught him to create simple gardens of rock and gravel. Ikkyū inspired another follower of his, Komparu Zenchiku, to write about the relationship of *wabi* gardens to Nō drama, of which Komparu was to become a leading exponent. The Nō's action of "no-action" stems from Zen and the *wabi* canon, which is basically the Zen Void worked out into material forms of artistic beauty. Ikkyū did not believe in giving certificates of enlightenment, or *inka*, to any of his followers, but he did give them samples of his own calligraphy, another form of recognition.

And to Shukō, who must have been among his favorites, he gave an ancient piece of calligraphy by Engo (Hsueh-tou in Chinese), the Sung author of *Hekigan Roku* (Blue Cliff Record), a rare gift and certainly an acknowledgment of the depth of Shukō's understanding of Zen.

Shukō is said to have used this in his tearoom *tokonoma* (alcove), and from this sprang the idea that calligraphy, especially by Sung- or Yüan-dynasty scholars of Zen, is the most appropriate art form for display at tea ceremonies. Today, when such ancient works are impossible to obtain, calligraphy by a Zen master from Daitoku-ji is considered a good substitute: it is thought to contribute a further religious dimension to the atmosphere of the tearoom.

In the *Shukō Mondō* by Ikkyū, it is recorded that Shogun Yoshimasa asked his official tea master, Shukō, to explain the essense of tea and the reply was as follows:

> On entering a tearoom, one should be free from differentiation between oneself and others. One should cultivate in one's heart the virtue of subtle harmony. It begins with a mutual communication between friends, and leads, eventually, to the ideal of universal harmony. One should be reverent, sincere, pure in heart, and quiet.

All these qualities reflect Zen and point to the reverential attitude of Shukō toward an essentially religious experience. In particular, his words "free from differentiation between oneself and others" are a simple expression of *satori*'s freedom from categories and discrimination.

Presumably Shukō's life at the Silver Pavilion in the service of Ashikaga Yoshimasa was quite a frustrating period in his life. He had acquired ideals of *wabi* from Ikkyū, worked out in a quiet country temple, but in this shogunal villa the atmosphere adulated everything sumptuous that was imported from China. Sketches exist of the arrangements for serving tea under Yoshimasa: the host sat in a chair imported from China, in front of a lacquered stand called a *daisu*, with various bronze vessels to hold water, and Chinese-style, multitiered, square lacquer boxes for sweets. A lacquer tray held six tiny wine cups on miniature stands, and beside these stood two larger-sized *temmoku* teabowls, also raised high on lacquer pedestals. In such an environment Shukō could only introduce his *wabi* ideas gradually. He discarded the Chinese celadon teabowls that had been a prized import, because their delicate jade green glazes made the powdered tea look muddy, and gradually the black-glazed *temmoku*, with golden iridescent "oil spots," came to be more highly valued in tea circles.

Even Yoshimasa, for all his extravagant tastes, seems to have caught glimpses of what "refined poverty" might involve. A poem has survived, attributed to him:

> If someone asks for me,
> Tell him I am leading a *wabi* life,
> In the mountains.

Yoshimasa's "mountains" were the wooded foothills of Higashiyama to the east of Kyoto, where his Silver Pavilion was located.

Shukō left five rules of conduct, which all suggest that he opposed the former pretentious style of tea and the gambling type, and gained his main principles from Zen temple life:

1. Be natural and quiet.
2. Sparse and simple decoration.
3. Simple incense.
4. Utensils in accordance with the guest's age.
5. Calmness and serenity, with "one-pointedness" for host and guest.

This "one-pointedness" is *zammai* in Japanese, from the Sanskrit word *samadhi*. It is a state of concentration that leads to *satori*.

The concavity of the teabowl, the hollowness that is formed by its clay walls, gives Void, to be filled and used. The emptiness of the tearoom is a Void to be filled with action. As Kobori Nanrei, abbot of Ryōkō-in, said recently, "The benefit of being is when non-being functions; this is the operation of Void or no-thingness."

While Zen tea was becoming popular among Kyoto's aristocracy, it was being given firm economic support by Sakai merchants. Ikkyū had been on intimate terms with leading Sakai merchants, perhaps because these men were more receptive than other Japanese. From the time of Ikkyū on, Daitoku-ji and Sakai port were closely connected. In fact, Nanshū-ji, the first Zen temple to be built in Sakai, was a branch of Daitoku-ji. A single chief abbot served both temples, with most of the donations for his inauguration coming from Sakai merchants. In return these wealthy cosmopolitan men realized that having a son become a Daitoku-ji priest opened up the most culturally advanced future to them. The early major tea masters were all from Sakai families, who studied Zen with Daitoku-ji abbots. The five most important tea masters in Japanese history and their connections with Daitoku-ji are:

Tea master	Zen master
Murata Shukō	Ikkyū Sōjun (forty-seventh chief abbot of Daitoku-ji)
Takeno Jōō	Dairin (ninetieth chief abbot)
Sen no Rikyū	Shōrai (hundred and seventh chief abbot) and Kokei (hundred and seventeeth chief abbot)
Furuta Oribe	Shun'oku (hundred and forty-seventh chief abbot)
Kobori Enshū	Shun'oku (hundred and forty-seventh chief abbot) and Kōgetsu (hundred and fifty-sixth chief abbot)

These five tea masters each introduced slightly different variations in their interpretation of *wabi*. Shukō talked of the "poverty of the natural" to a ruler who had been quite removed from such things in his earlier life. The chapter of tea's evolution represented by Jōō is obscure, but he acted as a bridge to Rikyū, who was deeply versed in Zen and studied it under two masters. Although not a priest himself, he was able to embody the essence of Zen into his refinement of the tea ceremony as he influenced architecture, garden art, and ceramics.

If Shukō had gone a certain way to translating Ikkyū's *wabi* aesthetics in Yoshimasa's time, it was left to Rikyū to fully realize this artistic symbolization of Zen's basic concept of emptiness. In its development from Shukō to Rikyū, the tea ceremony experienced a scaling-down of the size of the tearoom, an elimination of expensive imported ceramics, an abandonment of the *daisu* stand, and an evolution in garden design that resulted in it being little more than a pathway of stones with a hand-washing basin in Rikyū's time. All these tendencies reduced the sumptuousness of the ceremony, so that the guest was left with only the barest aesthetic framework and his concentration focused on a minimum of form.

The term, *cha-no-yu* means literally "tea's hot water," and this is the one act vital to the ceremony; symbolically a human being's whole life is concentrated into this single act of making tea with hot water. The Zen Void is the skeletal environment (the walls of the tea hut, the sides of the teabowl) and Zen immediacy is the creative act itself, which flows out from within this Void. The tea master is the Zen master of the moment and his guests are his disciples, and thus the personal relationship of master to guest is as intimate and as important as within a Zen temple. The tea ceremony becomes a type of religious experience and is truly an *upaya*, a "skillful means" of conveying Zen to those who cannot spend years within a temple. The closeness to nature that Zen absorbed from Taoism is represented by the *sabi* elements, those articles that have matured or aged in harmony with nature and are beyond man's control. The *wabi* elements are within his control and are shown in his choice of the simplest articles as opposed to luxurious ones, an application of the Zen concept of self-discipline, or *shugyō*.

For a brief period in the history of tea ceremony, this was the spirit in which it was performed, and learning tea was learning Zen. But as time passed, the ceremony became a dilettante's amusement or a vehicle for ostentation. The tearoom became a gathering place of social climbers, not enlightened beings.

Of the many sensory stimuli of the tea ceremony, the primary focus is on the teabowl itself. The term *wabi* is difficult to apply to a *temmoku* teabowl, specked with gold and reflecting the gorgeousness of a starry nebula at night. But in contrast to a Sung celadon bowl or a Ming bowl with blue and white painted patterns, it is *wabi*, since black represents Void, and the fortuitous effects of the glazing and firing are the only decoration of a *temmoku* bowl and could be considered natural *sabi* effects. Rikyū, however, desired a ceramic ware that more clearly epitomized these two qualities, a teabowl whose primary appeal was tactile and only visual secondarily.

He also wished to shift from Chinese imported ware, which was extremely expensive in the late sixteenth century to a native product and thus he began patronizing the potter Chōjirō and asked him to make teabowls more in keeping with *wabi* tea. Rikyū had used *temmoku* bowls many times, and recognized their two greatest disadvantages. First

their conical shape did not leave enough room for the bamboo whisk to move freely, and thus undesirable dregs were left at the bottom; the *raku* bowls that he inspired Chōjirō to make are much larger around the bottom. Secondly, instead of smooth, curving sides, *raku* ware's hand-shaped, straighter sides enhance the tactile potential; the guest can grasp the bowl more firmly and feel the irregularities that are a part of their *wabi*, their humble unpretentiousness. Furthermore, because of their shape, *raku* bowls retain the heat better than the open *temmoku* bowls.

Before Rikyū's time, the Seto kilns had tried making *temmoku* of a sort, since Chinese *temmoku* was scarce and Japanese pirates were the only means of obtaining them when relations between the two countries deteriorated. The earliest Japanese Seto-made *temmoku* teabowl was used by Ikkyū and Bokusai, the first abbot of Shinju-an, and it is still preserved there (Pl. 17). Another Shinju-an treasure is the thirty-five black *temmoku* teabowls made at a Seto kiln. These date from 1523 and show that experimentation to find a native-made bowl, preferably black like *temmoku*, was already underway before Rikyū found a solution.

After his death, Rikyū continued to influence tea taste in ceramics through pupils such as Hosokawa Sansai, who went to Korea at the head of Hideyoshi's army and brought back with him stone lanterns and teabowls. He was one of the most able of Rikyū's disciples and for many years harbored the desire to retire to Kōtō-in, a subtemple he built within Daitoku-ji for his father's retirement. The fact that leading generals were picking up Korean peasants' irregular rice bowls and treasuring this straightforward quality proves that the concept of poverty aesthetics had permeated the social fabric of Japan. It is not surprising that of the small number of these sixteenth-century bowls (known as *ido* ware) that survive, many are housed within Daitoku-ji; of these most are found at Ryōkō-in, founded in the memory of General Kuroda Yoshitaka (1546–1604), who led the vanguard when Korea was invaded in 1592. The son of Tsuda Sōkyū, who was tea master to Hideyoshi along with Rikyū, became founding abbot of Ryōkō-in under the Buddhist name of Kōgetsu. Since his father had been both a tea master and a Sakai merchant, Kōgetsu (1574–1643) had excellent taste in tea ceramics. He had studied Zen under Chief Abbot Shun'oku and at thirty-seven had become chief abbot himself. He proved such a dynamic leader that he was recalled to be chief abbot a second time and was instrumental in getting the main halls rebuilt at that time as part of Daitoku-ji's tercentenary. All of these buildings still stand today.

Although Kōgetsu added to Ryōkō-in's original collection of Korean ceramics, his main contribution to the subtemple's collection was its two most famous teabowls: a *yuteki*, or "oil spot" bowl (Pl. 19), and the *yōhen temmoku*, a bowl that will be called here "Starry Firmament" (*yō* referring to light, either sunlight or starlight, and *hen* meaning changing). No photograph can capture the beauty of this bowl in Ryōkō-in because it changes as one turns it in the light. It twinkles with a new and different beauty each second, creating a rarefied universe of its own, far beyond pottery's normal potential.

Some connoisseurs term Ryōkō-in's "Starry Firmament" teabowl (Pl. 18) "wealthy man's *wabi*" to distinguish it from the "poverty *wabi*" of Ikkyū or Rikyū, while purists say the two concepts (wealth and *wabi*) are incompatible. This bowl is wrapped carefully in three layers of brocade cloth and is lovingly examined about once a year. Ryōkō-in's famous Korean *ido* bowl also has an appreciative audience whenever it is unwrapped. Usually this occurs in October at Mushiboshi, when the Mu Ch'i paintings are also shown. These, too, are a legacy of Kōgetsu from the time of Ryōkō-in's founding.

Of Daitoku-ji's extensive ceramic collection, beside the "Starry Firmament" of Ryōkō-in, Kohō-an's Korean rice bowl was selected as an illustration because it enjoys a national reputation as being extremely *wabi* in taste. Made by an anonymous potter and probably used as an everyday household container before being brought back by a *wabi*-trained general, this simple stoneware bowl is the ultimate example of the discovery of beauty in what many would discard. However, this bowl (Pl. 20) may never even have been used in Korea because there is a horizontal scorch mark due to its being too close to another object in the kiln. It is warped and the lines of its simple outflaring lip are irregular. This is no "Starry Firmament" but a dull or pale loquat-yellow glaze. Its surface has an irregular shark's skin-like crackle produced by the shrinking of the glaze in the firing, and its bottom is irregular (Pl. 21). The Yabunouchi Tea School, founded by a follower of Rikyū, places this bowl at the very pinnacle of all tea ceramics in Japan, as do many other followers of "poverty *wabi*," as opposed to "wealthy *wabi*." In ranking it so high, the fact that it was made for daily use, rather than as a tea ceremony bowl, is an important element. The fact that this teabowl reflects the "instant moment" in its scorch mark, and that its glaze harmonizes with nature's colors all contribute to its *wabi* value.

The name of this famous teabowl is "Kizaemon-ido" and legend recounts that one Japanese owner was named Kizaemon. His wife contracted a facial tumor, so he sold it to Matsudaira Fumai, a man noted for his interest in tea. When the wife of this noble tea man also contracted a tumor, it seemed more than a coincidence. Fumai gave the bowl to his son Gettan, who subsequently suffered from boils and so, in 1804, it was given to Kohō-an, Kobori Enshū's memorial temple, in the hope that the sanctity of the place would counteract the malignant spirit that seemed to be residing in the teabowl. It is now too famous to be used in the tea ceremony, and the ghosts, Korean or otherwise, seem to have been laid to rest.

The craze for Korean ceramics reached its peak in the two campaigns of Hideyoshi in 1592 and 1597, and numerous potters were brought back to establish kilns in Japan, particularly in Kyushu. Indeed, this war is sometimes called the "Pottery War," since no soil changed hands and its only lasting effects were on the ceramics of Japan.

The whole country came to revere *cha-no-yu* in the decade from Hideyoshi's giant tea party held at Kitano in 1587 to the second Korean war and Hideyoshi's death shortly thereafter. The homage that Nobunaga, Hideyoshi and Tokugawa Ieyasu paid to their tea masters, all of whom had studied Zen with Daitoku-ji abbots, also gave Daitoku-ji added glamor in the public eye. There is no agreement on the date of the peak of the tea ceremony, but the American author feels that it probably came around 1585, at the tea party held at Daitoku-ji under Rikyū, when Hideyoshi was planning to make Daitoku-ji a sort of national Zen temple and *cha-no-yu* was the major preoccupation of his life. This would be before the rift between Hideyoshi and Rikyū, before the magnificence of the Juraku-dai, the "Palace of Assembled Pleasures," when *raku* ware was in its infancy, when the ruler's favorite tearooms were the two-mat Taian of Myōki-an and the "Mountain Village" of Osaka Castle, when Kokei was chief abbot of Daitoku-ji and the leaders of the nation looked toward *cha-no-yu* for their spiritual uplift.

After 1585, Rikyū gradually lost his battle to make *wabi* tea a pure Zen experience. Politics became hopelessly entangled with tea, and Daitoku-ji was almost destroyed amid the partisan rivalries. Rikyū committed suicide in 1591, but the decline of tea was prevented from becoming precipitous by two men,

Oribe and Enshū, who had studied Zen under chief abbots Kokei and Kōgetsu respectively. However, when the Tokugawa family was in power, they attempted to formalize every aspect of life according to rules, and this tendency was gradually to affect the tea ceremony.

Rikyū's leading pupil, Furuta Oribe (1544–1615), succeeded to Rikyū's position with Hideyoshi, and then served as tea master to the first Tokugawa shogun, Iemitsu, until Oribe, too, was ordered to commit suicide for disloyalty. Oribe is best remembered today for his influence on Japanese ceramics, for he supervised seven pottery kilns in the sense that he was their chief designer. His preference was for glazed areas of overlapping colors with geometric or floral designs painted freehand with iron-brown slip. His favorite color combination was a luminous olive green over a brownish cream with brown-black designs. In his search for novelty—perhaps a reflection of the ennui of the late Momoyama period—the clay slabs of the bowls were pulled into variations of round and square patterns, into angles, scallops, and other irregular shapes. The tea master had been drawn into active participation in the creation of tea ceremony utensils, a trend that was to increase as time passed.

Oribe also became interested in bending and cutting his own bamboo spoons rather than commissioning artisans, and the day of the wealthy amateur had arrived. A tea scoop now became a sculptural object, a major work despite its miniature size and the abundance of bamboo in Japan. The study of its visual curves became an experience akin to the tactile experience of cradling a hand-molded teabowl. Oribe learned his Zen at Daitoku-ji, but during his lifetime the tea ceremony seemed to have departed radically from the days of Ikkyū and Shukō.

To the last of the great tea masters associated with Daitoku-ji, Kobori Enshū, the term *wabi* meant something quite different from its significance to his earlier predecessors. Kobori Enshū (1579–1647) admired Rikyū as an old master of the previous generation. He studied under Oribe and learned his Zen at Daitoku-ji from the hundred and fifty-seventh chief abbot, Kōgetsu Sōgen. Enshū was the leading tea master during this period of prosperity in Japan's history, and his taste was that of a wealthy man, since he was born a noble and from his youth had associated with the imperial family and the shogun. Despite this background he respected Rikyū's ideas and his study of Zen under Kōgetsu deepened his insights. Ryōkō-in subtemple speaks for his taste, for it is usually assumed that he designed its Mittan tearoom and its gardens (Pls. 11 and 16). This tearoom, the most exquisite surviving example of "wealthy *wabi*," is discussed on page 67.

Kobori Enshū was a genius who gave the tea ceremony a final, authoritative, Daitoku-ji seal. He established a large body of complex rules that still govern it. In his aesthetics, he advocated "beautiful *wabi*" as opposed to Rikyū's more natural "poverty *wabi*," and his main patron was the Shogun Tokugawa Iemitsu. By this time tea ceremonies had become dramas of delicate appreciation of the subtleties of formalized beauty. The tea scoop, for example, originally a simple, utilitarian object of a natural inexpensive material, had become a sculptural object under Oribe's influence, and under Enshū's, it became virtually an object of veneration. In the Momoyama period, tea caddies, teabowls, tea scoops and iron kettles had acquired names derived from ancient poetry. This tendency continued in Enshū's time, and objects almost came to be personalities, whose genealogical tables were carefully recorded as they passed from one proud owner to another, carefully wrapped in costly silken fabrics.

By the mid-seventeenth century, when Kobori Enshū had codified the tea ceremony, the Tokugawa shogunate held the whole of Japan in tight control. Social mobility ceased, and a rigid form of feudalism was reasserted. *Cha-no-yu* could not remain free or unpretentious in such an atmosphere and inevitably it became the social pastime of the military and the noble classes. As a means of promoting Zen meditation or as a semireligious ritual, it almost disappeared, except when individual abbots used it in the privacy of the subtemple tearooms.

The age of the great tea masters passed with the seventeenth century, and, strangely enough, after this time there were no more famed chief abbots of Daitoku-ji. The eighteenth and nineteenth centuries are formalized and sterile in atmosphere compared with earlier periods. It could no longer be said that "To learn tea is to learn Zen." Rather, the possession of tea utensils became a mania, a perversion of Confucian materialism. The tea hut architecture still contained a Taoist-like vacuum with a Zen cleanliness, but the ceremony itself was fossilized. Only with the greater freedom of recent times is it beginning to return to the ideals of Ikkyū, Shukō and Rikyū. The tea ceremonies performed by the present abbots of Daitoku-ji, Tachibana Daiki and Kobori Nanrei, exemplify this.

Commercially, however, the tea ceremony has never been so successful as at the present time. In the *Nampō Roku*, a sort of diary written by Rikyū's disciple Nampō, there is a section quoting Rikyū, lamenting that within a decade after his death, *wabi* tea will have disappeared and *cha-no-yu* will have become a mere worldly recreation. The eighteenth-century tea enthusiast Matsudaira Fumai, who restored Daitoku-ji's Kohō-an after a fire, wrote during a trip to Kyoto: "When I requested Ura-senke's Sen Sōshitsu to arrange a tea ceremony, I was told that it would cost 50 silver pieces if it were an open tea party for a daimyo, 30 silver pieces for a private one, and 10 silver pieces if it were only for retainers to watch. This is very deplorable." This trend toward commercialism has continued unabated to modern times. Now there are a dozen important tea schools, one of which has seven million students, most of them women, since teaching tea was one of the professions approved for women in the Meiji period. To become a tea teacher requires a three-year course and the fees involved make the tea ceremony very big business indeed.

An idea of the extent to which the tea ceremony has become popular can be gained by a visit to Kyoto in the last week of October or the first week of November, when Daitoku-ji hosts a giant tea party, reminiscent of Hideyoshi's *chakai*, but with ten thousand guests. Sponsored by one of the larger tea schools, it lasts three days and disrupts the otherwise orderly schedule of Daitoku-ji to such an extent that some abbots tend to "go to Tokyo for a few days." Special trains, buses and even express streetcars run between Kyoto station and Daitoku-ji, so that tea teachers and tea devotees may be rushed with all possible speed to the site of the tea treasures, despite the fact that many have sat up all night in the train coming from as far afield as Kyushu or Hokkaido, and that many will sit up all that night for the journey back. Such enthusiasm can only be respected and such veneration of tea treasures must surely inspire their students in *cha-no-yu* during the following year.

On reaching Daitoku-ji, they are herded into queues by helpers with loudspeakers and they shuffle from temple to temple to see the treasures (the main rooms of twenty of the twenty-three subtemples are "leased"), or in the temples that have no tea treasures, they participate in a huge *cha-no-yu*, whose frothy drink restores them enough to be able to stand once more before the next subtemple.

All day long, these thousands of tea teachers enter each Daitoku-ji subtemple in turn, kneel on the wooden veranda, and inch along in lines to see a tea scoop fashioned out of a single node of bamboo by Master Enshū, or view a ceramic bowl brought across from Korea four centuries ago, or glimpse the elegant woodwork of a celebrated tearoom. The climax of the visit is to bow in reverence before the graves of Rikyū and the other tea masters.

For centuries now, tea has been a means of bringing culture to the middle class masses of Japan, and these ten thousand tea teachers, who make what may be a once-in-a-lifetime pilgrimage, are the local priestesses of the cult. Pursued with an almost fanatical devotion, the tea ceremony seems at times to border on being a religion in itself, and as such, an understanding of it is essential both to an appreciation of Japanese aesthetics and of Japan itself.

Tearoom Architecture

Daitoku-ji may be regarded as the tea architecture capital of Japan because it houses six of the most famous tearooms in the country, each distinct in its aesthetic character and each associated with a leading tea master. Taken together, these tearooms illustrate the full structural and artistic range, from the *wabi* "grass hut," or *sōan*, associated with Rikyū and his immediate followers, through the several stages of elaboration culminating in the elegance of Kobori Enshū's style which brought the *shoin* tearoom to perfection in the early seventeenth century. Thus tea enthusiasts from all over Japan visit Daitoku-ji to see both the graves of *cha-no-yu*'s great men (Shukō, Rikyū, Sōtan, Sansai and Enshū) and the tearooms that represent the peaks in the development of tea architecture.

Each of the different schools of tea has its particular favorite, though there is general agreement on the six leading tearooms. Of the "grass hut," or *sōan*, style there are:

1. Shinju-an's Teigyoku-ken (Jewel of the Garden); originally a lookout in the sixteenth-century Imperial Palace of Emperor Ōgimachi, it was designed as a tearoom in 1638 by Kanamori Sōwa, a well-known tea master.
2. Kōtō-in's Shōkō-ken (Facing the Pine); built by Hosokawa Sansai, the favorite pupil of Rikyū, in 1628, it has been rebuilt several times.
3. Jukō-in's Kan-in (Quiet Living); Rikyū is supposed to have committed suicide in this tearoom, which was later moved to the subtemple where he is buried.

Of the "nobility," or *shoin*, style there are:

1. Ryōkō-in's Mittan tearoom (named after a Sung

Chinese Zen master); it was designed by Kobori Enshū between 1606 and 1608 to exhibit the Zen master's calligraphy.
2. Kohō-an's Bōsen (Throw away the Net); originally constructed by Kobori Enshū in 1636, it was burned down in 1793 and reconstructed soon after by Matsudaira Fumai of Matsue.
3. Kohō-an's San-un-jō (Mountain Cloud Resting Place); built by Kobori Enshū, it is usually believed to have been burned down in the fire in 1793 and reconstructed, but records are vague and some believe that it escaped the fire as it is located on the northwest corner.

Several other Daitoku-ji tearooms are well known and can be seen, as they are located in the temples that are open to the public. The Sa-an (Straw Raincoat) at Gyokurin-in, for example, shows the Omote-senke school style of the mid-eighteenth century, designed by tea master Joshin. At Sangen-in, several Edo-period copies of old style tea huts are preserved, which can be viewed as one walks through the garden. Ōbai-in's tearoom, traditionally attributed to Takeno Jōō, can also be seen, as it is in an open temple. The six tearooms in the list above, however, are in closed temples and are not easily entered unless one ranks high in tea circles. Of these the easiest to gain admittance to and the most aesthetically rewarding is the Jewel of the Garden at Shinju-an. (This can be arranged by a prior telephone call, and a donation to the temple of a thousand yen or so is in order.)

To understand the significance of these Daitoku-ji tearooms, the general evolution of *cha-no-yu* aesthetics in relation to architectural forms must be grasped. The earliest recorded tearoom in Japan was built at the Silver Pavilion and is attributed to the first official tea master, or *chajin*, Murata Shukō, who had been trained by Ikkyū in the values of simplicity, frugality, and the beauty of the unpretentious. His master, Shogun Yoshimasa, had grown up in a building so elaborate that it was called the "Flowery Palace." In contrast to that, he found Shukō's four-and-a-half-mat tearoom (about nine square yards) full of the refinements of *wabi* aesthetics. This Silver Pavilion, however, has a nine-foot-high ceiling, the nobility sat on a higher level, and a Chinese lacquer stand was used for the arrangement of tea utensils.

The next generation, represented by Takeno Jōō, who was influenced by Daitoku-ji through the Sakai temple of Nanshū-ji, reduced the tearoom to three mats, with a ceiling that was only seven feet high. Instead of using only imported ceramics for teabowls, simple objects chanced upon in markets or farmyards were esteemed.

During the late sixteenth century, when the low-born Hideyoshi became military dictator of Japan and Rikyū was his leading tea master, the ultimate point was reached in *wabi*, as applied to tearoom architecture. Hideyoshi wielded a hundred times the power of the fifteenth-century Shogun Yoshimasa, and his wealth was incalculable. At the same time, he was one of the most brilliant men to rule Japan. He realized that man has more than one side to his nature and used his public face to impress his vassals. For that he had Rikyū design the fabulous "golden tearoom," knowing that its richness would become a legend. Since he was of humble birth, he must have relished the way the nobility, now his underlings, were impressed by its walls and ceilings covered with gold paint, and by its gilt-framed *shōji* covered with scarlet silk instead of the usual opaque paper. When he wanted to impress these powerful generals who served him, Hideyoshi used tea utensils of silver, and even the bamboo dipper was stained with purple dye.

Yet, in total contrast, within the same Osaka Castle, where Rikyū designed this golden tearoom, there was another tiny tearoom; only six feet square, it was called Yamazato (Mountain Village), and had ordinary opaque paper on the sliding doors, rough timber for the woodwork and mud walls.

Hideyoshi could enjoy each type of tearoom in turn, and Rikyū was able to design both since he understood the different purposes intended. However, the tearooms in Daitoku-ji, because they lie within a Zen temple compound, all incline toward austerity.

For a short time in the late sixteenth century, the men who reached positions of power were of humble birth, and the tea ceremony reflected this trend of vertical social mobility and became approachable to all, regardless of rank or birth. Soon Japan was to return to greater rigidity in its society, and the tea ceremony was again to become exclusive to the upper classes; but in the late sixteenth century a mixture of aristocratic richness and rustic simplicity occurred. As Rikyū said, the tea ceremony was represented by "a finely caparisoned horse tied before a rustic hut."

During the century from Shukō (and Yoshimasa) to Rikyū (and Hideyoshi), teahouse architecture showed development from elegance, based on imported Chinese taste, to naturalism and poverty aesthetics. The tearoom became smaller, the windows were made of bamboo grills and the *tokonoma* (alcove) post was of undressed wood, a tree trunk with the bark left on. The walls, too, changed. The white walls of Yoshimasa's time turned a darker gray and then a dull, earthen color, through which the participant could appreciate the dried rice straw, the only binder in the plaster. Whereas finished lumber and symmetrical design denote man's control over nature, these later modifications increased the feeling of intimacy in the tearoom, and, at the same time, by stressing closeness to nature, the guest was reminded of the passing of the seasons, the natural cycle and man's precious possession, time. Most of *cha-no-yu*'s patrons in the late sixteenth century were military men and their hold on time was precarious indeed. Thus this emphasis on the perishability of all things, on impermanence, must have struck a responsive chord in their minds.

Ideally, to follow the development of the tearoom, the visitor to Daitoku-ji would first visit the two "open" subtemples, Kōtō-in and Ōbai-in. Kōtō-in's small tearoom, though often rebuilt, has much of the *wabi* spirit about it as it is small in size and unpretentious, with a *nijiriguchi* (wriggle-through entrance) and a dim interior. Ōbai-in's tearoom is attributed to Jōō, and is worth inspecting, though it may be of a later date. Shinju-an is a "closed" temple, but its Jewel of the Garden tearoom is the most interesting. Finally the two Kobori Enshū tearooms, the Mittan at Ryōkō-in and the Bōsen at Kohō-an, are unfortunately almost impossible for the foreign or Japanese visitor to see, and in reality they do not quite measure up to their beauty in photographs.

Shinju-an's Jewel of the Garden is the most satisfactory of all the Daitoku-ji tearooms because it incorporates every architectural feature, recognizable even to a beginner in *cha-no-yu*. It is set, as its name suggests, like a jewel in a garden that forms a beautiful approach, with moss-covered stepping stones, a hand-washing basin and a stone lantern. By stooping on the veranda, one can see the eleven unusual, rather rough and high stepping stones inside the tea hut in a sort of vestibule with a skylight. This unique feature is attributed to the fact that the designer, Kanamori Sōwa (1584–1656), grew up in the Japan Alps and used the memory of snow to lessen the harshness of a winter *cha-no-yu*. This interior arrangement of stepping stones, which leads to a second hand-washing basin, has not been moved since it was set in the rough earth over three centuries ago.

Today the visitor approaches the Shinju-an tearoom from the west entrance, kneeling beside the host's three-quarter-mat alcove that adjoins the six-foot-square main tearoom. Emperor and Empress Ōgimachi looked through these windows a last time

on the fifteenth day of the fourth month in 1570, perhaps grateful that Nobunaga had brought a measure of peace to the country and was to repair the Imperial Palace. Surely their ghosts are happy that Kanamori Sōwa converted this palace lookout into a tearoom; the Japanese believe in re-using wood, and this Jewel of the Garden is an excellent example of the success of this procedure. It is a humble room, with a four-foot-wide *tokonoma* that has a reed-covered rectangular window in its north wall, a rather distinctive feature.

In this tearoom, one feels a measure of detachment from the outside world and this is the goal of tea architecture. Here one gives up the ordinary world for the beauty of a world of monochrome. In this tiny room, without strong colors, one perceives the subtle shadings in the centuries-old posts of red pine and chestnut and in the mud walls with their rice straw binder. Perhaps the room's "color" lies in the varied textures of the woven ceiling patterns or in the sheen reflected from the cuts of the axe as it hacked into the cedar log that forms the base of the *tokonoma*.

The outside world and its sensuous beauty of form and color are further shut out by the opaque paper windows. Northern light, steady and diffused, falls on the three-quarter mat upon which the tea utensils are intended to rest. At dawn the rising sun illuminates the vertical patterns formed by the cedar struts on the windows and, for a few moments, the plain opaque paper that covers them becomes rainbow-streaked.

Subdued music hangs in the air of this tearoom. One must be silent to hear the breeze of time through the cattails, now loosely laced on the ceiling, or the whiz of the axe across the cedar log, or the droplets of rain in the river bullrushes above one's head.

The Japanese term for this is *sabi*, the special quality that time adds to natural objects, and *wabi*, the beauty of the unpretentious. In the *sōan* type of tearoom, *sabi* and *wabi* should be so intermingled that while the mind is not superficially conscious of the cause, a loneliness penetrates to the marrow of one's bones. Even within the intimate space of a two-mat tearoom, one can feel immensely lonely and yet identify with all that is in the natural world.

In contrast to the *sōan* type of tearoom is the *shoin* style, epitomized in the Mittan tearoom in Ryōkō-in, designed by Kobori Enshū. Enshū admired Rikyū's ideal of refined poverty, but he lived in a prosperous period and had to accept the taste of the elite while at the same time try and elevate it. There is a story that he once designed a study for the ruler, Shogun Hidetada, but when it was finished the shogun did not like its rough plastered walls and ordered them "painted with country life and activities of the four seasons." The walls of the Mittan tearoom are all painted, but in a subdued way, with ink alone.

The Mittan is the only tearoom in Japan where the *tokonoma* was designed especially for a single special piece of calligraphy. This was written by a Zen patriarch in Sung China, and is the only known specimen from his brush. It came into the hands of Kōgetsu in the early seventeenth century, and since then it has always been highly honored, exhibited once a year on the anniversary of his death. It is said that Rikyū himself designed the silk brocade mounting for this *bokuseki*, as the calligraphy of Zen masters is called. In addition, Enshū is said to have designed this entire room around the calligraphy, so it has two *tokonoma*, one for the calligraphy in the east wall, and a conventional *tokonoma* in the north wall.

The calligraphy is not usually exhibited, and on the back wall of the east *tokonoma* are scenes painted in ink. A long tree trunk rises from brambles and fills the foreground, while sparrows either alight on the upper stumps of branches or soar into the sky. Below, on the perpendicular edge of the wall supporting the *tokonoma*'s base, is another painting showing a lakeside with boats sailing over an expanse of wa-

ter, with a treatment that is different in mood. These paintings are attributed to Shōkadō, who died in 1639. He was a Sakai priest who studied Chinese painting of the Sung dynasty and evolved his own style, specializing in birds and flowers.

Along the same east wall there is a three-quarter-mat projection, used by the host while preparing tea. The entire east wall is covered with an ink landscape in the Kanō manner, showing a vast expanse of water with a boat drifting in the middle, somewhat sheltered by a sandy bank. At the extreme lower right-hand corner, in the style of Sung "one-corner painting," is a large, twisted pine tree (Pl. 11). Its crooked branches are so placed that if one is seated on the *tatami* in a tea ceremony, the pine is perfectly framed by a rectangular space between the *tokonoma* and the supporting pillar of the partial wall. Furthermore, the host's movements as he prepares the tea are seen against the background of this pine. The style of the two paintings on the east wall is different enough that it is possible Shōkadō painted one when the tearoom was new and another when Enshū came to settle at Daitoku-ji. At about this time, Kanō Tanyū was staying as Ryōkō-in to paint the Headquarters Temple and the dragon on the ceiling of the Doctrine Hall. Both Enshū and Tanyū were eminently successful, the former as a builder and the latter as a decorator-painter. But Enshū was much older than Tanyū and may have influenced the younger artist. He may originally have left part of the walls unpainted and later, impressed by Tanyū's work, asked him to complete the decoration of the Mittan.

The conventional *tokonoma* is situated in the northwest corner, which is somewhat dim. Its back and side walls are painted in ink with a mountain scene almost devoid of forms except for vague shapes of mountains seen through clouds, with a pagoda silhouetted near the corner and a few trees.

The entire area of this tearoom is only four and a

half mats, plus the additional three-quarter mat on the northeast side, yet it seems quite large and airy. Part of this effect is due to the landscapes of distant views on the walls. Another reason is the arrangement of the lighting. The left half of the west wall and the right half of the north wall consist of three sliding panels each, with the upper two-thirds admitting light through the opaque paper. Words do not suffice to describe the effect. The workmanship cannot be excelled, even in the Katsura Palace.

In summary, the Mittan can be appreciated as Daitoku-ji's, and Japan's, best pre-Edo example of the *shoin* style of architecture compressed into a tearoom. It stands in opposition to the grass hut style with undressed trunks as pillars and many-angled ceilings. At the Mittan, all the wood is finely hewn and lightly lacquered as opposed to the rough logs in the small, dark, rustic tearooms of the *sōan* style.

Another way of expressing the difference between the *sōan* and *shoin* types of tearoom might be to make an analogy between these tearooms and Hinayana and Mahayana Buddhism. Rikyū's two-mat tearoom that he designed for Hideyoshi in 1582 was intended to be the ultimate in detachment from ordinary life and its cares. By rejecting class, rank, money, and the intellect, Rikyū stripped the tearoom to its bare essentials, and made the participants equal before their "original face" in the Zen sense. There was only enough light to perceive the teabowl and the utensils, a dimness that symbolized total emancipation from the real world and from attachment to things. Yet while this enhances the concentration of the participant, as in Hinayana Buddhism the emphasis is on the participant himself, on *his* enlightenment alone. The *shoin* style, however, has an aspect of Mahayana Buddhism in that the experience has a more social basis and the individual is subordinated to the greater happiness of other people. The tea ceremony is more integrated with life and society. The genius

of this style, Enshū, made his tearooms at Kohō-an, the Bōsen, and the Mittan bright and cheerful and large enough to live in, which he in fact did.

When he chose the name "Kohō-an," the "Single Boat Hermitage," he was referring to the passage of the individual through life. He elaborated on this metaphor by calling its principal tearoom Bōsen, referring to the injunction of the Taoist philosopher Chuang-tzu to throw aside the net after catching the fish, meaning that the enlightened man can cast aside the trappings that ordinary men need.

The Bōsen is nine mats in size with a partly screened-off alcove of three additional mats to the north, intended for the utensils brought in by servants. The real *tokonoma* is in the west wall, and its north supporting wall has an opening, below which it is papered with silver and gold. This seems too garish an idea for Enshū and must be a later innovation. The most unusual feature is the *shōji* that lifts vertically to reveal the garden (Pl. 15). The *fusuma* wall panels are said to have been painted by Kanō Tanyū and saved at the time of the fire that destroyed the building in 1793, though this is not certain. The ceiling is higher than in most tearooms and has been rubbed with white sand to bring out the grain of the wood. Vague, rounded mountains appear out of the mist on the north and south walls, with clumps of pine trees and, at the lowest corner, fishermen with nets, another allusion to the name of the room.

Matsudaira Fumai (1751–1818), who restored these tearooms after their destruction, wrote treatises on tea in which he suggested that the rules of tea could be applied effectively to the administration of a feudal estate. By that time, *cha-no-yu* had been institutionalized into a Confucian pattern to become another trapping of a feudal lord. Wealthy connoisseurs' *wabi* was a far cry from the ideas of Ikkyū, Shukō, or Rikyū. The intimate rustic hut had become the ultimate in elegance and luxury.

4

THE GARDENS

If a person thinks he understands Zen but doesn't know Zen art forms, he doesn't really understand Zen's mode of living.

Tachibana Daiki (1899–)
Founding abbot of the rebuilt Nyoi-an

In any country, gardens are a reflection of the culture and in Japan in particular the garden is a sensitive vehicle, an expression of the aesthetic atmosphere and concepts of the period in which it was created. Gardens in Japan were originally for the pleasure of the aristocracy alone, and, as so lovingly described by Lady Murasaki in her eleventh-century novel, the *Tale of Genji*, they reflected the sophisticated and sentimental delight in nature of the Heian aristocracy who used to walk and sit in them. The basic principle of these gardens was the selection and assembling of the most pleasant forms of nature—trees that flower in the various seasons, an artificial lake for boating, a miniature mountain made with earth excavated from the lake—and the enjoyment of them in an enclosed area. Kyoto was the home of this court nobility, and the surrounding hills and mountains supplied many streams that were diverted to meander through the gardens and even under the pillars of the mansion, which was always some four feet off the ground. It was all very idyllic and the function of the garden lacked any deep symbolism or stark philosophical confrontation with the Absolute. Indeed, it was not until Rinzai Zen took root that Japanese gardens began to discard their flowers and blossoming trees and running water.

During the early fourteenth century, Musō Kokushi (1276–1351) tried to give a Zen twist to the nobility's pleasure garden. He is credited with changing the shape of the pond in the moss garden at Saihō-ji into a Chinese ideograph meaning "mind," or *kokoro*, in 1339. With a great stretch of the imagination this character can still be read into the outline of the pond and its islands.

When Ashikaga Takauji was troubled by Emperor Go-Daigo's ghost, Musō advised the building of a Zen temple to quieten his spirit, and thus Tenryū-ji came into being with its lovely garden, said to have been designed by Musō in 1350. This garden was the prototype of the kind of Zen garden that recalled Chinese Sung landscape painting, with its elements evoking the "three distances" (near, middle and far). It has rocks, a pond, a bridge, and an artificial mountain on the further side of the pond, and the whole is set against the background of the Arashiyama foothills.

After this innovation, it was only in the poverty-stricken era of the late fifteenth century that Zen made further strides toward developing gardens that were completely distinct from secular gardens. In broad terms, the gardens that evolved may be divided into three categories, all excellently represented at Daitoku-ji. The first is the garden of the Tenryū-ji prototype, in which a landscape painting is rendered three-dimensionally. The second type was perfected in the late fifteenth century, and is a simple, meditative, gravel-based garden with rock groups arranged within a rectangle. Ryōan-ji has made this style world-famous, but Daitoku-ji also has outstanding examples. The third garden type is that around the path leading to a tearoom and seems to have developed in the sixteenth century under Jōō and Rikyū.

Some Daitoku-ji abbots feel that the gardens of the first sort are too crowded and too self-consciously constructed, while the intention of the gardens of the second category, usually known as *kare sansui*, "dry landscape," is far more serious. A garden of this sort is located along the side of the abbot's hall, facing south, so that it can be viewed by the abbot, his disciples and guests, and so that through it the abbot can be inspired to renew his closeness to *mu*, the Void; thus the design is a combination of form and formlessness, of the phenomenal and the noumenal. It is an aid to meditation, and it encompasses a fourth dimension, that of "time." For the waves of raked gravel taken from the bed of a river have the same matrix as the granite rocks set among them, even though they are at different geological stages and thus they appear different. It is Zen's ultimate lesson revealed in garden form: though things may appear different, everything is part of a continuum.

The exact point when river gravel was substituted for running water has never been established by garden historians, because the fifteenth century was one of extreme confusion and many records were destroyed in the disturbances. However, the American author believes that since Ikkyū taught *wabi* aesthetics to his disciples and one of them, Murata Shukō, is thought to have designed gardens at Shūon-an for the living Ikkyū, and at Shinju-an for the dead Ikkyū, the thread of development of *kare sansui* gardens may well originate from this time. The present Shūon-an garden has strange, powerful rock groups, but a well-meaning tea master in the eighteenth century "improved" it and moss was allowed to grow over the gravel. On Ikkyū's death in 1481, the subtemple of Shinju-an was built in his honor, and tradition assigns two of its gardens to Shukō. It was ten years, however, before the temple and the gardens were completed and during this period Murata Shukō was engaged by Shogun Yoshimasa as the first official tea master in Japanese history.

Since Yoshimasa obviously valued Shukō's judgment, what would be more natural than for him to consult with Shukō about the garden than he was building around his Ginkaku-ji (Silver Pavilion)? Basically Yoshimasa was copying the Saihō-ji moss garden, an Amida Buddhist temple garden with, as has been seen, the Zen idea of shaping the pond to form the character for *kokoro*. One feature of the garden has puzzled garden historians however: there is no other temple that has such a stretch of river gravel as the expanse just south of the Tōgudō pavilion. This pavilion contains the first tearoom in Japan, thought to be planned by Shukō. As tea master, he felt that a separate room was necessary for the ceremony, and so he designed a four-and-a-half-mat tearoom for Yoshimasa. It is probable that he also designed the part of the garden directly in front of the building that holds his tearoom. The irregular geometric expanse of raked river gravel could educate the shogun in true *wabi* aesthetics if he sat and contemplated it. The Silver Pavilion is adjacent to this expanse and is so arranged that it catches the full moon's rays as it rises above the eastern hills. Then the pavilion lives up to its name, painted with the real silver of nature, the light of the moon shining on this gravel garden. Ikkyū chose the name of his temple, Shinju-an (Pearl Hermitage), in reference to a poem by Yōgi, the Sung Zen master, which likened the snow falling through a broken roof to pearls. A parallel metaphor may be applied here, with the moonlight being nature's silver.

Of the two gardens that Shukō is credited with designing at Shinju-an before it was completed, one is the East Garden and the other is the South Garden (Pls. 22 and 25). He knew that Ikkyū's statue would look out over the South Garden and this he made totally *wabi* in taste: originally not a single form existed in the garden; there was only an expanse of gravel, an emptiness of which Ikkyū would have approved. Unfortunately, in the seventeenth century moss was grown on the gravel as this was thought to be more in accordance with tea taste. Perhaps it was easier to care for too, for keeping a gravel garden neat and free of moss in Kyoto's humid climate requires constant work. In order not to completely lose the Zen depth of this garden, a single pine tree was planted along with the moss. The idea derived from a certain *kōan*, "What is the meaning of the Buddha-mind?" An acceptable answer is, "A single pine tree growing in a garden."

Although this South Garden is much admired by visitors to Shinju-an, it is the East Garden that is the most like its original appearance. In 1491 it occupied twice its present-day area (in 1601, two rooms were added to the Main Hall and the stones were moved closer together), but the fifteen stones are the original ones selected by Shukō. Here too, though, moss was allowed to grow during the seventeenth century and the vastness of the raked gravel area has thus been lost.

At the time Shukō was designing this garden, Bokusai was painting sliding wall panels for the temple, translating *wabi* aesthetics into ink-flinging, or *haboku*. Shukō was also a *haboku* painter and if the asymmetrical blobs of ink on a rectangle of white paper are transposed into rock groupings on a bed of off-white gravel, Zen ink paintings metamorphize into meditation gardens. The immediacy and the challenge of a *kōan* can be transposed into a garden devoid of foliage and water.

If Shukō could convert the pastime of tea-tasting into a Zen tea ceremony of meditative calm and aesthetic awareness, he could accomplish the same with gardens, making them into deeper statements of Zen Void. At Shinju-an, because of his closeness to Ikkyū, Shukō had a free hand, and he had already had the experience of working on the Shūon-an garden with Ikkyū present and no doubt making suggestions. Thus the two gardens designed by him at Shinju-an seem to present the ultimate form of two types of Zen gardens, the brilliant result of Ikkyū's aesthetics and Shukō's genius. Both gardens have been tampered with, and to understand what the East Garden looked like originally we must study Ryōan-ji, built a few years later and commonly attributed to General Hosokawa. It seems odd that a general should conceive of such a stark, *wabi* type of design for a garden, and he might well have seen or heard of Shukō's arrangement of fifteen stones in Shinju-an's East Garden, and may possibly even have asked Shukō's advice. Ryōan-ji's rock groupings are reversed as regards Shinju-an's, because it faces west while Shinju-an's faces east. Another difference is that

Ryōan-ji's rocks are larger and more impressive, perhaps because of Hosokawa's wealth. It cannot be denied that time has been kinder to Ryōan-ji, yet Shinju-an's East Garden reveals a subtler aesthetic statement. After these two gardens, no further significant step in reducing garden design to minimal statement was possible, though one other garden, at Ryōgen-in, which is seventy-five square feet and has only five rocks, is counted as the smallest Zen garden in Japan.

After Shinju-an was finished, the chaotic conditions in the capital were reflected at Daitoku-ji, for it averaged one chief abbot a year for three decades before a strong personality with a wealthy sponsor appeared. Only then was a new subtemple with gardens built.

This man was Kogaku (1464–1548), and he, like Ikkyū, had a strong leaning toward the arts. He stayed at the hermitage of Nanshū-an at Sakai, steeped in tea and *wabi* atmosphere, and he sent his best disciple, Dairin, there as founding abbot (the temple's name became Nanshū-ji). One of Dairin's students of Zen was Jōō, who was to affect the history of tea garden design and of tea ceramics, and thus Kogaku's own interest in tea ceremony probably indirectly influenced him.

On his retirement in 1509, Kogaku had a subsidiary temple built just west of Shinju-an, called Daisen-in, "Retreat of the Great Sages." Though he surrounded his wooden Votive Hall with four gardens, all gravel-based, the present West and North gardens date from the present century and are not worth lingering over. The other two gardens at Daisen-in, the South Garden and the East Garden, are among the most often photographed in all Japan (Pls. 26 and 23-24). The South Garden may have been influenced by Shukō's garden at Shinju-an, for it is a rectangle of emptiness, with river gravel raked into a wave pattern. At some time in the past, two mounds of gravel that were left near the entrance vestibule, perhaps as a ready store of fresh gravel, became sanctified by tradition, and thus they are now permanent features. These mounds became part of the design elements of an originally formless garden!

Daisen-in's East Garden is in the tradition of the Sung landscape garden, started by Musō Kokushi at Tenryū-ji. There is a Daitoku-ji record that says: "Kogaku planted rare trees and placed strange stones to form a landscape," which indicates that Kogaku himself was the designer, although in later centuries, because of Sōami's landscape paintings just inside the temple, this artist's name became associated with the design. Daisen-in took four years to build and this gave Kogaku plenty of time to search for unusual stones in the sometimes abandoned mansion gardens of formerly wealthy men whom the Ōnin War (1467–77) had ruined. The East Garden is only twelve feet wide and forty-seven feet from south to north, but according to Shinju-an records it was originally six feet wider, a shape which approximates that used by the fifteenth-century masters Shūbun and Sesshū when they painted Chinese-style landscapes. And if studied carefully, the rock forms become an imaginative translation into garden design of the hard-outline (*shin*) manner of both Sung- and Muromachi-period painting. Seen as a three-dimensional version of a landscape painting, even the bluish color of the granite suggests *sumi* ink tones. The tall rocks simulate precipices, and the interval between them evokes the vertical waterfall so beloved of Taoist sages. The waterfall becomes a stream that widens to a river of raked gravel running under a bridge of granite. Large flat-shaped rocks suggest islands, and the effect of the swirling water is heightened by the junk-shaped rock called the "Boat Stone," which dominates the southern half of the garden. Unfortunately, a 1961 reconstruction placed a stucco bridge with a bell-shaped window almost on top of the Boat Stone, and

this slices the narrow, hanging-scroll-like garden in half. The original garden flowed directly into the South Garden, with its vast stretch of emptiness, and thus avoided the present overcrowded feeling.

From the late fifteenth century onward, the south garden in front of the abbot's quarters in any Zen temple came to consist of a walled rectangle enclosing an area of raked gravel, usually with a few trees or rocks. One of the most admired of these gardens in Japan is Daitoku-ji's Headquarters Temple garden (Pl. 27) in front of the Hōjō, which was rebuilt in 1636. It is also one of the largest of Zen gravel gardens, being 120 feet from east to west and 42 feet from south to north. In the south wall there is a Momoyama-period gate with a cedar-bark roof, originally built for Hideyoshi's Juraku-dai palace in 1587. It is called the Imperial Gate and is opened only if a member of the imperial family comes (the last was Empress Taishō in 1920). The design of the garden is attributed to various men, including Kobori Enshū and his friend, the one hundred and sixty-ninth chief abbot, Ten'yu (1586–1667). The garden takes into account the hills in the distance to the east, which seem to influence the tall, clipped shrubs in the southeast so that they suggest other hills, nearer at hand. A mountain cascade seems to fall from the three vertical rocks in the southeast corner of the garden. These are balanced at the northwest by the two low, flat rocks, reminiscent of islands, lying within the sea of raked gravel. The green moss that grows around these makes them strong enough to preserve the balance. Perhaps the best time to view this garden is around six-thirty in the morning, when three times a month sutras are chanted in honor of the founder, Daitō. In the cool dawn light, the gravel takes on a silvery sheen, and the ripples in the gravel seem almost to drift back and forth as the cantillating voices rise and fall.

The third type of Zen garden, the *roji*, is a type of

tea garden that must have evolved either at Sakai, in the courtyard garden of some tea master, or at Daitoku-ji, the early center of tea ceremony. By the time of Rikyū (1521–91), it had reached full development and contained moss, stepping stones, a hand-washing basin, a stone lantern to light the way at night tea ceremonies, and a bench or booth, where guests could wait while the tea master prepared the tearoom. According to the *Nampō Roku*, written by one of Rikyū's disciples, Nampo Sōkei, Rikyū said: "The *roji* is simply a path leading beyond this fleeting world." In other words, walking along this path enables one to cast aside the ordinary concepts of time and space associated with daily living, so that the tea guest is led artistically and psychologically into another world, and he is prepared for the experience of the tea ceremony.

At Daitoku-ji, twenty out of the twenty-three subtemples have one or more *roji* gardens (the exceptions being Daisen-in, Ryōgen-in, and Shōju-in, none of which has a tearoom). Among the tea gardens that are most admired are those of Kōtō-in, which suggests advancing into a mountain ravine; of Kohō-an, which conveys elegant rusticity; and that leading to the Teigyoku-ken (Jewel of the Garden) tearoom at Shinju-an (Pl. 14). All the Daitoku-ji tea gardens possess a serene clarity and one does not realize that they are so minute in scale. As a Zen priest wrote, "Thirty thousand leagues shall be compressed into a single foot." Indeed, on entering one of the gardens, Kyoto city, with its million and a half inhabitants, seems to recede that far. The garden becomes the moment's reality, sequestered by its warm, beige-toned walls, made of unadorned mud.

In the garden, the stones of the path are always too narrow for more than one guest, so conversation is discouraged and the guest is thrown back upon himself and his own reflections. No one stone is so assertive that it detracts from the assemblage, for the

function of such stones in the path is more important than any single shape or textural beauty alone. The path acquires a quality of dimness from shady trees and a feeling of length from the slight zigzags in it. Though relatively short, it is so totally enveloping aesthetically that the guest is removed from the distractions of his normal world. When used for the tea ceremony, a gracious welcome in the form of a previous sprinkling with water enhances the sense of freshness and the immediacy of the natural world, and a certain tranquil quality comes when water drips slowly like dew from the foliage and lies in partly dried pools on the stepping stones' irregular surfaces.

Each of Daitoku-ji's gardens is distinctive and well worth visiting. Some are famous for their granite lanterns (Ryōkō-in's is shown in Pl. 16), others for the uniqueness of their hand-washing basins, as at Kohō-an and Kōtō-in. Throughout their limited area, the art of the minimal is effected, and dramatic views, distorted pines or espaliered designs are not used, for they would be too conspicuous. Since most of the tearooms at Daitoku-ji are not separate huts (Sangen-in's is an exception) but attached wings, they have two entrances, one from the temple's raised floor and one from the lower, garden level, with an entrance through which one has to crawl (a literal translation of the Japanese term is "wriggle through"). The garden is not meant to be seen after entering the tearoom, with the exception of the Kohō-an tearoom, and so the gardens at Daitoku-ji are particularly austere and low-keyed.

The tearoom at Kohō-an, called Bōsen, was designed by Kobori Enshū and is one of the most famous. When its unusual sliding panel (that moves vertically instead of the more common horizontal direction) is lifted (Pl. 15), the visitor seems to be riding in a boat looking out over a lake, even though there is no water in the garden. A pine tree, its branches propped up, seems to be growing out over the simulated lake in the manner of the famous Kara-saki Pine on the shores of Lake Biwa, and a long granite bridge completes the illusion. The hand-washing basin is surrounded by black, oval stones that come from a lakeside at Odawara, three hundred miles from Kyoto. Tradition says that each stone was purchased from a peasant for a quart and a half of rice, then a day's wages, and that they were carefully wrapped in cotton and shipped by boat to Sakai and by river barge to Kyoto.

The elegant stroll gardens of the later seventeenth, eighteenth and nineteenth centuries are larger, more ostentatious descendants of Kobori Enshū's ideas, for his gardens generally stress elegance. Rikyū is said to have told his disciples that when laying rocks for a garden path, sixty percent consideration should be given to their usefulness and forty percent to their artistic appearance and that Kobori Enshū reversed these figures, an anecdote that neatly sums up the development from Rikyū's poverty aesthetics and his *sōan* style to Enshū's more sophisticated *shoin* style. Japan's urban courtyard gardens of this present century with stepping stones, lantern and modest shrubs are only remote descendants of Rikyū's *roji* garden in that they lead one from the street to the living quarters rather than to the tearoom, but they are nonetheless meant to suggest escape from the noisy world as much as they are intended to add light and ventilation.

A postscript should be added about two twentieth-century gardens at Daitoku-ji, both of which are normally open to the public. Sangen-in's garden was designed about fifteen years ago to combine the meditative gravel garden to the east with a *roji* garden to the north, whose stepping stones lead around a good Edo-period reconstruction of a teahouse. The success of this Zen garden design, despite its contemporary origin, is surprising. On the other hand, the garden at Zuihō-in designed by Shigemori in 1961, which attempts a raked garden design, has resulted in too many forms within the enclosed space and a loss of the Zen feeling of the Void. The visitor, however, is recommended to visit both gardens in order to realize the problems of this type of garden design and to understand that, while the elements of the design may appear very simple, the aesthetic principles involved are extremely complex.

8. The entrance pathway to Shinju-an, leading ▷ through the Chinese-style gateway, which is rarely opened, into the South Garden.

10. Kan-in tearoom, thought to be the scene of Rikyū's ritual suicide in 1591 and moved to Jukō-in after his death.

9. The Teigyoku-ken tearoom at Shinju-an. Before 1570 it was a lookout for the Kyoto Imperial Palace and was converted into a tearoom by Sōwa Kanamori, a follower of Rikyū.

11. The Mittan tearoom, designed by Kobori Enshū for Ryōkō-in between 1606 and 1608. The landscape painting is by Kanō Tanyū.

12. The Bōsen tearoom, originally designed by Kobori Enshū for his retirement temple, Kohō-an, built in 1621 and restored by Matsudaira Fumai in 1793.

14. The *roji* stepping stones leading to the Jewel of the Garden tearoom at Shinju-an.

16. The moss garden south of Ryōkō-in's ▷ Reading Hall, with its famous lantern brought from Korea by General Kuroda in 1598. At the extreme right is an ancient tree whose roots are watered with *sake* to keep it alive.

13. Ryōkō-in's entrance pathway, probably designed by Kobori Enshū around 1606.

15. The Bōsen tearoom with its horizontal *shōji* raised, allowing the guest to imagine he is in a boat on Lake Biwa. The pebbles simulate the shoreline.

17. The oldest surviving *temmoku* teabowl made in Japan. Probably dating from the 1480's, it was used by Ikkyū and Bokusai. Now preserved at Shinju-an.

19. The *yuteki* (oil-spot) *temmoku* teabowl, made in China in the thirteenth century. Now preserved at Ryōkō-in. The Chinese lacquer stand is inlaid with mother-of-pearl.

18. The *yōhen temmoku* teabowl from Fukien province in China, dating from the Southern Sung dynasty (thirteenth century). Now preserved at Ryōkō-in.

20. The "Kizaemon-*ido*" teabowl, brought from Korea in the 1590's and treasured ever since by tea enthusiasts. Now preserved at Kohō-an.

21. The foot of the "Kizaemon-*ido*," which is considered the ultimate in *wabi* ceramics. The rough, sandy bottom and the irregular surface are characteristics that are highly esteemed.

23. Daisen-in's landscape painting garden (East Garden), designed between 1509 and 1513 by Abbot Kogaku. Photographed from the Main Hall, the bridge that now divides the garden in half can be seen in the center. The Boat Stone is on the extreme right.

24. A view of Daisen-in's East Garden from the south, taken before the bridge was built.

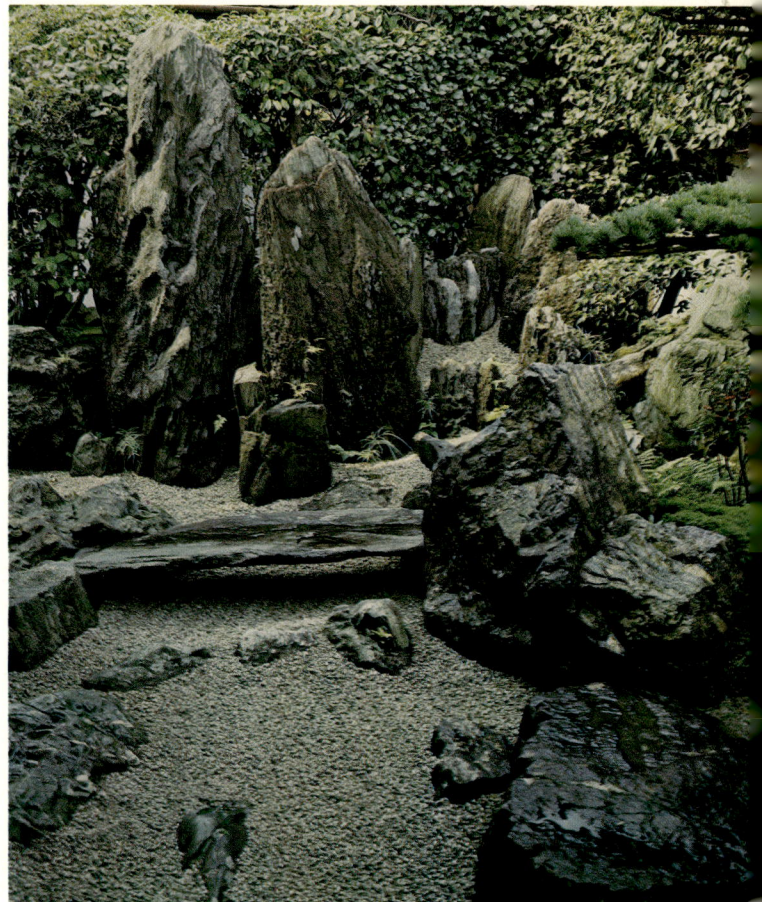

◁ 22. Shinju-an's East Garden in early November, showing the fifteen stones in three groups —seven, five and three. Designed by Murata Shukō before 1491.

⊲ 25. Shinju-an's South Garden dating from
1491, showing the Chinese-style gate and the
"single pine" alluded to in the *kōan* (see p. 72).

27. The South Garden, dating to 1636, of the
Headquarters Temple, Japan's largest Zen
gravel garden. The Chinese-style gate was
built in 1587 for Hideyoshi's Juraku-dai palace.

⊲ 26. Daisen-in's South Garden of 1513, with
the two intriguing piles of sand and, in the
background, the Chinese-style gate.

28. Shinju-an's Tantric treasure, the "Eleven-headed Kuan-yin," painted in the Kamakura period with calligraphy added later by Daitō Kokushi.

5

THE PAINTINGS

The experience of viewing Zen works of art must not be divorced from understanding their religious and cultural functions.

Kobori Nanrei (1918–)
Abbot of Ryōkō-in

The Chinese Paintings at Daitoku-ji

Although the Communist Chinese government, the Taipei Museum and the Tokyo and Kyoto Museums have been acquiring every ancient Chinese painting they can in recent years, they rarely display what they have, and from a Zen point of view none of them can rival Daitoku-ji's collection of Chinese ink painting. One might haunt the special exhibits of these various museums for years in order to see a few samples, but at Daitoku-ji, because of the temple's custom of airing its treasures one day a year as a precaution against silverfish and other paper-eating insects, the public can see many of these masterpieces at one time. The occasion is called Mushiboshi ("the day for airing to prevent damage by insects"), and it takes place in mid-October from nine in the morning to four in the afternoon. (It varies between October 10 and 15; inquiries should be made ahead of time at the Headquarters Temple.) In addition, the subtemple of Kōtō-in, which has an outstanding collection of Chinese Sung-dynasty paintings, airs its treasures on the same day.

The Headquarters exhibits a total of about three hundred hanging scrolls, perhaps one quarter from China, and the rest old Japanese paintings or calligraphy. Of the hundred scrolls of the "Five Hundred Venerable Disciples," painted in the Southern Sung dynasty and presented by Hideyoshi, five are displayed each year, the five being chosen from among the best and on a rotating basis.

The visitor to Daitoku-ji on Mushiboshi day might also take this opportunity to broaden his knowledge of a Japanese and Chinese art form that is difficult to appreciate and thus is little understood in the West, namely, calligraphy. For this is an art that Zen abbots have strived to excel in, and among the abbots of Daitoku-ji are the most famous calligraphers in Japan —Daitō Kokushi, Ikkyū, Takuan and many others.

The picture and calligraphy scrolls are hung in the three main Votive Rooms of the Headquarters Temple, and thus the eighty-four *fusuma* panels painted by Kanō Tanyū for these rooms may also be seen.

The ten Mu Ch'i paintings

Of the large assortment of art at Daitoku-ji, the world at large recognizes the Mu Ch'i triptych as the most important. The Daitoku-ji abbots seem to agree, for the paintings are hung in the central position on Mushiboshi day. If it is raining, however, although the originals of other paintings are shown, the Mu Ch'i is a postwar collotype copy. Many Japanese as well as foreign visitors do not know the difference, and this delights the abbots, who decide whether a stray cloud classifies that particular day as "rainy." October was selected as it is the driest time of the year, and yet about one time out of ten it "rains," so the public sees only the copies.

The Kuan-yin triptych (Pls. 29–31) and the "Six Persimmons" (Pl. 33) are the most often reproduced of all Zen paintings, and many Western art historians consider the "Kuan-yin" the greatest masterpiece in the entire history of Chinese painting. In size alone, the triptych dwarfs most other paintings that have survived from the Southern Sung dynasty and have found reverent care in Japan.

The exact route by which these Mu Ch'i paintings made their way from his temple workroom in Hangchou, China, to Daitoku-ji has a few missing links, but it is clearer than for many other important works of Sung art. The American author believes that the three paintings came to Japan in 1241 with Shōichi Kokushi (1202–80), and were taken to the temple that he founded, Tōfuku-ji. The Japanese author thinks they came to Japan in a ship from the temple of Tenryū-ji, which would place the voyage after 1349. Despite the debate over this period of the triptych's history, it is known that, once in Japan, it came into the possession of the Ashikaga family.

The third shogun of this family, Yoshimitsu, enjoyed more power than any of the previous shoguns and he was rich enough to erect a thirteen-building complex on the northwest side of Kyoto between 1399 and 1408 as a combination villa-retreat and Zen temple. Today none of the buildings remains, but when this Golden Pavilion compound was completed, Yoshimitsu invited Emperor Go-Komatsu (Ikkyū's father) for a housewarming party of great elegance, with music and dramatic performances, a variety of contests, and displays of the finest paintings in his collection. This imperial visit of 1408 lasted twenty days and it was, as is usual in Japan, the occasion of much gift-giving. It is recorded that the Shogun Yoshimitsu bestowed "five paintings by Mu Ch'i" upon his guest, the reigning emperor Go-Komatsu.

After Yoshimitsu's death, the Ashikaga became weaker and from their shrunken resources they failed to provide the emperor with enough rice and fabrics for his needs. At some point in history, one of Go-Komatsu's successors needed rice or silk more than the Chinese paintings and thus another exchange of gifts occurred, when a general (probably one of the Imagawa) presented the throne with the necessities of daily life. The emperor must have given him the Sung paintings in return, for it is recorded that in the mid-sixteenth century the Mu Ch'i paintings belonged to the Imagawa generals, who stored them at their Zen temple of Rinzai-ji. Around this time power in Japan was constantly changing hands and the Imagawa may have wanted to stand in well with the imperial family. The chief abbots of both Myōshin-ji and Daitoku-ji were appointees of the emperor and as such had direct access to him and could have introduced favored generals to the im-

perial court; this might have been the motivation for the Imagawa offering presents to both these temples. One present was a large sum of money and the other was the Mu Ch'i paintings. Since Myōshin-ji was the "mother" temple of Rinzai-ji in Shizuoka, the first choice fell to it. By tradition, Myōshin-ji deprecates art, in contrast to Daitoku-ji where it is highly esteemed. For this reason, and also because at this time Myōshin-ji needed money for a new Mountain Gate because the former one had been burned in the Ōnin War, Myōshin-ji accepted the money and Daitoku-ji was left with the second choice. This is how it came into possession of the Mu Ch'i paintings.

Many books in English refer to these paintings as completely monochrome, but they have occasional touches of color. All seven Mu Ch'i's in the Headquarters Temple are executed on the same type of silk, with silvery blue tones in the black ink. This is particularly conspicuous in the red topknot of the crane. Ashikaga Yoshimitsu himself must have pressed his big red seals at the bottom of the three scrolls of the "Kuan-yin," "Crane," and "Monkey," following the custom of Chinese emperors who thus endorsed works of art that they admired. The larger seal reads "Tenzan," or "Heavenly Mountain," a reference to the Ural Mountains; the smaller seal reads "Dōyū," or "Morality-preserver," which was his Buddhist name.

There seem to have been three pairs of "Dragon" and "Tiger" paintings in the shogunal collection at one time, but only one of the two at Daitoku-ji is both signed and dated. The inscription on the "Dragon" painting reads, "The dragon rises and causes clouds to appear," and that on the "Tiger" painting reads, "The tiger roars and the wind blows impetuously." Both are signed "Painted by Mu Ch'i in the fourth year of the Hsien-ch'un reign," which corresponds to 1269. The "Kuan-yin" is signed but not dated; some writers assert that it was painted around

1245 and predates the "Dragon" and "Tiger" paintings by some twenty-five years. The other three small paintings by Mu Ch'i in the Daitoku-ji collection are believed by the American author to be of an even later date than 1269 since they represent a more enlightened mind, one that is more deeply steeped in Zen. There seems little doubt that the "five paintings by Mu Ch'i" that Ashikaga Yoshimitsu gave the Emperor Go-Komatsu were the Kuan-yin triptych and the dated "Dragon" and "Tiger." Several pairs of flanking pictures of dragon and tiger were recorded by the sixteenth century and attributed to Mu Ch'i in Japanese catalogues, but at present only three survive: the two pairs at Daitoku-ji and one held by the Cleveland Museum. All are approximately the same size and all are executed on silk. It is noteworthy that the three smaller paintings in Daitoku-ji are on paper and are unsigned.

The cult of Mu Ch'i as the Zen artist supreme goes back to at least the fourteenth century. His "Eight Views of the Hsiao and Hsiang Rivers" have been owned through the centuries by powerful people in Japan, passing from the Ashikaga shoguns to their conqueror, Nobunaga, then to Hideyoshi, and finally to the Tokugawa shoguns. At present the museum of Japan's railroad king (the Nezu Art Museum) and the Tokugawa Art Museum in Nagoya have the largest part of these famous landscapes. The abbots of Daitoku-ji, for their part, are proud to have ten Mu Ch'i within their compound.

Mu Ch'i himself remains something of an enigma. For while the Japanese have accorded him the highest veneration, Chinese art historians, heavily imbued with neo-Confucianism, never ranked him highly. Chinese records are scanty and critical. Chuang Su, in his *Hua-chi Pu-i* of 1298, shortly after Mu Ch'i's death, criticizes the painter for lack of refinement and "failure to respect the tradition of ancient masters." This last phrase is the key to all Chinese criticism of

Mu Ch'i: he did not respect tradition but created new trends, tremendously influenced by Zen, which the orthodox historians did not relish. Two other works of 1330 and 1365 criticize him for his lack of elegance, an attitude that appears ridiculous if one stands in front of the Kuan-yin triptych.

Mu Ch'i is known to have spent the early part of his life in Szechwan province in southwestern China and the later part in Chekiang, particularly in the temple of Liu-t'ung-ssu, located in the Southern Sung dynasty's capital city of Hangchou in the hills bordering the shores of the beautiful West Lake. The *Sung-chai Mai-p'u* says that he was trained at court but later suffered persecution for criticizing a court favorite, Prime Minister Chia Ssu-tao (1213–57), for bad administration. He escaped to Yuen Ch'iu. This book also gives the date of his death as falling in the Chih-yüan era, which extended from 1264 to 1274.

Such are the bare bones of Mu Ch'i's biography according to Chinese records. Every Japanese version, however, links him to a Zen temple, a Zen abbot, or a Zen-inclined ruler, and such an affiliation may well have occurred in his later life although these early sources do not mention it.

Today the abbots at Daitoku-ji consider the Kuan-yin triptych as a religious icon, or *shōgon*, and they opposed loaning it for the Boston Museum's centennial in 1970 unless chanting was performed before it each morning. In Zen thought *shōgon* refers to the "flowering, a permeation of beauty on the way back from enlightenment." It represents the interior radiance of a person, which has no words and is transformed into art on the return to the world after penetrating the core of Transcendental Wisdom, or *Prajñāpāramitā*. This gives rise to an additional reason, besides their age and color, why the original paintings are not shown more often, for there is a danger of becoming attached to the "flower" alone, and the Zen abbots believe that to view the "flowers" of painting history without first going straight to the core limits one to a partial appreciation.

The "Kuan-yin" itself is sixty-eight inches high by thirty-nine inches wide, and the two flanking paintings are roughly the same size. Here is a mastery of Chinese tonal washes, the principal technique of the mid-thirteenth century. Background and foreground, forms and atmosphere are given a hitherto unequaled unity. Other Southern Sung artists, such as Ma Yüan and Hsia Kuei, had learned to express tremendous depths of atmosphere in their backgrounds, but their foreground forms stand out with a linear clarity that immediately presents a duality between these nearer forms and the formlessness of the vast universe that is hinted at in the background. Mu Ch'i, in these Daitoku-ji paintings, merges foreground, middle distance and far distance into a unity that gives the triptych a mystic quality. The deity is distinguishable from the rock he is on and the monkey is distinguishable from the pine branch upon which she perches, but there exists no duality. In Zen thought all form in the phenomenal world is permeated with the same energy-essence, the same Buddha-nature, the same Buddha-mind. The Zen artist, being neither conceptually oriented nor intellectually motivated, uses art to hint at philosophical oneness.

The flanking of a Buddhist icon, such as "Kuan-yin," with a pair of animals or landscapes instead of with two other deities as is customary in older forms of Buddhist art, was a means adopted by Zen to express this idea of oneness or non-discrimination between the energy-essence of a deity and of natural objects like animals, trees and rocks. It is impossible to say whether this combination of animal and bird with the "Kuan-yin" originated in China, or whether it is the result of selection by some fourteenth-century Japanese, but it had become a set of five by the time of Ashikaga Yoshimitsu. One unifying factor in each of the paintings is the use of an evocative mist around the dominant figure, though this mist, or Void, is more noticeable in the "Dragon" and the "Tiger" paintings than in the triptych.

In ancient Chinese mythology, the dragon represents the heavens, or the male element, and also east, sunrise, spring and rain. He is the highest-ranking of the four supernatural animals. The tiger represents the earth, or the female element, and also west, sunset, autumn and wind. Although the dragon is superior because of its association with the heavens and the fructifying powers of rain so essential to life, these two animals are correlative and are not thought of in opposition. In Zen art, if only one animal is to be represented, the dragon is chosen as representative of all. Most major Zen temples have a dragon painted on a ceiling, and Daitoku-ji's was painted by Kanō Tanyū in about 1636 and stretches across the Doctrine Hall's ceiling. (This dragon can be made to roar by standing directly under it and clapping one's hands, since there is a double ceiling that forms an echo chamber.)

The symbolism of the Kuan-yin triptych is open to several interpretations, but Abbot Kobori of Ryōkō-in suggests that one is paramount. In the *Hekigan Roku* (Blue Cliff Record), written by Hsueh-tou (980–1052) and commented upon by Yüan-wu (1062–1135), there are two often quoted lines of poetry that present a visual image. These lines were used to expound Zen teachings among the literary circles of Sung society, and Abbot Kobori feels that they certainly influenced Mu Ch'i, who was probably in the court circle when he painted this work.

Monkey embraces child, blue cliffs at the rear.
Bird holds flower in its beak, blue cliffs in front.

Broadly stated, the crane symbolizes the intellect and the monkey represents a human being's emotional nature. The crane walks alone, as a scholar should, head erect, long legs raising its body with its white plumage high above the ground. The bamboo, too, is associated in the Chinese mind with the gentleman scholar.

The mother monkey is painted with a baby monkey around her neck, suggesting the closeness of family ties, the pull of one's emotional side. But Kuan-yin merges the seeming opposites of intellect and intuition in its all-embracing character. By means of ink distribution, this unity is hinted at, and just as these ink tones unify intellect and intuition, form and the formless, into a singleness, so the final stages of Zen enable the individual to abandon discrimination.

In Mahayana Buddhist iconography, the crane represents Mañjuśrī (Monju in Japanese), or the principle of Transcendental Wisdom (*Prajñā*), and the monkey is Samantabhadra (Fugen in Japanese), or the principle of Compassion (*Karuna*). Wisdom and compassion must merge for religious awakening. Compositionally the "Crane" and "Monkey" paintings (Pls. 30 and 31) complement each other in a subtle way. The predominant sweep of the composition in the "Monkey" is a pine-tree trunk that stretches from the lower right to the upper left, with a crossing diagonal in the branch that ends in a pine-needle spray. The compact form of interlocking ink strokes of mother and baby monkey dominates the composition by the darkness of the ink, but they are slightly above dead center. The "Crane," on the other hand, has verticals and horizontals of various sorts. The crane's open beak "drinks in the universe" in a Zen manner, but its long, smooth, sharp lines are suggestive of the sword associated with Mañjuśrī. This deity's image presides over Zen meditation halls because his sword cuts off delusions that the individual meditator may harbor. The direction of the bird's beak is noticeably upward, just as the paths in a Zen landscape usually ascend a mountain. The upwardness is associated with the search for enlightenment.

In the upper left-hand corner of the "Crane" painting the bamboo leaves dissolve into misty atmosphere in a manner parallel to the pine needles in the lower left-hand corner of the "Monkey" painting. In viewing these scrolls sometimes the misty atmosphere seems more real than the animals and at times the reverse is true. In Zen thought, form leads to Void, and then Void is realized as form. Mu Ch'i is a noetic painter. The calmness and strength of Kuanyin is instantly felt, but the activity of the crane seems to merge into Kuan-yin and be an extension of the deity. If Zen can be rendered with intellectual understanding via ink tones, then the Mu Ch'i triptych is the ultimate in art.

Mu Ch'i painted these three scrolls while he was still associated with the government elite, while his understanding of Zen was intellectually complete, and he used the tonal washes of the Southern Sung Academy as his medium. He had not himself experienced Zen's "great death" nor reached his own awakening. He was, however, a technical genius and the stupendous calm emanating from the "Kuan-yin" comes from a soft and fluid treatment that is basically circular. Each brushstroke in the central part of the painting is a quiet curve, from the drapery folds of the headdress cowl which droops over the deity's diadem as for a meditative Buddha Śākyamuni, to the longer loops of the Indian-style earrings and the wide, flat necklace, composed of many partial circles. Even the ringlets of hair that escape from under the white cowl frame the ears in semicircles. The lines that suggest a tiger skin, part of the Kuan-yin iconography, curve and bend, lacking any suggestion of a tiger's harshness and ferocity. Not even the rocky background of a shallow cave and the crag upon which the deity is seated are angular, as would be normal for rock forms in Southern Sung-dynasty landscapes. These are quite different from the strong right angles and cross-hatching diagonals of ink in

Hsia Kuei landscapes, which were famous around Hangchou city when Mu Ch'i painted this.

Later Chinese critics who disparage Mu Ch'i were literati and enjoyed "ink play." There is no playfulness here, but a very serious elegance. The form of Kuan-yin (Pl. 29) has a certain solidity, in contrast to the darker rocks and cloud-laden atmosphere. The white form of unpainted silk is the same basic triangle as the *zazen* posture, softened by the curves of the robe's outline. There are numerous places that evidence painterly expertise, for example, the vertical of the vase of water with a sprig of willow branch seen through the translucent vase. This is not an amphora with supernatural powers as in Esoteric Buddhist icons but a natural willow branch in a translucent vase; thus the stem is clearly seen too. The Kuan-yin and the willow branch are equally stable, equally upright, both full of Buddha-mind, as is all nature. In the Chinese mind the willow is associated with spring and the freshness of a new season, the ever-renewing cycle of life. And the Zen man, after enlightenment, is "reborn," a phrase emphasized by the Chinese Zen master Lin Chi (Rinzai in Japanese), whose words must have been known to Mu Ch'i.

Thus, philosophically, the composed form of Kuan-yin expresses the union of Transcendental Wisdom and Compassion, placed outdoors in the vastness of nature. This composition had tremendous influence on subsequent Japanese artists. Even though many have disappeared, perhaps fifty ink paintings still survive in Japan of the White-Robed Kuan-yin (*Byaku-e* in Japanese). Most of these were painted in the fifteenth, sixteenth and seventeenth centuries, when the Mu Ch'i painting was in Japan. None have the presence of the Daitoku-ji "Kuan-yin," but several are quite strong.

As time passed, Kuan-yin became more feminine, although sometimes a painter adds a mustache to suggest double sex, for the deity originated in India

as Avalokiteśvara, a male deity. Mu Chi's depiction strikes a balance between masculine and feminine and thus takes on a certain universal quality. Everything about this painting suggests a marvelously trained artist at the peak of his skill, the supreme master of tonal washes, the hallmark of Sung painting.

Mu Ch'i lived about three decades after reaching such technical excellence. He suffered disgrace, fled, knew "the great death," and emerged a non-intellectual who discarded elaborate subtleties.

Rather than considering the "Dragon" and "Tiger" as late, weak works by Mu Ch'i's hand, the American author considers them transitional to the small paintings about to be discussed. In the history of Oriental art it is not unusual for an artist's last years to be his best. Three small paintings attributed to Mu Ch'i's hand are treasured at Daitoku-ji, and have been there for about four hundred years. Hideyoshi's two tea masters considered them perfect works by Mu Ch'i.

After the visitors on Daitoku-ji's Mushiboshi day have viewed the several hundred scrolls hanging in the rooms of the Headquarters, they reach an airy tearoom and are served ceremonial tea by monks-in-training at the Sōdō. Only one painting hangs in the *tokonoma*, the "Hibiscus" by Mu Ch'i (Pl. 34). The guests kneel reverently before the alcove to gaze at the painting and examine the calligraphy displayed below. It is a letter in Sen no Rikyū's hand, saying that this art work will be given the next day to Daitoku-ji. It was given to Nobunaga's mortuary temple, Sōken-in, and the gift is thus datable sometime between its foundation in 1582 and 1591, the year of Rikyū's death. Possibly Rikyū had located this painting through his connections with Sakai merchants. Hideyoshi had another tea master, of equal rank with Rikyū, Tsuda Sōkyū, whose father had been a tea master and whose son became chief abbot of Daitoku-ji and founder of Ryōkō-in subtemple in 1606. Presumably Tsuda Sōkyū acquired the other two small ink paintings, "Six Persimmons" and "Chestnuts" (Pls. 32–33), through his Sakai overseas connections, and left them to his son, Kōgetsu, at Daitoku-ji.

The tea ceremony, as such, was not known to Mu Ch'i, but tea masters of Daitoku-ji feel that Mu Ch'i reveals his enlightened state best in the small paintings. The Kuan-yin set is too ponderous and bulky for the intimate surroundings of a tearoom and is better suited to the walls of a high-ceilinged Chinese temple. The small, unsigned works cast aside complexity to explode into Zen core. They suggest "voiceless poetry" in ink expressing the depths of Zen-mind. The large-scale Kuan-yin suggests unity with nature through its ink washes. But it is an intellectual concept; it reveals an architectonic building-up of association-steeped forms. But in the small paintings, the artist paints Kuan-yin and all it stands for by means of a simple flower or a fruit. He no longer needs an imposing deity, for he now realizes that the humblest nut is a manifestation of the same energy-essence. He is, then, unhampered by intellectual complexities. The Void, which is "nothingness," represents everything through a flower or a fruit. These ink studies on paper spring from a different plane of reality than the world of appearances. Yet the noumenal, the formless, is revealed and interpenetrates the world of form, and so the species can be recognized and the unenlightened can enjoy these paintings without reference to their religious implications. Perhaps it is helpful to realize that these are austere icons, without color, without inscriptions, uncompromisingly stark and simple, without a ground line. The almost staccato rhythm of the ink strokes produces emergent forms, absolute and positive. From a *satori*-born "flow" comes an assemblage of ink strokes which, almost in the manner of accidents of the kiln creating glazes of great subtlety, results in an art work that remains as an indelible record of the artist's awareness, his Instant Now.

A fruit, a flower, a Kuan-yin—they differ in outer appearance, but any subject can be used to convey the religious experience in painting. As one sees islands and an ocean in the rocks and raked gravel of a Zen garden, so one can feel the whole of nature in a single blossom or spray of flowers, or in a fruit. The whole of nature, the total experience of enlightenment, is distilled into this. Any further distillation reaches the abstract level of calligraphy, another means of communicating the continuous flow of the universe.

In the painting of persimmons, the six specimens of fruit may be read as emblem-allegories of stages of Zen enlightenment, dominated by one central persimmon, totally black. In Zen, darkness means wisdom or enlightenment; light represents ignorance. The lampblack persimmon in the center, wisest and most enlightened, is created with a bold ink statement, circled back on itself, not tangent to any other form. This central absolute can represent the Zen master, or *rōshi*, who can guide others in their meditation.

To its right is a nearly black piece of fruit, its stem depressed. Its nearness to the central dark shape suggests its dependent relationship to the master. This emblem of a partially-enlightened one overlaps a totally white, unripe, rounded fruit made with a single circular brushstroke, an emblem of the ignorant beginner.

On the left side of the central dominant persimmon there is a distance between it and the half-aware fruit that overlaps the unaware, rounded one at the far left. And the small persimmon on the lower level? The distance, the empty area between this small one and the central fruit is pregnant with interpretative possibilities. It is also aesthetically essential in order to avoid a static row of fruit.

Two further avenues of approach open to the Westerner probing the allegory of the "Six Persimmons." The Historical Buddha had five disciples, and the tea master usually invites five guests (at a maximum). This small painting is now the most honored of all "tea ceremony paintings," and outside of an unscheduled airing is only used for a tea ceremony.

Out of an artist's totality of awareness flowed six persimmons, four chestnuts and two hibiscus blossoms. The flow of energy or flashes of ever-renewing, now-energy, which created these ink paintings, reflects the flow of the universe, just as drops of water flow with the sea. The use of ink lends a universality to the depiction; for example, while the hibiscus in nature is a highly colored flower, here it is shorn of its character because it is rendered in ink alone.

Such paintings should not be signed, because the artist's selfhood should be left far behind. In Zen thought there exists no enduring self. Rather, the self is ever-new, reborn from instant of energy to instant of energy. Thus, there is no enduring individuality. This is the exact opposite of Christian theology which glorifies the individual self and seeks to perpetuate an individual "soul" after death. Such ink paintings of fruit or flowers represent a stage attained by the man of Zen when all the world seems at spring and all forms are transcendent with beauty. About fourteen inches wide, and a little taller, these three paintings, can be interpreted as microcosms that bespeak the macrocosm. But they are not passive comments, for they emanate a tremendous sense of energy, constantly being renewed.

The Sung paintings at Kōto-in

From a Westerner's point of view, Zen temples do not seem to be overly concerned about historical dating, but when a temple's tradition claims that a painting is very old, it usually turns out to be of importance. Two ancient landscapes (Pls. 35–36) held by Kōtō-in for hundreds of years and attributed to the T'ang master Wu Tao-tzu proved, under recent infrared ray testing, to have the signature of Li T'ang (active 1050–1130) hidden among the leaves of the painted trees. This painter worked for Emperor Hui Tsung of the Northern Sung dynasty. When the emperor was kidnapped in 1126, Li T'ang fled south and soon joined the new court set up at Hangchou, south of the Yangtze River, to rule a shrunken empire. Since the elderly Li T'ang had already received the "Golden Girdle of Merit" from the former imperial court, the new emperor asked him to become the director of a revived Imperial Academy of Painting. Its emphasis was on landscapes, perhaps because the capital was situated among beautiful surroundings and perhaps because in times of trouble landscapes are relaxing themes.

The composition of these two scrolls at Kōtō-in displays the Northern Sung dynasty type of landscape, wherein the painter is interested in suggesting extreme height for his mountains, in contrast to the size of the human figures. No particular mountain or man is portrayed, but rather a generalized type. There is progression into space on a gradual diagonal uptilt, from foreground to middle distance, and then a visual jump to the sheer mountains in the distance by means of mist or unpainted silk.

However, the height of the mountains is not so extreme as in earlier Northern Sung works of art and the mountain top is cut off, indicating a tendency that was developed by the artist's pupils, Hsia Kuei and Ma Yüan, of portraying a fragmented vignette of landscape on a vertical scroll, rather than a vast panorama. The Kōtō-in examples are thus transitional works between the Northern and Southern Sung dynasties, and were probably painted around 1128 and brought to Japan during the following century. When China was conquered by the Mongols, many Zen artists from the mainland sought a better life in

Japan and knew the advisability of bringing paintings with them.

In these works at Daitoku-ji, Li T'ang has focused on certain sections of the landscapes with greater attention than others, particularly on the foreground rocks in both paintings. The axe-hewn surfaces created by the cross-hatching seem to delight the artist and this same technique was adopted by Hsia Kuei, his pupil. In the fifteenth century it was a technique admired by the Japanese painters Shūbun and Sesshū, who worked for the Hosokawa lord while he was living in Kyushu and undoubtedly saw original landscapes of Li T'ang and Hsia Kuei. In fact, Sesshū painted several axe-hewn rock scenes for the Hosokawa generals, and labeled them with both his own pseudonym and that of Li T'ang and Hsia Kuei, so he may have been copying Chinese paintings in the Hosokawa collection. Kōtō-in is a Hosokawa mortuary temple, established in 1601, and this might explain why these paintings reached the temple so early. In contrast to Sesshū's paintings, the Li T'ang rocks have more volume; on the other hand, toward the top of the composition, the mountains are only slightly modeled, not enough to escape being a mere backdrop, and this is a mannerism that Sesshū was to adopt often.

If there were color originally, it has faded away in eight centuries. At most there could have been only light tints around the foliage, as any more color would have disturbed the contemplative nature of this scene. Li T'ang had lived through turbulent times, but he sweeps all these troubles aside to deal poetically with mountain solitudes, placing human beings on the path as symbols. The viewer can vicariously identify with them and, through them, wander beside the stream and compose his own poetry. The eye is not led outward by any strokes but rather remains within the composition and is turned inward to contemplation within the mind.

Shinju-an's Tantric Treasure

The oldest Japanese painting within Daitoku-ji according to the Japanese government's art commission is, together with the Mu Ch'i paintings, among the most treasured there. This "Eleven-headed Kannon" is in Shinju-an, and has probably been there since the subtemple was founded in 1491. As it is a religious icon of Tantricism, which retains iconographic forms unchanged, it is difficult to date but probably belongs to the late Heian or Kamakura period. This vertical scroll has been attributed to Kanaoka, Japan's leading painter of the ninth century, because of its masterly execution. Kanaoka began the Kose school under the patronage of the imperial family and he is recorded as having painted Chinese subjects for the walls of the Imperial Palace's Enthronement Hall in 892, unfortunately destroyed by fire.

The scroll (Pl. 28) is small in size, about thirty-nine inches high by nineteen inches wide, and this suggests it was commissioned for a private altar rather than for a large temple. Only the imperial family or the top nobility could have hired such an excellent painter.

These multiheaded deities represented the personification of Compassion. Later, Zen painters were to portray this deity, Kuan-yin, outdoors in a natural setting and with only one head, as Mu Ch'i did. In Tantric Buddhism the heads are multiplied to increase the power of the image and this bears the influence of India's multiheaded deities. Tantricism brought this idea from India through Nepal and Tibet to China and Japan, where it arrived in Nara times and was especially popular from the ninth century onward. In China also, during the ninth century, this deity became important and was associated with water and with helping fishermen. An island, Pu-t'o-lo-shan (Potalaka in Sanskrit), stands near the coast of Ning-p'o, historically the principal port in the China-Japan trade. There, in 848, an Indian Tantric monk was praying in one of the caves and saw a vision of Kuan-yin. Thereafter this spot became famous as "The Cave of the Roar of the Billows"; Kuan-yin's name literally means "one who hears sound," and thence comes the idea of helping those who cry out from a shipwreck. A hundred temples sprang up around this cave. Dramatically situated, it is dry at low tide, but when the breakers come thundering in from the China Sea, they surge upward into the cave. Many Buddhist pilgrims have been inspired to hurl themselves into the ocean at this point in order to join Kuan-yin in the Western Paradise quickly, or else they have been moved to cut off a finger or an ear and toss it into the waves (the Communists have placed the cave off-limits).

In this scroll, Kuan-yin is atop the mountain of the world in one sense, but undoubtedly stories of an actual location in China inspired the artist. Kuan-yin stands over a rocky cave, with two small human figures near the entrance; the young and somewhat effeminate figure of one on the left is kneeling in prayer while riding on a porpoise; the taller human is guiding a boat by means of his bright red oar. He rides out the waves even though these foam-topped billows rise as high as the rail on both sides of his craft. The mast is cinnabar red with bluish wooden supports across its front. The centrally positioned Kuan-yin, huge in proportion to the human figures near the bottom, levitates on a multitiered lotus, whose pinkish red petals separate the deity from the top of the cave.

The grotesqueness that might have resulted from eleven heads on one body is entirely bypassed because of the small scale of the multiple heads; they appear to be more like brilliant jewels, since each bears a golden crown. The topmost head shows the face of the Historical Buddha, framed by a small golden halo, while on the forehead is Kuan-yin's spiritual father, Amitābha (Amida), dressed in a monk's red robe. Flames emerge delicately from the golden rim of the lower golden crown and there is a large, all-encircling gold halo. This rises from behind the shoulders to add another golden gleam, and on the right side of it, in mid-air, a vessel of holy water floats upon a double-tiered pink-gold lotus pod, behind which rise golden flames.

In the Tantric tradition, gold signifies omnipotence and blue represents the subordination of all evil forces, while red denotes strength. The colors in this painting are remarkably well preserved because the artist not only painted the surface of the silk with layers of paint but also applied color on the reverse side to heighten the depth of his color. This gives a very rich effect, in spite of the passage of many centuries.

The elaborate golden jewelry—necklaces, heavy earrings, bracelets, bands on the upper arm, and even toe rings—all suggest Indian influence. The silken scarves that float about Kuan-yin's standing figure are meticulously painted to suggest red, brown, blue and green embroidered patterns on gauzelike Indian material. Threading in and out among these thin draperies are fragments of golden chains, and a few links here and there sparkle in the candlelight of the altar. The rosary in the deity's right hand is also highlighted with golden light.

This silk painting probably functioned as an altar piece from Shinju-an's foundation in 1491, though it is strange that a Tantric Kuan-yin should have been used on the altar instead of a Zen deity. When the Votive Hall was enlarged in 1601, this painting would already have been four or five centuries old and showing signs of wear, and a wooden statue of Kuan-yin was ordered to replace it as the main image in the east niche; the scroll was put in the storehouse and a Momoyama-period copy was ordered which now hangs in the west altar niche. The original is only seen on the October Mushiboshi day.

It is interesting to find a touch of Esoteric Buddhism so near the wooden effigy of Ikkyū. In his later life he held the Esoteric Buddhist belief that the body is the real Buddha, and when he realized his Buddhahood in Zen fashion, he practiced it in the body as well as in the mind. The American author believes that Ikkyū himself knew this painting and that is why it is enshrined in this temple. Furthermore, it seems probable that it had some connection with the imperial family in its early days and that is how it came into Ikkyū's hands, for he was the son of the hundredth emperor, Go-Komatsu.

The Ami School

Sōami, the third generation of the Ami school that served the Ashikaga shogunate during the fifteenth century as personal advisers in artistic matters, apparently worked for Daitoku-ji in his old age, after his master, Yoshimasa, had died. The garden of Ryōgen-in is attributed to him and the garden of Daisen-in was formerly assigned to him. In the field of mural painting, the tradition that Sōami painted for Daisen-in is of major importance in Japanese art history. At Daitoku-ji, also, two rooms in Shinju-an's Tsūsen-in are said to be by Sōami. In both Japan and the West, many small paintings have been attributed to him, but most of them are somewhat dubious and thus the connection of Sōami with Daitoku-ji plays a major role in establishing the exact nature of his painting style.

The word "ami" is generally thought to stand for a member of the Amida Buddhist sect who served the shogunate. They were personal servants to the *de facto* ruler, but though they shaved their heads in youth, in fact they were not priests; rather they were members of an intimate group with ready access to the shogun, and may sometimes in youth have been his paramours. As adults they were the curators of his art objects. The phrase "Ami school" refers specifically to the three-generation clique (Nōami [1397–1471], Geiami [1431–85] and Sōami [?–1525]), that was especially respected for its knowledge of painting in the Chinese manner. Sōami's grandfather, Nōami, had been the first curator of the Ashikaga shogun's collection of imported paintings and had commenced a catalogue and evaluation of them. Sōami finished this work, known as *Kundaikan Sō-chōki* (Research Notes for the Monarch), Japan's first book of art criticism, in which painters were ranked and methods of arranging hanging scrolls were explained and illustrated.

Sōami was thus more familiar than anyone else with the Chinese paintings in Japan's oldest and best collection, and it is interesting that he agreed with contemporary Ming-dynasty Chinese literati in preferring the Southern school to the Northern school technique. The latter used bold and angular outlines and Sesshū's *shin* style incorporates this. The Southern style, on the other hand, had soft ink washes and rounded forms. Many authors state that Sōami follows the style associated with Mu Ch'i, but he seems also to have been influenced by the Yüan master Kao Yen-ching, sometimes known as Kao K'o-kung. Muromachi-period writings praise the works of "K'o Nenki," who was probably this same artist. Sōami, after classifying the works of over a hundred Chinese painters of the Sung and Yüan dynasties, seems to have felt that the soft ink wash technique lay closest to his heart and he avoided the angular outlines and harsh contrasts of ink values associated with Hsia Kuei and Ma Yüan of the Northern school. (During the Sung dynasty when these men painted, these two divisions were not used but are the distinction of later critics.) In Sōami's technique there is also some reference to the ink dot style made popular by Mi Fei during the eleventh century. This had been simplified and refined by the Yüan dynasty in the landscapes of Kao Yen-ching. In landscapes, Sōami selected the softer, gentler aspect and seems to have particularly liked to depict mountains and trees in rain, a not unnatural selection since Kyoto, where he spent his entire life, has such a damp climate; in all the mural paintings of Sōami at Daitoku-ji, the sun is never felt to be shining, but rather the weather is cloudy, rainy or snowy. The "Eight Views of the Hsiao and Hsiang Rivers" (Pl. 44) appear to have been Sōami's favorite theme, and these views emphasize misty, rainy landscapes at twilight.

All the paintings at Daisen-in attributed to Sōami have a dreamlike quality. The mountains are not overwhelming by their sheer height or massiveness but are unsubstantial and shadowy. Entirely absent is the bustle of the world, the strife of battle, the clap of thunder, or the pounding of breakers on the shore. It is difficult to realize that Sōami lived in a battle-torn country and saw most of the works of his predecessors go up in the flames of the Ōnin War.

Many seventeenth-century artists such as Kanō Tanyū and Kanō Naonobu often painted landscapes with the same restrained quietness, and the mural paintings at Daisen-in were undoubtedly seen by them and perhaps influenced them. On the inauguration day in 1513, the subtemple of Daisen-in surrounded its altar in the central Votive Room with panels which portrayed the "Eight Views of the Hsiao and Hsiang Rivers" and which are considered to be Sōami's masterpiece. The panels are unusually large for the Muromachi period for they are sixty-nine inches high and four feet across. Presumably the choice of subject was decided by consultation between the painter and the abbot, but since Mu Ch'i's sets illustrating the same subject were in the Ashikaga collection, it was already established as an appropriate theme for a Zen temple.

On the Daisen-in panels there is a remarkable consistency in the soft, rounded forms, so that at first glance it is not easy to identify which of the eight views the artist had in mind, but an examination of details gradually reveals which specific theme he wished to illustrate. Water or mist occupy most of the extreme foreground and the forms of the small-scale hills and trees become dominant about a quarter of the way up from the bottom. Passages of mist with trees, gradually diminishing in size the further up the hillside they are, take the eye into the landscape.

In the fortieth year of the Meiji era, Daisen-in was in great financial trouble, for the suppression of Buddhism had been going on for a generation and few visitors came with donations. Thus it was decided to sell the mural decoration of the entire Main Hall, or Abbot's Quarters, in order to raise the money to celebrate the four hundredth anniversary of the death of the founder. In the end, the Tokyo National Museum purchased the paintings of the four smaller rooms attributed to Kanō Motonobu and Yukinobu (now mounted as twenty-two *kakemono*) and the Sōami paintings were loaned to the Kyoto National Museum, which in return pays a yearly rental fee for preserving them in their basement storerooms. The museum suggested that Kanō Shurei and his pupils at the Tokyo Art School copy the original, and these copies were installed in Daisen-in and are the panels on view now.

There exists no document earlier than the Edo period that attributes these Daisen-in panels to Sōami. As in other subtemples at Daitoku-ji, traditions at Daisen-in were not recorded but handed down orally. If, however, Sōami did not paint for Daisen-in, then his whole style must be reconsidered, because most art historians hold these landscape panels to be the touchstone of his manner of ink painting. When Daisen-in was founded, Sōami was the leading landscape artist in Kyoto and the chief abbot of Daitoku-ji was Kogaku, the strongest personality in the temple since Ikkyū. Sōami himself was not a Zen follower in the strict sense, but at this time, that is after the fifteenth century, the rule that allowed only Zen priests to decorate the temples was relaxed. Sōami, however, must have imbibed much of Zen taste from his youth at Yoshimasa's court and by handling the treasures imported from China; he was thus the logical choice as artist when Kogaku was supervising the erection of his retirement subtemple, Daisen-in, between 1509 and 1513.

One room at Daitoku-ji that is attributed to Sōami's brush remains in its original splendor. It forms the eastern corner room of Shinju-an's Tsūsen-in

(Pl. 45), which was part of the Imperial Palace until 1570 when Nobunaga offered to rebuild the palace and Emperor Ōgimachi is said to have given six rooms to his physician, who bestowed them on Shinju-an. How one of these rooms came to be covered with murals in the Sōami manner is not documented, and the style is somewhat different from the Daisen-in murals. There is more use of the dot technique of Mi Fei and greater application of light tints, so that the landscapes are more lively, even though they still have a dreamy and restrained quality. They appear a little more secular in taste and it is quite possible that they were originally commissioned for the Imperial Palace while Sōami was still alive, or before 1525.

Daitoku-ji's Influence on Japanese Ink Painting

During the first century and a half of its existence, Daitoku-ji was not an important art patron because at this period Zen was establishing itself in Japan and art was of secondary importance. From the time of Ikkyū, however, Daitoku-ji had a strong effect on painting, as well as on the tea ceremony and other art forms. The earliest painted sliding wall panels (*fusuma*) in Japan are preserved at Daitoku-ji (within Shinju-an), and the major painters of the sixteenth and seventeenth centuries left the products of their skill on its walls. Indeed a list of the original mural painters for its subtemples reads like a history of Japanese art. Beginning from the Ikkyū school (fifteenth century), there is the Ami school (late fifteenth, early sixteenth centuries), the Kanō school (late fifteenth through early seventeenth centuries), the Unkoku school (sixteenth century), the Hasegawa school (sixteenth century), the Tosa school (seventeenth century), and other *fusuma* of the eighteenth and nineteenth centuries.

However, when the subtemples lost all financial support in the late nineteenth century and were urged to sell their buildings and painted wall panels, a number did so. Later on, the Japanese government reversed this policy; the paintings became "National Treasures," or "Important Cultural Properties," and museums took to removing screens and panels for their "better preservation." Daitoku-ji's losses as a living museum of five centuries of Japanese mural painting can never be replaced. Perhaps as much as eighty percent of its original priceless heritage is now housed in museums or private collections and will not be returned to the temple.

In spite of this, enough remains to give a good idea of the evolution of Japanese ink painting from the fifteenth century through the seventeenth. Some of the more important examples will be discussed here, particularly with regard to their function, for they were not mere decorations and seeing them on the pages of an art history book or in a museum violates their essential character. These paintings were intended to augment and deepen the quality of Zen-type living within the monastic walls. As Abbot Tachibana Daiki said recently, "If a person thinks he understands Zen, but doesn't know Zen art forms, he doesn't really understand Zen's mode of living."

Zen art is mainly didactic. In the orthodox portraits this is readily apparent: the sterling qualities of the leader are to be emulated by his followers. The mural landscapes are similar in intent. At first sight they appear to be setting a calm mood for daily life, but their real purpose lies much deeper, in the ontological realm. Those who know little of Zen principles can find solace in the tranquillity of its landscape paintings and this may well speak for the universality of the Zen message. The medieval artists, however, were not creating these scenes for today's casual visitors but rather for the priests who would perform memorial services within these rooms. In a sense these landscapes are timeless and not limited to a particular locale, and yet they were executed with a certain time of day in mind, that of dawn, when the light is muted. To see them in full daylight is to misunderstand their original intention. When chanting services are held, as they are each daybreak, the rice-paper-covered *shōji* panels of the outside walls are never opened and thus no direct daylight enters. Incense has been lighted before the service begins and the priest and acolytes are in a world of their own—a painted environment to be sure, but symbolically ancient, with an echo of seasonal progression. In the chanting, the priests renew their link with the past, their pledge to carry on a tradition is reaffirmed, and this the artists knew.

The artists who painted the panels were Zen priests in the early days but later this was not the case. Kanō

Eitoku was totally secular in his point of view, and yet his works for Daitoku-ji are more subdued than those he did for the dictator Hideyoshi. On the whole, the tradition of restrained ink painting was so well established at Daitoku-ji that it held in check the more ostentatious talents of later painters who worked there.

The Ikkyū school

During the late fifteenth century, a style of ink painting was emerging in Japan that was quite unattached to any large temple at the time, but was loosely clustered around the dynamic personality of Ikkyū Sōjun (1394–1481). He spent much of his life traveling, and his vibrant personality seems to have inspired many men he met. He was a master calligrapher and poet, but he did ink painting not as a professional but on the spur of the moment, as the mood struck him. His style was not based on any particular formula imported from China, although he was famous for composing Chinese-style poems. Rather, Ikkyū's landscapes and bird paintings are an expression of his sense of union with the life force of the universe. In Ikkyū's ink painting, the brush of the painted form and the brush of the calligraphy of the poem that he usually wrote above the form are difficult to distinguish apart.

He was to greatly influence his oldest and most persistent disciple, Bokusai, who became the first abbot of Shinju-an and who in the brief year he lived there, painted several pieces that qualify him as the most expert in "ink-flinging" (*haboku*) in the late fifteenth-century. Beyond this direct master-disciple influence, Ikkyū in his wanderings met a samurai known as Soga Jasoku, who had studied painting under a Korean named Ri Shūbun. From his extant

works, Ri Shūbun seems to belong to the same pedantic school as the more famous Shūbun of Shōkoku-ji.

Due to Ikkyū's influence, Soga Jasoku ceased being a samurai and, under the pseudonym Bokkei, came to paint Zen Buddhist subjects, of which a number remain at Shinju-an. He also painted an orthodox portrait of Ikkyū at fifty-nine. He died about the same time as Ikkyū, but his son was already a talented painter by then and decorated the three major rooms of Shinju-an for its official opening in 1491. This Ikkyū-influenced line of painters was connected with Shinju-an for over four generations: Soga Jasoku I (Bokkei), Soga Jasoku II (Sōjō), Soga Jasoku III (Jōsen), and Soga Jasoku IV (Sōyo).

The three rooms in Shinju-an that Jasoku II painted are those in the Hondō, or Main Hall, and he followed the Sung-dynasty Chinese manner, which was admired by Japanese Zen painters of the fifteenth century. For the Central Votive Room, he adopted the manner of Mu Ch'i, for the Guest Room, the manner of Hsia Kuei, and for what is now the Incense Room, formerly the Abbot's Quarters (see plan on pages 196–97), he chose the manner of Yu-chien. With these basic painting styles, Jasoku II composed his own symphony of black and white, his tribute in *sumi* ink to the memory of Ikkyū and the aesthetic ideals of his *wabi*.

This symphony in ink has three movements. Its core is the andante of moderately slow tempo for the Central Votive Room, where bird and flower forms flow slowly from the southeast, past the altar niche and back to the southwest corner in a progression of spring, summer, autumn and winter that covers sixteen panels. This slow flow is in keeping with the fact that this room is the religious heart of the whole memorial subtemple, and that the sutras chanted here are rather slowly cantillated.

The brush melody changes to an allegro movement in the Guest Room, adjacent to the west, where the same seasons, embodied in landscape motifs, move more rapidly over eight panels. Finally there is a subito forte, with sudden, strongly emphatic areas of splashed ink in the northwest corner room, through which the incense is now carried in. Abbots and acolytes walk swiftly through this room; in the Votive Room they bow and chant in much slower tempo, and the Guest Room never sees them unless they are cleaning it, for it is the secular room. Perhaps for this reason, the paintings there (Pls. 40–41) are the easiest for the ordinary person to appreciate. In styles of calligraphy or the handling of ink, these three rooms would be classified as: formal, or *shin*, for the Guest Room, with clearly outlined forms; semiformal, or *gyō*, for the Votive Room, with less distinct outlines and abundant use of tonal washes; informal, or *sō*, for the Incense Room, which displays the ink-flinging technique.

Since the Guest Room has the most understandable forms, its panels are the most often reproduced in art history books, but, even here in the most secular sequence, the sensitive critic will find spiritual touches. Yashiro Yukio, who is the grand old man of Japanese art historians and who writes in English, says of the Shinju-an Guest Room:

> The austere spirit of Ikkyū still seems to dominate the temple and especially this room which houses these screens. The painting . . . is, in its composition, the essence of simplicity worked out with a minimum of brushstrokes and nuances of dark ink. The result at the hand of a great artist is a masterpiece of spiritual landscape . . . a world untouched by any taint of the commonplace and far removed from that of man.

For his composition Jasoku II used mountains and water, buildings and boats, the same as every other fifteenth-century landscape painter. But here he

stretches his lake across the whole room, while the forms of mountains rise from its banks and subside into mist. At the extreme right edge or beginning from the southeast corner of the Guest Room, nature is seen close up in the form of a brushwood gate standing ajar, inviting entry, and there are several boats, one with passengers in it moving into the next section where a tall mountain with a temple retreat represents the middle distance. At the corner, where the two walls of the room meet, the lake takes over completely and the observer's eyes traverse miles, although on the near bank is a waterside hut with a thatched roof, two philosophers and a boy attendant. Geese bank in a lazy diagonal above this lakeside pavilion, while autumn haze takes over the north wall's panels, from which emerges a mountainside clad in snow, an effect achieved by the white of its unpainted paper.

The illusion of a vast panorama is so complete that the landscape seems calm and peaceful and almost devoid of forms, yet careful attention reveals thirteen different boats painted in various aspects and with different speeds of movement. The five boats within the winter section on the north wall have their hulls covered with straw, while the lone boatman sits shrouded in his rice-straw raincoat and broad-brimmed hat. This section reverberates with references to Ikkyū's poetry, which was known to the artist, and with nuances of loneliness and *sabi*, that quality that comes from aging. It suggests year's end and the lonely life of a boatman in winter, and it also evokes Ikkyū's last years.

Guests, sitting in this room and hearing chanting that they do not understand, can let their eyes wander over the details of the ink landscape. They see that hidden among the tree branches and tucked behind cloud banks are nine structures for the guest to delight in discovering. These structures are vague, however, and so the overall impression is of a peaceful, almost unpopulated landscape, despite the humans present: a fisherman, two priests gazing at the vast empty spaces, one gentleman standing in the pavilion, his hand on its post as his friend mounts the bridge that links it to nearby land; another gentleman is seated by himself in a pavilion, anticipating his tea being brought by a servant boy.

When Yashiro writes that this Guest Room of Shinju-an is a "spiritual landscape," it is difficult to believe that he ever saw the Central Votive Room. For the ink paintings in this room are created by soft ink washes, ink strokes and also intentional non-painting, that is, the leaving of areas blank so that the form is conveyed by the ink washes around it (Pl. 42). To see these paintings at dawn makes it seem mere pedantry to say they are in the manner of Mu Ch'i.

Jasoku II understood Zen Buddhist rituals; he was himself a Zen Buddhist priest. He knew the dawn chanting that takes place every day of the year in this room, whose walls he covered with birds and flowers of the four seasons. When these daily services begin at five in the morning, at first the light is too dim to see the panels. Gradually the dawn seeps in through the opaque-paper-covered *shōji* and reveals the paintings. The sounds of the sutras, too, are "form" that structures the inaudible mysteries of life. While the whole room resounds with chanting and incense seems to penetrate even the forest background of the birds, the visual mystery of ink which is itself all things and Zen's "no-thing" becomes a totality. Almost as recounted in the first chapters of Genesis, the world seems to be unfolding anew. It is a Zen awakening to reality: form becomes formlessness and then form and formlessness interpenetrate. And in a state of non-discrimination, ink, unpainted paper, cantillating, and incense all merge beyond any one sensory perception into an ontological experience of the totally inexpressible.

In the Central Votive Room no human beings appear in the landscape. The Buddha is within each bird and bud, and not separated off into a person. Each breathing creature is divine and part of the sacred continuum that is simultaneously the every-day routine of this world. Thus the religious subjects are birds and flowers in a seasonal progression that conveys the passage of time and suggests the timelessness of the natural world. This quality of continuity is felt with each sutra chanting at daybreak, wherein the individual links himself with the past and renews himself with each day's dawning.

If one returns in full daylight to analyze the painter's technique, one can see that the right-hand, or east, wall starts with a close-up of nature—birds on a branch—and becomes more distant as the eyes move to the left. The north wall, which partially screens off the altar niche, has birds in the distance. By the time the eyes reach the southeast corner where winter is shown, the painter is again painting in close-up—a white goose under a pine tree through the branches of which a winter moon is glimpsed. One of the two most unforgettable sections of non-painted form show three herons on the north wall, left of the altar niche, one bending down, one with head raised, and one in flight; the other scene shows the winter moon, conveyed by the washes of ink, while below it stands a white goose, created by the application of ink washes around the unpainted form, and by black ink that indicates the beak, the eye, and the webbed feet (Pl. 42).

This mastery of ink as a medium and this depth of Zen understanding places Jasoku II above Shūbun as a skillful painter and makes him almost as versatile as Sesshū. Then, when one sees the third room at Shinju-an he is seen to surpass the renowned Sesshū in total ability.

This third room is somewhat of an enigma. Now only eight *fusuma* panels remain, but they are unparalleled in Japan. In no other temple is ink-flinging displayed over such a large area at this early date. Ikkyū had painted with this method, and small *kake-mono* scrolls remain from his hand. Apparently inspired more by him than Yu-chien, Jasoku II used this small room to create an entirely austere mood. This is the space through which the abbot and the acolytes pass with offerings of flowers and food and with incense for the dawn ceremonies.

This fifteenth-century artist has stopped just short of total non-objectivity (Pl. 43). After the viewer recovers from the initial dramatic impact, he recognizes semiabstract ink blobs that suggest mountain slopes, two river banks connected by a bridge, and lonely stumps of trees. Areas of unpainted paper force the viewer to interpret them as water, cloud, and mist and thus become himself a consummator of the landscape through his intuition. Rooftops and two flags that are only vertical black lines suggest man's presence. A flight of sparrows seemingly moves out of the room on the far west, suggesting the passage of time. Yet this composition is so far from the objective world that it is beyond seasonal progression as indicated in the other two rooms. This landscape is even more totally wrapped in an eerie, unworldly light. Instead of suggesting a definite scene, a real landscape, this is the painter's own inner world, as he felt Ikkyū's mind to be.

Confronted with this special type of intuitive unorthodox art, Chinese critics try to categorize it as untrammeled and say that it contains "spirit harmony." Here ink, in one sense, expresses the spiritual quality of the artist's attainment. This is what Yashiro should have called "spiritual landscape." Here the ink blobs have their own timeless rhythms, ecstatic expressions of the cosmos. This room is more in the spirit of Ikkyū's own ink paintings than any of the others, and so appropriately it is the passageway to the altar bearing his wooden statue and his spirit tablet and those of the abbots and benefactors of his memorial temple.

Thinking back over the three rooms that Jasoku II painted in three quite different manners, it is clear that he chose each to correspond with the religious use of the space. Ink-flinging is the most Zen, the least secular. If the dimness of the tea garden is to prepare the guest for his spiritual experience within the tearoom, the otherworldliness of this ink-splashed landscape serves a similar purpose, preparing the priest chanter as he enters Shinju-an's Votive Room from the west. It creates a somber, serious mood, far removed from the ordinariness of life, as the black-robed figure passes through it to embark on a new day of devotion.

29. Mu Ch'i, "Kuan-yin," c. 1245, 67-11/16″ × ▷ 39-1/4″, Headquarters Temple.

30. Mu Ch'i, "Crane,"
c. 1245, 68-7/16″ × 38-7/8″,
Headquarters Temple.

31. Mu Ch'i, "Monkey,"
c. 1245, 68-7/16″ × 38-7/8″,
Headquarters Temple.

32. Mu Ch'i, "Chestnuts," c. 1270,
13-3/4″ × 13″, Ryōkō-in.

33. Mu Ch'i, "Six Persimmons," c. 1270, ▷
13-3/4″ × 11-7/16″, Ryōkō-in.

35. Li T'ang, "Landscape," c. 1127,
38-9/16″ × 17-1/4″, Kōtō-in.
36. Li T'ang, "Landscape," c. 1127,
38-9/16″ × 17-1/4″, Kōtō-in.

◁ 34. Mu Ch'i, "Hibiscus," c. 1270,
13-9/16″ × 14-7/16″, Headquarters Temple
(formerly in Sōken-in).

37. Bunsei, portrait of Yōsō, c. 1452, 46-3/4″ × 20-3/8″, Headquarters Temple.

38. Soga Jasoku II, portrait of Ikkyū, c. 1491, 38″ × 18-5/16″, Shinju-an.

39. Soga Jasoku III, portrait of Ikkyū in his eighties (detail), c. 1475, 25-3/4″ × 13-7/8″, Shinju-an.

40. Soga Jasoku II, "Landscape" (running
from top right to bottom left), *fusuma*, 1491,
Guest Room of the Main Hall of Shinju-an.

41. Soga Jasoku II, "Landscape," detail of ▷
fusuma, 1491, Guest Room of the Main Hall
of Shinju-an.

42. Soga Jasoku II, "Birds and Flowers,"
fusuma, 1491, Central Votive Room of the
Main Hall of Shinju-an.

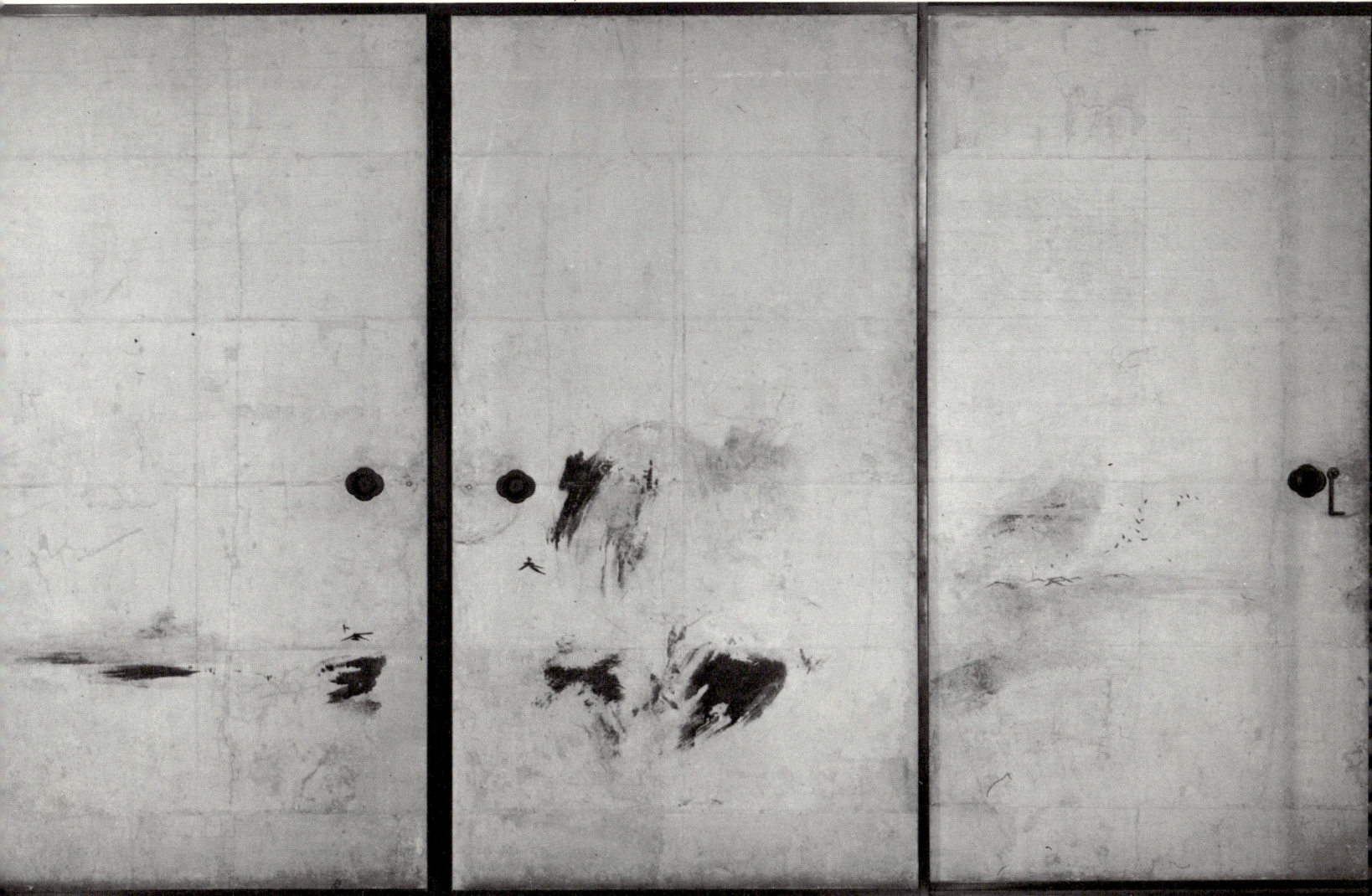

43. Soga Jasoku II, "Ink-flinging Landscape,"
fusuma, 1491, Incense Room of the Main Hall
of Shinju-an.

44. Sōami, one of the "Eight Views of the Hsiao and Hsiang Rivers," detail of *fusuma*, c. 1513, Daisen-in.

45. Sōami, one wall of a "Landscape," *fusuma*, early sixteenth century, Tsūsen-in, Shinju-an.

47. Kanō Motonobu, "Birds and Flowers," ▷
detail of *fusuma*, c. 1513, Daisen-in.

46. Kanō Masanobu, "The White Crane,"
four panels of a six-panel screen, c. 1491,
Shinju-an.

48. Kanō Eitoku, "Birds and Flowers," *fusuma*, 1566–69, Jukō-in.

50. Hasegawa Tōhaku, one of four "Angels," ▷
painted in 1590 on the wooden ceiling of the
Mountain Gate.

49. Hasegawa Tōhaku, "Pine Trees and
Sages," *fusuma*, 1601, Shinju-an.

51. Unkoku Tōgan, "Landscape," *fusuma*,
1588, Ōbai-in.

52. Unkoku Tōgan, one of the "Seven Sages ▷
in a Bamboo Grove," *fusuma*, 1588, Ōbai-in.

53. Kanō Tanyū, detail of one of eighty-four
fusuma, 1636, Headquarters Temple.

The Kanō Dynasty

Nothing in Western art history parallels the impact of the Kanō school of painting on Japan's aristocratic art, an impact that lasted from the fifteenth century through the eighteenth. And no place in Japan better displays all the leading Kanō painters at their best than Daitoku-ji. A brief list of the school and its work at Daitoku-ji is as follows:

Kanō Masanobu (1434–1530), who painted for Shinju-an.

Kanō Motonobu (1476–1559), who painted for Daisen-in, Nyoi-an, Shōgen-in and Kōrin-in.

Kanō Shōei (1519–92), who painted for Jukō-in and Zuihō-in.

Kanō Eitoku (1543–90), who painted for Jukō-in and Tenzui-ji.

Kanō Kōi (c. 1569–1636), who painted for Ryō-sen-an, Jukō-in, and Shōju-in.

Kanō Tanyū (1602–74), who painted for Ryōkō-in, the Headquarters Temple, Tokuzen-ji, Hōshun-in, Kōtō-in, and Kohō-an.

Kanō Einō (1634–1700), who painted for Jōraku-an of Kōtō-in.

The founder of the school, Kanō Masanobu appears to have studied with Shūbun's pupil, Sōtan, whom the Ashikaga rulers paid a stipend as their painter and whom Masanobu eventually succeeded as chief decorator of the shogunal residences. This made him head of what might be called the "Ashikaga Art Academy." His predecessors, Josetsu, Shūbun, and Sōtan, had all been Zen priest-painters. Kanō Masanobu began a secular trend, for he did not live in a Zen temple. His work may be termed "art for decoration," as opposed to the painting of religious icons for didactic or ritual purposes that had engaged Josetsu and Shūbun.

Family ties are exceedingly strong in Japan, and the Kanō family exemplifies this in painting history. Masanobu and his descendants managed, either by training their sons or by adopting their most talented pupils as sons-in-law, to be able to monopolize the major commissions for the Ashikaga shoguns from the eighth, Yoshimasa, to the sixteenth, Yoshitane, and his de facto boss, the Miyoshi warlord. Then they proceeded to supply the military dictators Nobunaga and Hideyoshi with temple and castle decorations. After these men, when the Tokugawa became powerful and moved their military headquarters to Tokyo, the Kanō family moved too and continued to decorate the Tokugawa palaces while this family was in control of Japan from 1693 to 1868. Furthermore, through the numerous branch families of the Kanō or through subordinate schools, Kanō school painters decorated the castles of the generals subordinate to the Tokugawa. The Kanō remained secular, but although they were originally Nichiren Buddhist followers, they turned more toward Zen. Motonobu studied Zen at Myōshin-ji in the sixteenth century and Tanyū studied at Daitoku-ji in the seventeenth century. The latter was given a Buddhist name as an honor, and this became the custom with later Kanō men, even though they remained laymen.

In this way, their artistic control lasted from around 1480, when Masanobu began to work for Ashikaga Yoshimasa at his Silver Pavilion (on the recommendation of Sesshū according to history books written by later Kanō) until the last of the line, Hōgai (1828–88), laid down his brush. Even this was only after he had influenced both Okakura Tenshin (the author of *The Book of Tea*) and had taught ink painting to Ernest Fenollosa and thus inspired, if not dictated, the trends of the major collections of Japanese art in American art museums, such the Boston Museum of Fine Arts and the Freer Gallery. Consequently it is possible to refer to a Kanō dynasty, which controlled both artistic talent and art taste among Japan's ruling classes for more than three centuries.

Kanō Masanobu (1434–1530)

The first generations of the Kanō were the most talented, since it was they who established the dynasty, but even later on there was no lack of painters with adequate ability and, under the static feudalism of the Tokugawa shogunate, no new or original ideas were desired from artists. Later generations became weaker, copying the formulas perfected by their predecessors and this was especially true during the eighteenth century when the full effect was felt of the Tokugawa's isolation of Japan from outside influences.

The founder, Kanō Masanobu (1434–1530) was officially a member of the Nichiren sect of Buddhism, but from the fifteenth century onward aristocratic taste inclined toward Zen subject matter, Zen moods and the style of ink painting begun in Sung China; both the military leaders and the imperial house were mostly practitioners of Zen. Thus the Kanō painted for their patrons the Chinese-style landscapes of the Shūbun-Sesshū manner and bird and flower themes made popular by Sesshū after his visit to Ming China. Since it was beyond their understanding, the Kanō discarded the depth of Zen symbolism, and the mystic mood of the Void is replaced by a decorative handling of space.

Since Daitoku-ji lay at the heart of Japan's aristocratic circle, it had patrons who employed Kanō school painters, and thus in this temple is preserved a remarkable record of their abilities. This record is unusually comprehensive as Daitoku-ji has not suffered from total destruction by war or by fire since 1467, while the castles that Kanō painters decorated for Nobunaga and Hideyoshi have all been destroyed except for Nijō Castle and Nagoya Castle, where murals have survived.

In all Japan, perhaps the most splendid work attributed with relative certainty to the brush of Kanō Masanobu belongs to the subtemple of Shinju-an, and its present condition is a tribute to the care of the abbots during the four hundred years it has been in the temple. A study of its composition suggests that this six-panel folding screen once formed one of a pair, and it may well have been originally commissioned for the Shinju-an's Reception Room, where it is known to have been in use during the nineteenth century. Around 1878, when all of Japan's Buddhist temples were threatened with dissolution, this screen was removed to the recently constructed Kyoto National Museum for safekeeping. Presumably, the other of this pair was pilfered at this time, for if extant, its whereabouts now are unknown. It is interesting that the Kyoto Museum pays Shinju-an a rental fee of about twelve dollars a year for the right to preserve this folding screen in their humidity-controlled basement storerooms.

There is a tradition that, around 1480, when the aging Sesshū (1420–1506) refused to leave his retreat in the far west of Japan and come to Kyoto to decorate Ashikaga Yoshimasa's Silver Pavilion, Kanō Masanobu was nominated in his place by Sesshū. This "White Crane" screen (Pl. 46) at Shinju-an makes one believe that this may be true, for Masanobu's style seems influenced by Sesshū, particularly in the manner in which certain rock formations are presented by areas of cross-hatching. There is also a somewhat similar vertical assertion of silhouette values that Sesshū used in his bird and flower screens, but the bright colors of Ming China that Sesshū employed are missing. Masanobu's screen has only ink washes, with the exception of the red topknot of the crane that is placed near the center and that dominates the composition. Masanobu cannot equal the three-dimensional solidity of Sesshū's rocks, and he uses less heavy ink strokes to outline forms. Instead he prefers to use ink washes, giving a softer, less staccato effect. Furthermore, in his desire for clarity, Masanobu uses fewer forms in his six panels than Sesshū ever used in his bird and flower screens. Indeed, Masanobu's two right-hand panels present the illusion of an ink-washed pond, cattails, and a wagtail on a crag of rock and nothing more, whereas the Sesshū screens in the Maeda and the Ōhashi collections are crowded with forms. Possibly the painter felt in this Shinju-an screen that he was painting in the manner of Mu Ch'i, because he had seen the bird and flower panels of Soga Jasoku II in the Central Votive Room.

This leads to the point of when and under what circumstances Kanō Masanobu painted this screen. Perhaps it was commissioned for the opening ceremonies at Shinju-an, which occurred on July 6, 1491. The patron of this subtemple, Ōwa Sōrin, had enough money to engage any painter he desired, and he had chosen as the chief artist to paint the *fusuma* panels Soga Jasoku II, who was of the Ikkyū school. A decorative screen to be placed in the abbot's Reception Room, where he entertained important visitors, was a more secular matter and did not require Zen depth.

In 1491, Kanō Masanobu was fifty-seven years old and his official patron, Yoshimasa, had died the year before. The Ashikaga family were losing power daily and Masanobu needed to look about for new patrons and other commissions. After the horrors of the Ōnin War had destroyed so many buildings and so much of the best painting in Kyoto, the opening of Shinju-an was an important art event, and Masanobu would have been glad to participate.

If, indeed, this screen was commissioned by Ōwa Sōrin to honor Ikkyū's memory at the dedication of the Shinju-an subtemple, it is understandable why Masanobu did not use color. Soga Jasoku II used no color in any of the *fusuma*, since Ikkyū was a man of ink and the Kanō tended to follow the tastes of their employers. Jasoku was a painter of greater versatility and depth than Masanobu. In the Central Votive Room he used ink washes to outline the birds instead of color and instead of ink strokes, two techniques that Sesshū's bird and flower screens display. Here Kanō Masanobu follows Jasoku's lead in his use of ink washes, but retains Sesshū's style of crosshatching on the rocks.

In this screen, there still exists the suggestion of three distances (foreground, middle and far distances), a concept Sung landscape painters adopted and Muromachi-period Japanese priest-painters tried to follow. Masanobu's son, Motonobu (1476–1559) was to move toward eliminating the middle distance and his grandson, Kanō Eitoku, was to stress only the foreground in his compositions.

Twelve painted *fusuma* also survive at Shinju-an (forming three sides of a six-mat room from the Imperial Palace of 1570) that are attributed by oral tradition to Kanō Masanobu; they represent a snow scene, with mountains in the distance and temples or pavilions beside a lake. Once they must have been very beautiful, but in the lean financial years of the early Meiji period the roof of Shinju-an leaked and could not be repaired, so water has hopelessly damaged the paintings. Enough remains, however, to confirm their late fifteenth-century date and to make one wonder if Kanō Masanobu's connection with the early Shinju-an might not have been stronger than is now recognized.

Kanō Motonobu (1476-1559)

The two most important sets of *fusuma* paintings of this artist are those in Daisen-in at Daitoku-ji (Pl. 47), which were probably executed before the 1513 dedication of the subtemple, and those at Myōshin-ji, painted a few decades later. These works alone assure his position as an artist of genius, and they exemplify the success of the grafting of sixteenth-century decorative trends onto the trunk of fifteenth-century Zen ink painting.

The strong bounding line of Sesshū is still present in this second-generation Kanō artist, but his attitude toward space is different, and he tends to isolate a few forms in the foreground and silhouette them against a distant view. In the illustration selected here (Pl. 47) from Daisen-in, a sturdy foreground trunk curves across the vertical sheet of a waterfall, while three birds add some life to the otherwise static and patterned tree trunk. The bird forms, however, are also only design patterns and even the foam that shoots up as the waterfall crashes onto the rocks is a flat, two-dimensional motif.

Kanō Motonobu may be considered as a link, as an artist who took the decorative pairs of bird and flower folding screens of Sesshū, which that fifteenth-century artist had adopted from Ming China during his visit there, and adapted them into a Yamato-e or Japanese manner. This style is partly based on the Tosa school tradition of line and color, but it also incorporates the strong ink outlines dear to the Zen school and includes the literary associations that the Kyoto aristocrats found as pleasing as the Peking court had.

In a Zen temple, the innermost rooms were usually painted in ink alone, without color, while color could be used for the outer rooms designated for sleeping or for guests. At Daisen-in, the Sōami paintings cover the walls of the central rooms, while the panels of the outer rooms were decorated by Motonobu and his brother Yukinobu (see plan of Daisen-in on pages 194–95).

Besides birds and flowers, always a safe theme in troubled times, Taoist sages were included as motifs. This was especially appropriate since Daisen-in translates as "Retreat of the Great Sages."

Kanō Eitoku (1543-90)

In Japan, it was the custom for a painter to undergo twenty or more years of apprenticeship before he was considered a master. But the mid-sixteenth century was turbulent and thus the rigidity of custom became slightly softened. In addition to this, the natural genius of Kanō Eitoku was so great that his ability had been recognized by the time he was twenty years old. In 1566 he and his father, Kanō Shōei (also sometimes called Naonobu), were commissioned to paint the murals for the Votive and Guest Rooms of Jukō-in's Main Religious Hall. This subtemple was established at Daitoku-ji in memory of General Miyoshi Chōkei (1523–64), who had ruled Kyoto with an iron hand from around 1550 until 1564. He had been a patron of the tea ceremony and had built Nanshū-ji, a Sakai branch of Daitoku-ji particularly famous for the tea ceremony.

The Jukō-in rooms were large and the decoration was to be luxurious. It was to be paid for by Miyoshi's son, and the Miyoshi family was rich enough to supply the artists with powdered gold, which was just then coming into fashion for aristocratic commissions. Flowers and birds were the most acceptable subject in this politically unstable period. According to Jukō-in's tradition, these two Kanō painters spent three years on the project, but this probably means all the paintings within the temple were done over a three-year period, with Kanō Shōei beginning the work and his son Eitoku finishing it (Tōhaku painted two rooms at Shinju-an in ten days and Eitoku's design is only a little more complex than

Tōhaku's). Shōei was the best at details, and his touch can be seen around the altar where small panels of fishes and flowers abound. Next he probably worked on the panels for the southeast room, painting sages in landscapes, in the Chinese manner used by earlier Kanō painters. But the Central Votive Room and the room on the west of it reveal the much bolder, more dextrous hand of the son, Kanō Eitoku, who was to become the favorite painter of both dictators, Nobunaga and Hideyoshi, and who would decorate or design the decoration of their castles until his untimely death from overwork.

The tearoom where Rikyū committed suicide was moved to Jukō-in so that it would be close to his grave in the subtemple's cemetery. Consequently there is a constant stream of tea devotees to this temple. The present abbot feared that so many visitors would endanger the Kanō paintings and so he had them stored in the Kyoto National Museum. Although this is supposedly only a ten-year loan, whether these *fusuma* panels will ever again stand as the artists intended them is a moot point. However, they will be described as they were studied, in their original position in the temple.

Normally a Japanese painter in undertaking a bird and flower picture of the four seasons starts at the southeast corner with spring and moves around the room panels from right to left, dividing the seasonal progression into four parts, as Jasoku II did in Shinju-an's Votive Room. Kanō Eitoku pays scant attention to the progression, however, and concentrates more on the lightness of effect. In the central room, he used only *sumi* ink, in the manner of the preceding period. In the Central Votive Room he worked out the formula for the Momoyama "grand manner" style. He seems to have begun on the west wall, where a pine tree with a contorted trunk dominates the area, along with a crane and wild geese in reeds at the far left. Faint gold clouds thrust the geese into the foreground

and stress their importance, while vague ink-washed mountains suggest the far distance. This west wall (Pl. 48) is, in fact, not too far removed from Kanō Motonobu's work at its best. The north wall, adjacent to the altar, has eight narrow panels, representing summer, with a cooling waterfall and a red-headed crane. Each separate panel is self-contained and a perfect composition in itself, while leading the eye beyond.

The east wall, which represents spring, has four wide panels. Here Eitoku extended a flowering plum tree across the entire width of the wall, almost twenty feet, and omitted all the mountains in the background. Gold mist obscures all distant forms except for one smudge of ink strokes near the northeast corner, a last concession to the Muromachi period when ink alone was used to convey landscape forms. The stylistic change from southwest corner to southeast corner is so gradual that there is still unity, but one can see the artist growing bolder as he works.

During these same years of the Jukō-in commission, Nobunaga gained supremacy over Kyoto and a new resurgent Japan was in the making, proud in its nationalism and willing to overthrow the Chinese-based style of ink painting. Kanō Eitoku was to supply artistic leadership by using the formula he had devised at Jukō-in. Basically it was to spread one large tree form across many panels, to eliminate the background and fill in with gold dust or gold leaf, and to give a dramatic foreground placement to a few forms. Subtleties of Zen symbolism were dropped as leadership in painting passed from Zen priest-painters to secular artists employed by the *nouveau riche* military. Most of the wall panels and screens that Eitoku painted for the wealthy and all the thousands of square feet he designed for Nobunaga's Azuchi Castle and Hideyoshi's Osaka Castle have disappeared. Fortunately, through the Jukō-in panels of 1566–69, one can witness the birth of the Momoyama "grand manner" and see Eitoku's genius reaching toward bold, innovative designs, devoid of Zen symbolism, even within the confines of a Zen subtemple.

Kanō Tanyū (1602-74)

Kanō Tanyū was the darling of the Tokugawa shogunal court in the mid-seventeenth century and was placed in charge of the decoration of the Nijō Castle in Kyoto and most of the important new residences in Tokyo. While still in his twenties he had mastered the style of his grandfather Eitoku and could paint birds and flowers in the boldest of the Momoyama "grand manner" style. By the time he came to live at Daitoku-ji in his thirties, he was the most sought-after painter in Japan, a fifth-generation giant of the Kanō and the leader of three major Kanō schools. He had also become the leading art appraiser in Japan and many valuable paintings passed through his hands; he had seen the Sesshū "Long Landscape Scroll" and had been much impressed. This painting seems to have influenced him when he came to paint the eighty-four panels in the three large Votive Rooms of the Headquarters Temple (Pl. 53). Another factor may have been the subdued atmosphere of Daitoku-ji.

For the eighty-four panels, he seems to have taken various aspects of Sesshū's scroll, which was only seventeen inches high, and expanded them to cover six-foot-high panels. Originally he may have intended some seasonal progression from spring in the southeast corner to winter on the far west wall, but, if so, it is difficult to follow now. The slight tints he used on foliage and the blue for water have faded due to sunlight. A few areas still show a dull reddish hue as though the painter meant to suggest maple leaves in bloom.   Tanyū also covered the east, west and north walls of Tokuzen-ji's Votive Room with *sumi* ink compositions. This subtemple is the oldest and most respected of Daitoku-ji's subtemples. First built around 1340 with the financial assistance of the imperial prince Kajii-no-miya, it burned in 1467 and was rebuilt just south of the Mountain Gate.

Instead of the usual three rooms, the subtemple has one large room of one hundred and two *tatami* mats, and for this room Tanyū chose a very simple subject. On the eastern wall he painted waves in *sumi* ink, from which a dragon emerges, and on the west wall he painted panels showing a bamboo grove in which tigers sport. The composition starts slowly at the open or southern end of each wall and reaches a crescendo of forms as it approaches the north. The northern panels display a mighty waterfall in *sumi* ink and a dragon thrusting his head through the clouds, not unlike the dragon that Kanō Tanyū spread over the entire area of the Doctrine Hall's ceiling. According to Daitoku-ji temple records, Tanyū also painted *sumi* ink landscapes for Gyokurin-in and for Kohō-an, as well as decorating the walls of Hōshun-in with colored paintings. All have now disappeared or been destroyed in fires except some landscapes that he painted on the wall of the Mittan tearoom in Ryōkō-in and two other rooms with bird and flower ink *fusuma* in that subtemple.

This tearoom was first constructed when Tanyū was an infant and was painted by Shōkadō (1583-1639), but when Kobori Enshū moved to Daitoku-ji to retire in the 1630s, he seems to have given the painting of the room fresh consideration. Though Enshū was much older than Tanyū, both had worked for the Tokugawa shoguns. Kanō Tanyū must have absorbed what he could of Daitoku-ji's Zen quietness and this is reflected in his later works, even though the end of his life was spent entirely in Tokyo at the bidding of the Tokugawa shoguns, whose gaudy taste is exemplified in their mausoleum at Nikkō.

Hasegawa Tōhaku (1539-1610)

This painter was born in a family of Nichiren Buddhists and in maturity he made his home in the Nichiren temple of Hompō-ji, near Daitoku-ji. On reviewing the list of the many painters who worked for Daitoku-ji, it is noticeable that Tōhaku received more commissions than any other, and these might have come to him through his friendship with Rikyū. His early training had been under a Sesshū school painter, Tōshun, and when he was middle-aged, he quarreled with Unkoku Tōgan as to which of them best deserved to inherit the leadership of the Sesshū school. Unkoku Tōgan followed Sesshū's technique quite closely, while Tōhaku seems to have been more interested in his spirit. Tōhaku must also have had some training in the Kanō manner, for when its chief artist, Eitoku, died, Tōhaku succeeded to some of his commissions. His most often reproduced work is the floral mural he did for Chishaku-in, originally a memorial chapel to Hideyoshi's first child, a son, who died in infancy. Though Chishaku-in was a Zen temple, Tōhaku's murals for it are brilliant in coloring and design, and totally different from the commissions he undertook for Daitoku-ji. Perhaps in the latter case he was somehow influenced by the Mu Ch'i paintings that he must have seen there.

Most of the Kanō artists were capable of painting in monochrome, as well as in the Momoyama "grand manner" of color on top of gold foil, just as Tōhaku was. The Kanō ink strokes, however, seem mannered exercises rather than expressions of a profound meaning. From Tōhaku's paintings, one would judge that he had gone far in Zen study, and, indeed, in the twenty years between 1580 and 1600, almost every major figure in Japan studied Zen in some fashion. Tōhaku went deeper than most, and if one traces his career of commissions at Daitoku-ji, it reveals an increasing awareness.

Tōhaku's major commission at Daitoku-ji was for the second story of the Mountain Gate, the ceiling of which he decorated with angels and a dragon. This commission was around 1589–90 at Rikyū's behest (Pl. 50). Later, in 1601, Shinju-an asked him to decorate two of its rooms (Pl. 49), when the Main Religious Hall was being enlarged. Other commissions that Tōhaku received were from Sōken-in (1582), Sangen-in (1588), Kinryū-in (1591), Daiji-in (1603) and Ryōkō-in (1606). Kōtō-in, which was established in 1603, asked Tōhaku to handle the decoration of the entire subtemple, so highly was he respected. Later, in 1606, both Tōhaku and Unkoku Tōgan were invited to share the decoration of Ryōkō-in. Alas, of these numerous commissions, only the *fusuma* panels for the subtemple of Shinju-an and the Mountain Gate paintings have survived.

For the second story of the Mountain Gate, Tōhaku painted a dragon with heavenly beings on either side and guardian figures on the surface of the round pillars, so that the whole building was symbolically protected from any evil. The recent five-year restoration of this gate has endowed the Momoyama-period color with its original brilliance. Most decoratively appealing is the being illustrated in Pl. 50. Tōhaku has followed the plump-cheeked, amply proportioned ideal of T'ang China, signifying prosperity. His outer bounding line is extremely lyrical as it flows in and out, suggesting draperies moved by the wind. The angel holds a censer in its right hand and delicately touches the mound of incense with its left middle finger.

While the Mountain Gate painting is marked by its sinuous curves and its beautiful color, the Shinju-an *fusuma* panels are full of angular ink strokes, and are devoid of color, with large unpainted areas. Tōhaku's most famous work is the pair of six-panel folding screens that the Tokyo National Museum treasures, and rarely exhibits. This pair shows pine trees in mist. In the Tokyo screens, however, the pine trees loom like black phantoms out of the mist, while the three pine trees painted for Shinju-an are less obscured by mist, particularly the one illustrated here (Pl. 49). Tōhaku was over sixty when he painted this, and his lone pine tree, almost bare of branches, the weathered survivor of many storms, might have been a reflection of thoughts about himself. Beside this single tree, with zigzag, lightninglike diagonal branches, the artist has painted three other trees on this wall, but they are just whispers of muted ink on otherwise empty paper. Tōhaku handles the space of the wall with extreme asymmetrical balance, but by carrying the ink line of the branches of the pine across three of the wall's four panels, he unifies the space. Two Han-dynasty sages, presumably Taoists, advance toward the tree from the shelter of a rocky cliff.

In another room in Shinju-an, one that has eight mats, Tōhaku painted Tang-dynasty masters of Zen at the moment of their enlightenment. One of them is being bitten by a crayfish and wears an ecstatic expression on his face.

The sixty-two-year-old painter temporarily moved into Shinju-an on October 10, 1601 and had finished the sixteen panels he painted for the two new rooms before the memorial service to Ikkyū held on October 21. The extensive Shinju-an library still has a record of how much rice and *tōfu* bean curd the painter consumed and how much *sake* he drank. In addition he was paid 86 *momme* of silver, perhaps equivalent to five hundred dollars today. Presumably Tōhaku did the paintings as much to honor Ikkyū as to receive money, but these commissions led to further ones for him, and it is possible that the "Pine Forest" folding screen that is at the present time preserved in the Tokyo National Museum was once part of the pine sequence he is recorded as painting for Daitoku-ji.

Unkoku Tōgan (1547–1618)

One of the few sixteenth-century artists to withstand Kanō domination of an entire epoch was Unkoku Tōgan, who found his inspiration in Sesshū, the famous Zen priest-painter of the fifteenth century. The turning point in Tōgan's career was executing forty-four *fusuma* panels for four rooms at Ōbai-in, the extensive Daitoku-ji subtemple founded in 1588. Ōbai-in's Main Hall is said to have been first ordered as his mother's mortuary temple by Hideyoshi, who then rejected it because it was too small to do her honor and gave it to the Mōri family. It is ironic that Ōbai-in still stands while Hideyoshi's more grandiose buildings have vanished. In this way Ōbai-in became the mortuary temple of the Mōri, as well as of the Hatakeyama and the Kobayakawa, all of whom were military clans located in the far west of Honshu, the main island of Japan. For the mural decoration of the temple, the Mōri chose an artist who lived in Yamaguchi, some three hundred miles west of Kyoto, Unkoku Tōgan, though it is unknown whether he painted them in Yamaguchi and had them transported or whether he made the journey to Daitoku-ji himself.

For the East Room of Ōbai-in, Tōgan employed the bird and flower theme, somewhat in the Mu Ch'i manner. Unfortunately insect damage has been serious and in many of the sections it is difficult to realize the original effect, except that it was subdued and reflects Mu Ch'i. If Tōgan had come to Daitoku-ji to paint the murals, he might have seen Shinju-an's Soga Jasoku II panels, which may have influenced him.

It is in the Central Votive Room that Unkoku Tōgan showed his real strength, in the "Seven Sages in a Bamboo Grove." In this series, Daitoku-ji holds the best remaining evidence of Unkoku's skill with a brush. His theme is the Taoist sages who lived in China around A.D. 260 and met in a bamboo grove for wine-drinking parties. They congregated on the outskirts of Lo-yang, the capital of the Wei dynasty, and were really rebels in a political sense. Over the centuries the "Sages in a Bamboo Grove" had become safe as a theme. Kanō Shōei had used it in the southeast room at Jukō-in, but his sages were smaller and flecked with gold dust. Tōgan's figures tower three-quarters life-sized, seven sages spread over twelve *fusuma*, each panel being almost four feet wide. In scale alone Tōgan projects an expansive Japan!

If one analyzes Tōgan's organization of forty feet of horizontal mural painting, one sees that he commences in the right-hand, or southeast, corner and moves from right to left, as though painting a horizontal handscroll. The east wall shows two Chinese sages, accompanied by two serving boys. Further to the left, two more panels have another pair of sages, plus a kneeling servant. These three figures were just to the right of the altar area. The servant boy is kneeling, presenting a bamboo staff to the aged sage. This permits Tōgan to portray drapery folds for a fully erect elder (on the right), a sage who is bending slightly (in the middle), and a servant's figure bent in humility. The bold ink of these draperies carries the major interest of the composition on the east wall.

Then, for variety, Tōgan depicts only bamboo trees and leafy foliage on the big panels to the left of the altar. In his suggestion of atmospheric depth through misty clouds prevading the bamboo, Tōgan has no rivals except for Hasegawa Tōhaku. Now, turning the corner onto the west wall, Tōgan portrays two more sages of the bamboo grove conversing with one another. These two Chinese elders are crowded together towards the northern corner to allow for one very wide panel of paper almost devoid of form. Space is thus its chief ingredient, or the suggestion of space through non-form. Finally the two southernmost panels contain the painter's climax, a single sage with a calligraphic brush in his right

hand, attended by two servants to his right (Pl. 52). The boy on the left holds an ink stone in a box and an ink stick, and the other servant carries the cover to this lacquer box. The box is open, ready for the master to dip his brush into. Its long tapering point is shown against the wall, with a faint trace of ideographs. This sage, isolated by himself and dominating an entire wide panel with his peculiarly dramatic stance, is the most unforgettable of Tōgan's seven sages. The servant figures are rendered shorter, in the Chinese manner for showing less important people. They, together with the foreground rocks and sprig of bamboo, form a frame, accentuating this sage, who brush in hand, is posed in the instant of revealing his wisdom.

Tōgan, in presenting his seven figures, chose different angles for their bodies to face the viewer. A few "nailhead" strokes occur in the drapery but not as many as would be seen in the contemporary works of the Kanō school. These sages are also less static than Kanō school sages would be. Perhaps because of Sesshū's influence, Tōgan reflects more philosophic depth within the subject than Kanō Eitoku, or perhaps this impression lies in the fact that Tōgan uses only ink. Tōgan's brush reflects the energy of the 1580s, but he also seems to feel the solemnity of a commission for a Zen temple, so there is nothing gaudy or garish in the pictures.

The fourteen panels in the West Room, adjacent to the Central Votive Room, are landscapes (Pl. 51). Here Tōgan uses some color, particularly green for the foliage, blue on the passages of water, and brown-yellow on the thatched roofs of the buildings. The various panels seem to be directly inspired by passages from Sesshū's fifty-two-foot-long horizontal scroll, here blown up to five-foot-*fusuma*-panel size. Furthermore, Tōgan's foliage is more hazy than Sesshū's, his ink outline more repetitive. It is as well to remember that at about this time Tōgan and Tōhaku were vying in a court of law for the honor of signing "Sesshū of the Third Generation" to their paintings. Unkoku Tōgan won the lawsuit and Tō- haku, allowing for Tōgan's son, Tōeki (1591–1644), thereafter signed himself "Sesshū of the Fifth Genera- tion." It must be admitted that Tōgan's landscape is much closer to Sesshū's scroll mentioned above, and that Tōgan must have had a chance to see and copy that.

The Mōri were so pleased with Tōgan's work that he was permitted to live at Unkoku-an, Sesshū's temple residence for many years, and to study from the paintings Sesshū had left behind there. In fact, the first syllable of Tōgan's name, tō, derives from Sesshū's name "Tōyō." The panels Tōgan did for Ōbai-in reflect his assiduous study of the Sesshū style, with the addition of mist composed of minute gold flecks, which give a decorative touch in keeping with the sixteenth century, but which is something the older Zen master would not have permitted.

6

LIFE
AT THE TEMPLE

*Zen lives in the present moment and therefore this world is
the Buddha-paradise.
When an abbot cleans his garden, he is simultaneously
cleansing his mind-heart.*

Yamada Sōbin (1920–)
Twenty-sixth abbot of Shinju-an

The Daily Life at One Subtemple

The day commences, almost invariably, shortly before four-thirty in the morning, when the younger disciple stirs, lights the kitchen fires, and unlocks the front gate; it ends before ten at night, when the oldest inmate is through with her bath. On Sundays, the disciples have no classes and are allowed an extra thirty minutes of sleep, but once awake they work harder than ever. Except for the sweets served with the tea, the calorific intake of the adults amounts to less than one thousand five hundred calories daily. Miniscule portions of fish or meat are eaten occasionally as "medicine," but the energy that runs this subsidiary temple comes from an inner determination, each consciously or unconsciously challenging the others not to be slackers.

At four forty-five in the morning, the disciple who is to chant slips into his white cotton underrobe and puts on the priest's black outer robe, or *koromo*. The disciple who is on kitchen duty, dressed in blue jeans, is already busy making *miso* bean soup, cooking rice, laying out pickles, and preparing four breakfast trays for the wooden statues in the Votive Room of the Main Hall, or Hondō.

The abbot, who entered Daitoku-ji's walls more than four decades ago and has chanted sutras at fifteen thousand dawns, has two privileges, which he frequently exercises: he can brush his teeth beside the courtyard's five-century-old well and bucket-splash its cold water over his face; and he can be a few minutes late.

The older disciple has been chanting or preparing breakfast trays for the departed spirits at every single daybreak during his entire six years' residence in this subtemple, but only lately does he know all the sounds, Chinese, Japanese and Dharani, by heart. He sits cross-legged on a raised *tatami* platform which skirts the wood-planked floor of the Votive Room to form a transitional stage between the wooden floor and the paper-paneled walls of *fusuma*, or sliding wall partitions, about six feet high. These panels were painted with *sumi* ink and ink washes almost five hundred years ago and are of major importance in Japanese art history, but the disciple seems to pay them no heed as he chants, signaling the progressive stages of the sutra by striking a small chime with a miniature mallet and hitting a big bronze drum with a larger felt hammer. The abbot usually accompanies him as he chants.

At the conclusion of this dawn service, which lasts about forty minutes, the abbot rises from his mat and spreads out the rectangle of silk that he carries over the sleeve of his left arm. Three prostrations on the wooden floorboards honor Ikkyū, the Zen saint in whose memory this temple was built, and by extension every other sentient being. The central altar has a fifteenth-century life-sized effigy of Ikkyū, while side altars contain wooden votive tablets of Ikkyū's father, who was the hundredth emperor of Japan, and of Kannon, embodiment of compassion, with additional tablets representing former abbots and benefactors.

Shortly before the ceremony finishes, the acolyte who has been working in the kitchen appears in the altar area, carrying four black lacquer trays. These are set before Ikkyū's image, and before his father's tablet, and before "Kannon and all that is." These trays contain the same breakfast that the temple inhabitants will eat—*miso* soup, rice, pickles, and a slightly bitter tea known as *bancha*. The tray portions are smaller, since the honored ones only consume the "essence" and the substance is later added to the inmates' fare. This custom of serving food to departed ancestors was practiced by China's nobility from the second millennium B.C. and became part of Zen Buddhist ritual in China in the seventh century.

After the service, the temple's four inhabitants, the

abbot, two disciples, and the eighty-year-old lady caretaker, sit down to breakfast before a table that almost fills the nine-by-nine-foot Eating Room. First they chant the "Five Reflections," as in the Training Hall, and then, in silence, they eat. The abbot, with six years spent in a Training Hall, can consume his meal silently in less than three minutes. The boys, too, have learned to eat fast. Only the old lady caretaker seems not quite reconciled to total silence.

With breakfast finished, everyone drinks a bowl of stimulating powdered tea, for there is much work to be done. Before six-thirty the two disciples have cleared the dishes, washed and dried them, fed both the front-gate dog and the back-gate dog, and are already out hand-raking the emerald green carpet of the eight moss gardens. There are also eleven hand-washing basins of granite to be scrubbed with stiff, bristle brushes, and sweet water drawn from the well to be poured in them. Three times a month everything must be swept: this means fifty-eight *tatami* (a *tatami* equals eighteen square feet) in the Main Hall and forty-seven in the rooms that formerly belonged to the Kyoto Imperial Palace. Furthermore, all horizontal and vertical ridges and wooden surfaces must be dusted as well as all the statues and ancestral tablets. These chores are additional to the daily sweeping and dusting of the Living Quarters' forty-odd *tatami*, the mopping of its floorboards, the cleaning of the three toilets, and the emptying of the big wooden tub for the nightly hot bath.

After breakfast, the abbot listens to the early morning weather and news on color television. Then he dry-mops countless square feet of corridors and verandas in the three main buildings. On the days the statues are dusted, he cleans the principal altars, hopping upon the three-foot-high platforms with an agility appropriate to one born in the Year of the Monkey. The technique of dusting the temple is to

have the cloth not too wet because in time the moisture would rot the wood, and yet it must not be perfectly dry or it will not pick up the dust. If one corner was overlooked or not cleaned, no one would know, and yet the abbot and his disciples feel a personal responsibility not to let this happen and they are scrupulously careful.

By nine o'clock the acolytes have finished their chores and have gone off to school (one to the Zen college of Hanazono and one to a senior high school). The subtemple—after four hours of work—is now more or less officially open. Now come delivery boys, bill collectors, and those sightseeing visitors who have managed to make appointments. The abbot has a second bowl of green tea, and then proceeds to the veranda linking the Living Quarters with the Main Hall.

From this strategic post he can supervise all temple activities while seated at a low table, piled high with dictionaries and religious genealogical charts. He can keep an eye on the rooms with the ancient murals and the gardens; he can hear the telephone ring; he can also hop over to the excellent library in the rear, where more books on Daitoku-ji's history are kept than in any other place in the world. During the early sixteenth century, the fifth abbot of this subtemple, who became Ikkyū's disciple at the age of five, started a historical library, and it has constantly been added to over the centuries.

By eleven o'clock two hours of intellectual work have been accomplished, and having eaten so little for breakfast, lunch is needed. This is the big meal of the day, consisting of heated-over white rice, vegetables, pickles, followed by a dessert made of bean-paste.

After lunch comes a short rest. The abbot lies down on any convenient mat and goes to sleep immediately. Zen considers dreams a waste of time! An hour later, the boys return from school. The abbot is already up, and it is time for a third cup of green tea to energize everyone for the afternoon's work. This usually centers on the backyard, and the tasks vary from day to day and season to season—hoeing and watering vegetables, repairing the damage of the last rainstorm. When a typhoon has passed, the abbot clambers up onto the roofs, trowel in hand, to replace broken ceramic tiles. In mid-August he is cutting branches off trees for firewood to heat the daily bath, or felling bamboo for the Obon festival flower vases. (This festival requires 235 new vases and 235 leaf and branch arrangements placed before the graves on August 12.) Around three-thirty there is a ten-minute rest, and in summer the three male workers come in out of the sun to drink ice-cold powdered tea, a needed restorative in heat that is over eighty degrees and in humidity that averages ninety percent.

On August afternoons, also, the process of making *nattō* begins. This Chinese use of soybeans was brought to Japan in the late fifteenth century by the Sakai merchant, Ōwa Sōrin, and it was incorporated into the Zen diet by Ikkyū. To make it, gallons of Hokkaido soybeans, wheat flour and salt must lie in the sun of the back garden for about two months, fermenting and slightly drying out. The soybeans are transferred from tubs to wooden crates and dried for several days on the southern verandas, each bean being carefully turned several times by hand. Thousands of man-hours go into making these *nattō* beans, but it has become part of the temple's tradition and so no one questions this annual backbreaking work.

After tea, another two hours of farming work remain in the back garden. For the abbot this is one of the happiest times of the day; he was born a farm boy and he easily enters into a *zammai* state while performing the garden chores, letting the world and its problems remain in another realm.

The disciples leave the garden at about five in order to light the fire for the bath and to prepare dinner by six. After a light dinner of noodles dipped in soy sauce, it is time for all the inhabitants to take their daily bath. The first to bathe is the abbot, followed by the disciples in order of seniority, and then the other servants, who are female. The caretaker lady comes last, but meanwhile she has watched two hours of samurai movies on television. After bathing, the abbot retires to his study to work with his books or his accounts.

Nine o'clock is locking up time, when all the gates are barred, double-checked, and then the nine o'clock evening news may be watched, while a snack of fruit, if some has been donated to the temple, is eaten. By ten all are in bed and only the low night lights glimmer.

A note might be added about the ability of the abbots to assume various roles during the day simply by changing their costume and demeanor. Robes of varying degrees of formality hang on clothes hangers in the open passageway to the rear of the Living Quarters. If an important visitor should arrive while the abbot is dressed in his baggy farmer's trousers, he can slip into the rear entrance, assume the clothes that are fitting to the visitor's position and the occasion, and in less than five minutes be sitting erect on his purple silk cushion in the Reception Room, worlds removed from the farmer or stonemason of a few minutes before.

Zen emphasizes living in the "now-moment." Thus the abbot totally experiences the magic of sound as the sutras are cantilled; he is completely involved with eating when he eats, or dusting when he dusts (having removing his outer robes of course); he becomes the stern abbot when a museum director wishes to borrow a painting; he can be a building overseer when talking with a carpenter about repairs. The robe, the personality, the bearing, the tone of voice, even the grammatical forms of language vary according to the situation.

By total attention to each of the day's many demands, by concentration on the business at hand, the Zen abbot retains his composure despite the fact that there is scarcely a minute when he not active in some way. Thus the strain of living in multiple worlds within the same day is less wearing, because he does not try to live in more than one sociological pattern at once. When he rakes the leaves that have fallen on the garden overnight, he knows approximately how long it will take, and allows for this in his schedule. Nothing extraneous floats into his mind or distracts his body while he is performing this leaf-raking duty of the day. This is the "one-pointedness" that early training is aimed at, and that becomes so engrained that it becomes a lifelong and automatic habit.

The Sōdō

However hard it may be, life within a subtemple is easy compared to life within the Sōdō, the training hall that is dedicated to making the young monks lose their ego and their emotional attachments. It is slightly ironic that the site of the present Sōdō of Daitoku-ji was originally a temple built by Hideyoshi for his mother, for there can have been few such egocentrics in Japanese history as this dictator.

All large Zen temples have a Sōdō, and Daitoku-ji's is only medium-sized. It is more severe than most, and is now called a "devil" Sōdō, one that is extremely strict in its treatment of the young monks studying in it. Though it can be regarded as a sort of college, the Sōdō is a place where all the worldly values of the monks' former lives are discarded to make way for a new mode of living.

The whole repetitious routine of life within this Training Hall is devised to remove the young monk's individual will, to eliminate conscious purpose from his life pattern, to stop him playing his interior tape recorder, that is, his memory. The routine tries to keep him from living in the "unreal" world which his logical mind projects and to cause the "great death" of his ego. To attain this state his emotions need to be neutralized, and so the routine is planned to cut through his thoughts and reactions that are conditioned by his former life at home, in school and at college.

The young monk's mornings are filled with hard physical work, an open-eyed form of meditation, and during the evenings he sits cross-legged for five hours, the half-closed eyes form of meditation. As a member of an almost automatized group, he learns to "empty out," both in his activities and when sitting motionless. His body may be racked with pain, but gradually it adjusts. At first, as he meditates, his mind races restlessly with other thoughts which he obliterates by counting his breathing or by examining the thoughts that are dominating him and realizing that they only sustain his ego. Gradually his mind becomes less restless, less agitated; his emotions shrink, then they become neutralized. And yet the biggest trap that may still lead him astray is to hold *satori*, or freedom from attachment, as a goal.

The Training Hall's routine eliminates the necessity for making choices. Assertive thinking is superfluous; the monk acts with the group, participating in its activities of the moment, and, hopefully, being released from the chains to past or future. Ideally he is reduced to a non-reflective being, to non-analytic thinking and, instead of squandering vital energy on emotional attachments, it is channeled into concrete actions. This is the routine that was worked out in T'ang China, and was polished and refined during the Sung dynasty.

In this walled subtemple, one man, who is called the *rōshi*, "elderly teacher," and who is celibate by tradition, holds sole authority for the Zen education of the monks in his charge. To the lay public, the Sōdō is, of course, off-limits. At Daitoku-ji, even the other abbots do not normally enter the Sōdō grounds except to participate in the chanting for special ceremonies.

The average term of training is three to six years. In fact, "a thousand days" is the minimum requirement, and this is the length of time that the sons of abbots of country temples who are to succeed to their fathers' positions usually stay. Half of the Sōdō monks have this background and if in three years they do not manage to attain complete egolessness, they do learn humility, a sense of responsibility, and a respect for hard work. The other monks in the Sōdō come from Daitoku-ji subtemples; if they survive life in the Sōdō for four, five, or six years, they may be selected as successor in their subtemple and someday become the abbot, or they may become

abbot of another subtemple if their own temple has more than one disciple.

Zen is full of paradoxes, not the least of which is that to enable future leaders to reach beyond the world of phenomena and experience *satori*, the monks must discover their natural state, their "before-born" face. Sōdō life *trains* them in the discovery of this natural state. Originally, in China, it was much simpler: the Zen monk threw off the Confucian regulations and discovered a Taoist type of freedom. But life has become more complex since then, and Zen has become more institutionalized. Universities have strengthened the hold of the logical mind on the individual; *satori* is less frequent now than in former days.

The training in the Sōdō involves supervision of every moment during several months of the year for many years, with about three months of annual vacation in what is the rainy season in India, where Buddhism originated. In Japan this coincides with harvest time, when the monks can help their legal father at his country temple, and with Obon, when respects are paid to one's ancestors at their graves. Years of hard physical work toughens the bodies of the monks and the *rōshi* probes their minds almost daily as they strive for the natural state that children know and that society educates out of them.

The Zen term for a monk is *unsui*, which means "drifting or floating like clouds and water." This reflects the ideal state of unattached young monks, for, in earlier centuries, Zen monks would travel around, spending several years in one monastery after another. In the 1970s, the personnel shortage has affected even Zen, and those monks with a minimum period of training are quickly employed at some temple.

Since unnecessary talking is prohibited in the Sōdō, the schedule is directed by bells and gongs, commencing when the monks get up at three-thirty (four o'clock in the winter) and continuing until eleven at night, when they go to bed. Little time is wasted on meals. They are eaten quickly and in silence, except for the chanting of sutras before and after. The grace that is recited before eating is called the "Five Reflections":

1. We reflect on whence this meal comes.
2. Weighing our merits, we accept this offering.
3. We must first overcome all greed.
4. We take this medicine to cure our bodily weaknesses.
5. We now eat this food to assist in attaining enlightenment.

Food ranks among Zen's three necessities, the other two are sleep and clothing. In contrast to some early Buddhist sects, Zen does not believe in extreme asceticism. The Daitoku-ji Sōdō diet is nearly identical with other Zen temples in Japan and is based on eighth-century Chinese fare. Meat and fish are prohibited, so that animal fat and protein are missing. During the three months of vacation, however, monks are free to eat anything they wish, and on their one day's monthly holiday from the Sōdō, secular sympathizers feed them meat, beer, and cheese.

The Sōdō meals are largely rice, barley, and vegetables, with pickles and the ever-present green tea. Vegetables are quick-fried in Chinese style with vegetable oil. Cubes of bean curd (tōfu) furnish protein, and are used in the miso shiru, the bean paste soup that is the basis of the evening meal, eaten around four-thirty in the afternoon. Breakfast consists of okayu, a mixture of rice, barley and water that is drunk, perhaps with a handful of soybeans in it. Pickles add flavor, and the whole is washed down with tea. Lunch is at around eleven in the morning and consists of vegetables, or vegetable soup, rice, pickles and tea. At any meal, second helpings and

even third helpings are allowed, but they must be completely finished as nothing is permitted to be wasted.

There are two monks who do the cooking, and the job is rotated each month. When the unsui goes to the dining room, he carries his five bowls with him in his cloth belt. After the meal a bucket of hot water is held in front of him so that he can rinse each bowl in it, thus eliminating the chore of washing up. The rules of silence and of eating noiselessly are observed in the dining room, and only lifted when the monks are given a "treat," which means a late evening meal of buckwheat noodles, boiled and dipped into bowls of diluted soy sauce, flavored with mushroom stock, with bits of seaweed, sesame seeds and grated radish. (In summer the noodles are eaten cold, in winter hot.) Only on these occasions are the monks allowed to enjoy the food noisily, as they slurp up the long strands of noodles.

Autumn is pickling time. Daitoku-ji's one hundred and fifty-fourth chief abbot, Takuan, invented a means of utilizing the always plentiful crop of long white radishes. They are hung out to dry in November; after two or three weeks in the sun they are gathered, packed into giant wooden tubs, with a lot of salt, nuka powder made from rice husks, and the dried stems of garden vegetables. The latter gives the final nuance to the flavor of the pickle and symbolically the dead vegetables live again; in Zen thought, positive benefits can come from the negative. As the pickles begin to ferment, the lids of the tubs would be forced open by the pressure of the gases, so huge rocks are placed on them to weigh them down. Chinese cabbage is treated in the same way as the radish and the pickled vegetables are able to be kept from season to season without refrigeration.

Since Zen also admits the necessity of sleep, each monk is assigned one tatami mat, an area that is six feet long by three feet wide, as his "home" for the duration of his stay. He sleeps on it at night and meditates upon it during the *zazen* periods. Indeed, any monk must bow and ask permission before standing on his neighbor's mat. The monks are allowed four to five hours' sleep, though the more eager may go into the garden for further *zazen* after the lights are out. In spite of the five hours' sleep allowed them, whenever the *unsui* monks appear in public they appear drowsy, and at the dawn services in Daitoku-ji's Buddha Hall, at least half demonstrate how well they have learned to sleep while standing upright.

On one occasion in the year, during the first week of December, the monks are urged to forego sleep. This is called the *Rōhatsu Daisesshin*, and it commemorates the anniversary of Gautama's enlightenment in the sixth century B.C. If the monk must sleep, he is encouraged to sleep at this time in the *zazen* position. (This is quite possible physically and one Buddhist monastery above San Francisco never allows its inmates to lie down at night.)

Zen believes that the average human being is malleable in mind and body to an almost infinite degree. Ideally the young Zen trainee reaches a point of maximum efficiency and self-reliance, able to meet any situation and expend just the right amount of energy to accomplish it. Neither excessive passion nor the threat of physical danger needs upset him. He can dwell in the Void, with every sense alert. There should be no intermediate state between the will and the act. Thus action becomes effortless; it is "one-pointed," or *zammai*. It is this type of dynamic simultaneity of mind and body that the *roshi* tries to impart to his charges, but, in fact, to acquire this to a high degree normally requires maturing in the fires of life.

The first week of each month is special in the Sōdō, for it is a time when most activities are suspended and all hours devoted to *zazen* meditation and to *kōan* counseling, or *sanzen*. During this week,

called *Sesshin*, lay Buddhists, if they can sit cross-legged and if they have a sponsor among Daitoku-ji's abbots, may sometimes be admitted to the Sōdō. *Sanzen*, which is face-to-face confrontation with the *roshi*, is a feared moment to many, and it occurs about three times a day. The *roshi* sits in a room and the monk seeks admission by ringing a bell. The way in which he rings it may indicate to the practiced ear of the *roshi* just how far the monk is from *satori*, and he may well be sent flying back from the door with verbal curses or with physical blows of the *keisaku*, the stick the *roshi* carries, or he may be questioned. Since the monk must experience the "great death" of his former ego-centered world, any tactics are acceptable if they are felt to be beneficial. The *roshi* wears a heavy scowl, and must be especially severe. He cannot socialize, has his own servant-cook, must take his meals in private and must prevent casual contacts, lest the magic of the *sanzen* conference be lessened by intimacy.

Thus the loneliest man within Daitoku-ji's walls is the *roshi* of the Sōdō. At the dawn ceremonies in the Buddha Hall he is accorded the honor of occupying the second highest place, even though many abbots are older than he. Only during August, when his charges have gone home for a vacation, does the strain leave his face. He represents total dedication to Dharma, or Truth; he must be a model and must die in Dharma in order to inspire others.

At the rear of the Sōdō is a large cemetery, which furnishes some economic support through the donations received from the families of people buried there. In addition the *unsui* go out and chant in homes, especially at the time of Obon, and receive contributions (perhaps the equivalent of ten dollars) toward the temple's upkeep. But for the daily expenses the centuries-old custom of begging, called *takuhatsu*, is relied upon and this forms part of the monks' training. In the summer, the monks may be seen filing out of the Sōdō's gate at about six-thirty in the morning; in winter months, an hour later. Daitoku-ji monks wear black robes over their gray inner garment, bind their legs in white lacings, and wear straw sandals (*waraji*) on their feet. At first the straw gives their bare feet callouses, but three excursions for *takuhatsu* a week soon accustom them to this hardship. On their heads they wear a hat, broad-brimmed, made of woven wicker, to protect them from the sun, rain, and the occasional snowstorm.

The monks walk in groups of three, with the ideographs of the monasteries printed in white on the black begging bags that hang from their shoulders to their waist. It is usually children who give coins today (coins of small denominations), encouraged by their parents as a lesson in charity. And it is usually the last monk in the line who gets his bag loaded first, since children are shy and hesitate to approach the leader. The monks are usually out two or three hours in the morning, and when they return they give the money, which belongs to the community, to a treasurer monk.

More important than the money is the mood that, hopefully, is instilled into the *unsui*. For the begging teaches him humility, and binds him to the ordinary people upon whom he may depend in the future. The single syllable that is chanted with each step soon becomes automatic, and so the earnest monk can concentrate on his *kōan* at the same time as walking and chanting. When someone puts money in his bag, he bows. No words are exchanged; the giving of money, the receiving of money are both illusions, and, in a religious sense, the Void lies between the monk and his financial benefactor. Money itself is an illusion. The bow reflects this, and not the amount of the gift. The money collected in this way pays the gas and electricity bills, buys vegetable seeds for the garden, rice and barley. Although the lifestyle is frugal and nothing is wasted, there is never a surplus at the Sōdō.

At present, Daitoku-ji monks go begging in the mornings on days that have the numbers two, five or seven in them and on days that are multiples of ten. Days of the month that have the numbers four and nine in them are reserved for cleaning. This cleaning is total; every corner of the Sōdō is meticulously swept, dusted or wiped, and on these days the monks take a bath and may shave their heads. For this they use a cut-throat razor, with hot water but no lather. Some of these razors are ancient and must be sharpened each time. The head shaving is considered a religious rite and is held in the Zen Meditation Room, in silence. Bathing, too, is in silence.

The harsh routine of the *unsui* monks in the Sōdō prepares them to conduct a life where hard work of the body (*samu*) is combined with the discipline of the mind (*shugyō*), and at the same time instills in them dedication, self-effacement and humility. This is epitomized in the words of one abbot who spent six years in a "devil" Sōdō and forty years at Daitoku-ji. "I am the sweeping, mopping servant of the wooden statue of a Zen master whose memorial temple this is, nothing more."

Shutō: The Dawn Ceremony

On the first, fifteenth and twenty-second day of each month, and on special occasions, there is a dawn ceremony lasting about three hours in the Buddha Hall and the Headquarters Temple. This ritual involves group chanting by all the abbots of the twenty-three subtemples, and includes the walking-chant known as *gyōdō*. In form, the ritual dates back to twelfth- and thirteenth-century China when Zen was transmitted to Japan, although the origins of Zen in China can be traced back to the eighth century. In the Shutō ceremony all types of meditative Zen are combined. The eyes are semi-closed so that worldly distractions are shut off and the Void is reached. In chanting, the communal voices are performing a verbal form of meditation, and in the walking-chant, the bodies practice a moving meditation. This is the vigorous culmination of Zen principles in action, when mind and body become one and the individual is kinetically and aurally manifesting oneness with the cosmos.

The Shutō Ceremony held at Daitoku-ji on January 1
At five-twenty in the morning the fifty acres of Daitoku-ji lie in pitch darkness and the three miles of irregular cobblestone paths are barely visible to the eye. Yet the Temple of Great Virtue is not really as asleep as it seems from the outside pathways. At five-thirty a woman in her fifties, with a kitchen apron over her black-knitted dress, emerges from the Headquarters Temple gate and walks the two hundred feet toward the Buddha Hall, carrying an ancient, foot-long metal key in her hands. She struggles with the lock, then swings both portals back on their creaking hinges. She makes the journey back and forth, carrying trays of vegetable offerings: carrots, cucumbers and turnips, washed and tied together with ceremonial red and white cords; some rice, a mound of salt, some spongecake and tangerines.

These she arranges in front of the four altars in the freezing half-light of the Buddha Hall. Lastly, she pours *bancha* from a pewter pot into the empty *temmoku* teabowls placed on all four altars.

Fifteen minutes later a scowling young abbot with heavy, horn-rimmed glasses appears from the western side of the compound. He strides toward the open portals of the Buddha Hall, discards his wooden *geta*, and steps into the pair of slippers which bear the ideograph of his subtemple. These waiting slippers (Pl. 55) at the Buddha Hall, wider and longer than usual ones, are hand-fabricated of red or black felt and embroidered with Chinese patterns, similar to those seen in T'ang and Sung portraits of Buddhist leaders.

The young abbot cursorily inspects the altars, especially the central altar in front of the twenty-foot gilded wooden statue of Gautama Buddha, or Shaka as he is called in Japan. The rice, salt, vegetables, spongecake and tangerines are all arranged, and in the center stands the ceramic jar for incense, in between the two teabowls on their lacquer stands, awaiting their role in the ceremony. He lights the candle to the right of the altars.

The dawn light grows increasingly stronger through the three open-grilled doors on the south side and the unglazed bell windows in the walls. From a distance comes a low, dull boom, timed so that the abbot farthest away from the Buddha Hall can arrive on time if he walks briskly. All Zen abbots if they are under the age of eighty walk fast; they have a way of gliding over the cobblestone paths reminiscent of a Nō actor on a wooden stage.

The abbots begin to arrive, singly or in pairs. They also change into the Chinese-style slippers and then take their places in a double line on the west side of the hall. Each abbot is dressed in a white under-kimono, a colored over-kimono (*koromo*), and a colored silk ceremonial cape (*kesa*), draped over the left shoulder. This silk piece is the insignia of a priest, but abbots wear colored *kesa*, largely based on seniority, purple ranking highest, then red, yellow, brown, green, with black being the humblest. One subtemple has a five-century tradition of wearing only black *kesa* to express a poverty aesthetic. Since it is winter the abbots wear a winter headgear over their shaved heads. This is a foot-high, twin-eared, conical silk hat, also seen in ancient paintings. These hats are removed and held in the hand when chanting to an emperor or the Chinese founder is performed, but are replaced for the chanting before Shinto gods or Chinese folk deities, such as Fu-an.

Since it is almost time to begin, the scowling abbot from the "Dragon Spring Hermitage" walks to the northeast corner and grasps the rope to sound the bell. With this insistent boom the last abbots straggle in over the slate-blue pathways.

Puffs of vapor emerge from their mouths in the semidarkness of the unheated hall and occasionally an abbot wipes his nose with a piece of white paper. All are present except for one, who arrives, by tradition, five minutes later. The chanting begins, slow and mournful, to pay homage to the emperor and the whole country, led by the ceremonial chief who is dressed in purple silk. The ceremonial chief for the Shutō rituals rotates each month among the higher clergy of Daitoku-ji, and his position is distinguished by the purple color he wears during them.

The present chief, who is eighty-four, is surprisingly spry and has attended more than 2,000 Shutō rituals. When he can no longer kneel on the stone floor, unspoken pressure will force him to retire. His adopted son is already an abbot and his grandchildren are of school age, yet he still clings to his position of prestige. It is the only world he knows. He begins the ceremony by burning incense before the gilded statue and then, one at a time, he passes the *temmoku* teabowls over the curl of smoke from the incense, passing it with a circular movement three times from left to right.

He moves back and a jeans-clad boy steps quickly forward with a straw mat which he spreads on the stone floor. The ceremonial chief takes his prayer silk from his left forearm where it is draped carefully in folds and covered by a four-foot-long rosary. With a quick movement he is out of his huge slippers and his toes have anchored down the silk rectangle. As he sinks to his knees, he spreads out the silk with his right hand, then prostrates his whole body three times, lying lengthwise on the *tatami*, his hands rising slowly above his head in a worshipful gesture. The other abbots chant slowly and solemnly in low, monotonous voices. The chief gathers up his prayer silk, steps back into his slippers and adjusts his cape and rosary.

The other abbots cease chanting. One abbot answers, echoing the chant. Everyone then files in front of the altar slowly and shuffles sedately to the northeast corner, to group before two wooden statues that are sheltered in an altar niche. They represent Shinto nature gods, the *kami* of this locale, and many Indian deities transmitted through China. This altar, too, has teabowls and a guardian statue on either side which looks like Śiva or a relative of Shingon Buddhism's Fudō figures. The chief once more burns incense while a bell tolls. The echo-abbot chants, a little faster this time. In front of these foreign deities the ceremonial chief does not put his head on the floor and the abbots do not remove their conical hats. The echo-abbot chants for a long time.

After this the abbots move over to the northwest corner of the hall where three wooden figures, one-third life-size, are arranged. They are Daruma, the legendary founder of Zen, in the center; Rinzai, founder of this sect of Zen, on the left; and Hyakujō, who laid down regulations for China's first Zen monasteries, stands on the right. To the back there is a small effigy of Daitō Kokushi. Along the sides are wooden memorial tablets to all the chief abbots of the past, with their ideographs inscribed in gold on a black lacquer surface. These dignitaries receive the full honors, including obeisances that involve the chief abbot lying prostrate on the floor and the removal of the abbots' hats.

The next part of the ritual is performed at the rear of the Buddha Hall with the chief facing south and all the abbots grouped around the screen wall behind the gilt image. This is the altar to Fu-an, god of prosperity. He is honored with the same teabowls, candlestick, vegetable offerings and incense, but the abbots keep their hats on. They want protection and prosperity but as Buddhas they cannot bow too low before a Chinese folk god.

The abbots then retire to their starting positions to assemble for the walking-chant. The four *kōzō* disciples and the twelve student monks from the Training Hall join in at the rear. They walk in a meandering pattern at right angles along the stone floor, stopping at the end of certain sutras to wait for the echo-abbot's response, and then continuing with their walking-chant. The younger monks carry their sutra books and read from them as they walk, although most of the trainees appear to be sleep-walking.

Suddenly the abbots snap back into the everyday world with incredible speed. They are already proceeding southward toward the portals of Tokuzen-ji, the earliest of Daitoku-ji's subtemples. There ceremonial tea is made to honor Tettō, the first disciple of the founder. One sutra is chanted in front of his statue and then they walk back to the Headquarters Temple for the third ceremony of the new year.

Their capes swinging as they walk, they enter the ceremonial heart of the whole temple compound, the Hōjō, or Abbot's Hall. This whole wing in the Head-quarters temple is rated as a National Treasure and considered as more sacred than the Buddha Hall. It is

here that they will pay tribute and give thanks to Daitō Kokushi.

The most sacred room in Daitoku-ji, which is always kept padlocked, is the northeast room of the Abbot's Hall. The moment the abbots arrive on the Hōjō's wide verandas, the higher-ranking ones spread out their prayer silks and stretch themselves out three times, facing a northern direction. The ones who do not rank so high make the same salutation on the wooden planks of the veranda to the south. All are paying reverence to Daitō's statue, which sits inside the Holy Room. The image carries some traces of damage from the Ōnin War of 1467, when it was carried north for safety, and it is supposed to date from the year of the founder's death. This salutation is followed by silence with the abbots facing east while two abbots are inside.

While the abbots are kneeling on the floor in hierarchical positions, the ceremonial chief and his assistant are in the Holy Room. The former lights incense before Daitō's effigy while his assistant pours hot water from the copper ewer he carries with him into a *temmoku* bowl. He whisks the tea and hands it to the chief who offers it before the wooden statue. The assistant replaces the tea utensils upon a lacquer side table and carries the ewer to the kitchen. Incense is also burned before Daiō's portrait and the spirit tablets of emperors Hanazono and Go-Daigo. The ceremonial chief also salutes all the emperors from Go-Daigo down to the father of the present emperor. He steps down one level and burns incense in front of the Konoe family's spirit tablets, Daitoku-ji's only official "member," and then to the two generals Hideyoshi and Nobunaga. Retreating to a lower position still, spirit tablets representing wealthy sponsors from all over Japan are honored with incense, and the country as a whole is blessed in the same way.

It is now six-forty-five. Just as the abbots and monks begin their walking-chant, the sun rises from behind the dark blue outline of Mount Hiei in the distance. When this is over, all the abbots retire, in hierarchical order, to a room on the west and sit in two rows, their backs toward the *fusuma* painted by Kanō Tanyū three and a half centuries ago. Young monks from the Sōdō carry in red lacquer trays laden with *temmoku* bowls on gold stands. Besides the ceremonial tea, each abbot also receives a number of *manjū*, or bean cakes, served on black lacquer trays.

The tea ceremony is suddenly over, and they have ten minutes to smoke a cigarette before the fourth ceremony of dawn is called for in the Buddha Hall. This is the bizarre sutra reading, when the *Prajñāpāramitā Sutra* (the Sutra of Perfect Wisdom), called the *Hannya-kyō* in Japanese, is given a complete symbolic reading. Every abbot is seated behind a stack of the ten volumes of the sutra, each volume bound in the traditional way so that it opens like an accordion. First there is an initial chanting. Then with a great shout they attack the pile. Each abbot picks up the first volume, stretches it out full length, about three feet, in front of him, and then shouts out several phrases at random from it. With twenty-three abbots, who are all accustomed to barking orders in loud voices, and a dozen monks-in-training grunting in different keys, the Buddha Hall is a scene of bedlam.

After the first volume has been stretched out and closed again three times, it is put aside while the second volume is attacked and devoured symbolically in the same way. One abbot controls the cacophony with a chime so that everyone is reading and grunting from the same volume, or approximately so. The younger monks usually fall behind since it takes years of practice not to lose hold of a seventy-two page book that is three feet wide when opened. The most memorable performance is put on by the monk in charge of the Training Hall, the *rōshi*, who seems almost to eat the words, so close is he to the pages in front of him. And for about ten minutes these men

of Zen express their understanding, amazement and delight at the contents of these volumes, so erudite that few people alive can even read them. It becomes just another paradox of Zen that the ceremony pays symbolic homage to the time when the Chinese priests could actually read these books.

This symbolic reading occurs only four times a year, apart from January, when it is performed on the first, the second, the third, the eighth and the fifteenth days. On New Year's Day, this reading is the last of the four ceremonies of the morning, and at about nine o'clock the abbots return quietly to their subtemples to prepare for the other twelve days of ceremonies held in the month of January.

SHUTŌ:
THE DAWN CEREMONY

54. The gilded wooden statue of the Historical Buddha, whose enlightenment exemplifies the state toward which each abbot strives. In front of this statue, which is in the Buddha Hall, are the votive tablets for the present emperor, for Katoku, the god who protects against fire, and for the patrons of the temple.

55. Felt slippers, made in the eighth-century Chinese style, awaiting the twenty-three abbots before the dawn ceremony in the Buddha Hall.

56. Despite spring rain or winter snow no healthy abbot misses the dawn communal ritual. Here they are leaving the Buddha Hall on their way to the Headquarters Temple for the second part of the ceremony to honor the founder, Daitō Kokushi.

58. The chief abbot paying homage before Daitō Kokushi's wooden effigy.

57. The present chief abbot approaching the high altar in the Doctrine Hall at the beginning of the year's most solemn ceremony.

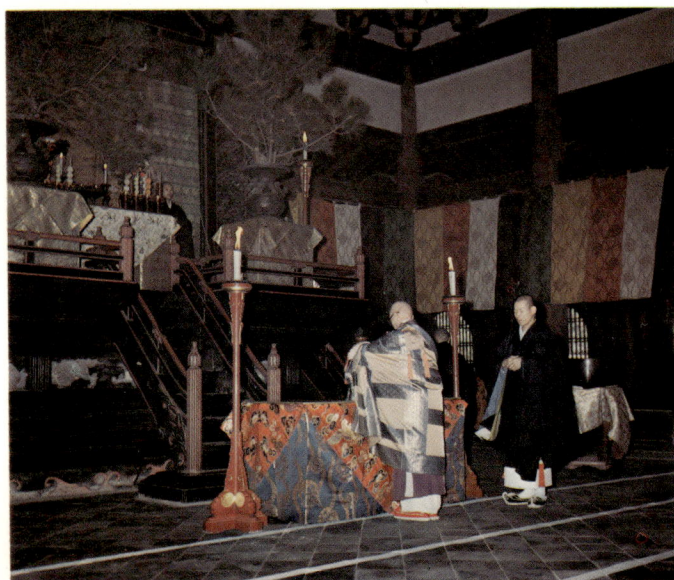

59. A *temmoku* teabowl is passed over the burning incense with a circular clockwise motion before being presented to the statue.

60. Abbots in ceremonial robes walking from the Doctrine Hall to the Headquarters Temple by way of an open corridor that is only used once a year, for this ceremony.

BUDDHA'S BIRTHDAY: April 8

JIZŌ FESTIVAL: August 26

62. At the Jizō Festival, the abbots chant outdoors in honor of this folk Buddhist deity of children. Sōdō monks are also present.

61. Buddha's birthday is the only ceremony in the year in which the public participates. Dippers of cold, sweet tea will be poured over the small gilt statue of the baby Buddha, which is flanked by cherry blossoms.

63. A few of the five hundred statues of Jizō at Daitoku-ji.

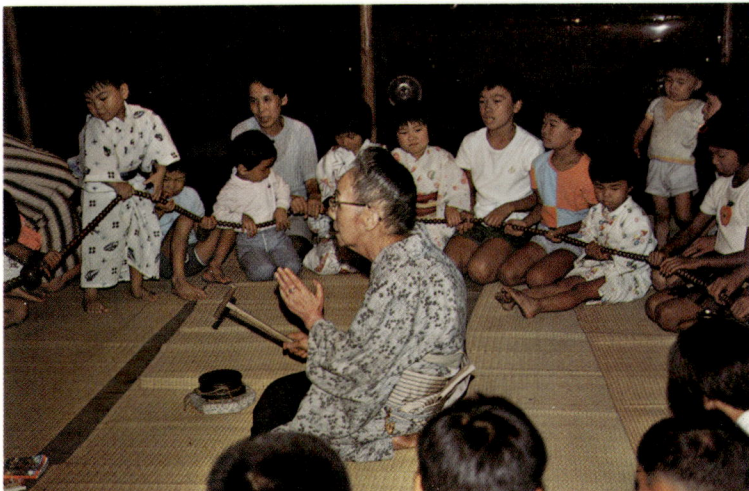

64. An old lady beats time at the Jizō Festival as she teaches the children to chant while they pass along a giant rosary.

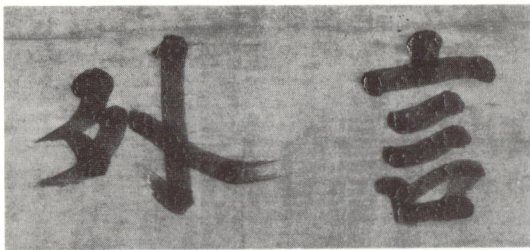

Gongai, "Beyond Words," which characterizes all "action Zen."

65–66. Seventy-five-year-old Tachibana Daiki, now abbot of Nyoi-an, performing tea ceremony (*left*) and creating calligraphy (*above*) on the veranda of his former temple, Tokuzen-ji.

67. Every abbot sweeps and mops after the morning chanting.

68. Fresh flowers being arranged to honor Ikkyū's statue by the abbot of his memorial temple, Shinju-an.

69. Plastering a wall, calligraphy, and painting are equal expressions of an enlightened mind.

70. The twenty-sixth abbot of Shinju-an seated before the Soga Jasoku II paintings in the Central Votive Room of the Main Hall.

71. 5:00 A.M. Opening the gates.

72–74. 6:30–8:30 A.M. The period for tidying
up the gardens and refilling the hand-washing basins.

75. 6:30–8:30 A.M. Sweeping the tea garden.

76. 8:30 A.M. Arranging flowers for the altars.

77. 8:00–9:00 A.M. The abbot sweeping the Central Votive Hall.

78. 10:30 A.M. Getting out the pickles for lunch.

79. 11:00 A.M. Eating lunch.

80. 3:00–4:00 P.M. Hoeing the vegetable garden.

81. 3:00–4:00 P.M. Watering the garden.

83. 4:30 P.M. Minor repairs are carried out in any spare moments.

84. 5:00 P.M. Preparing dinner.

82. 4:30 P.M. Lighting the fire for the evening bath.

85. A disciple placing flowers before the communal grave of the abbots of Shinju-an. The circle represents *satori*.

86. Pouring water (a Buddhist custom to refresh the spirits of the dead) over the rock of Murata Shukō's grave.

87. Ruth Sasaki (1892–1967), abbot of Ryōsen-an and the only woman ever to become an abbot at Daitoku-ji, walking in her garden.

88. Once a year, in the autumn, ten thousand tea teachers descend on Daitoku-ji to pay their respects at the "shrine" of the tea ceremony. Before entering each of twenty subtemples they remove their sandals—and probably have difficulty finding their own again when they come out!

89. A few of the tea teachers take a welcome rest.

90. The cedar bark roofs of the temples need to be replaced every thirty years. The old roof is removed in sections and the exposed area is covered with a tarpaulin during the night in case of rain.

91. Narrow, yard-long strips of cedar bark are put on in layers.

92. The strips are overlapped gradually until the thickness is built up to about four to five inches. For this thickness about sixty layers are needed.

93. The curve of the Chinese-style gate consists of about one hundred layers of cedar bark, which are neatly trimmed with a knife as a final touch.

94. Each autumn the temple's *shōji* are re-papered. The white translucent paper is cut to the exact size of the wooden skeleton. A standard module, about six feet high by three feet wide, is used throughout.

95. The wooden struts and framework of the sliding panel are moistened with a brush dipped into flour paste and then the cut sheets of paper are applied before the paste dries.

96. The abbot begins from the bottom and works up. The sheets of paper must be pulled taut and they become tauter as they dry. Any tears that occur during the year are mended with patches, as can be seen on the *shōji* behind the abbot's head in plate 94.

98. The abbot of Shinju-an unwraps a precious calligraphic scroll by the founder of Daitoku-ji, Daitō.

99. The abbot of Ryōkō-in wrapping up the ▷ Kuan-yin triptych of Mu Ch'i for another year's safekeeping.

97. Mushiboshi is the day in mid-October (the middle of the dry season) when the treasures in the Headquarters Temple are taken out and aired to prevent damage by insects or mildew. Here the wooden boxes that hold the scrolls are laid out in the sun to dry. In the background is the Headquarters Temple garden.

100. Each subtemple has its own Mushiboshi apart from that of the Headquarters Temple. Here the abbot of Shinju-an is hanging up its treasures to air.

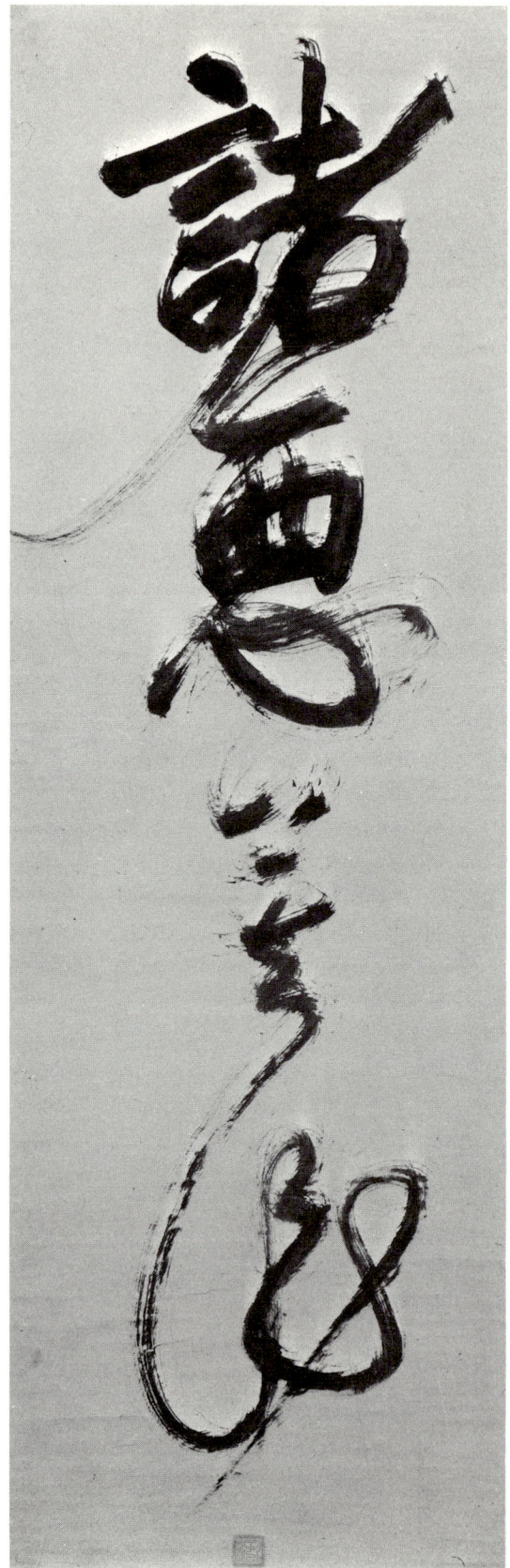

101–2. Calligraphy by Ikkyū. These are hung on the right and left of the altar in his memorial temple on the anniversary of his death. They are examples of the four-character sayings popular with Zen abbots, and together they may be translated, "Let your actions be good and beautiful, not the opposite.

The Annual Calendar

Buddha's Birthday (April 8)

Although the actual birth date of Buddha is unknown, in Japan it is celebrated on April 8 and is called Hana Matsuri, or "Flower Festival." Since Zen is mainly concerned with the enlightenment of the living person, it only pays courtesy respect to the historical figure that other sects make much of, and the ceremony is over in half an hour.

At seven in the morning the abbots gather in the Buddha Hall and, after a preliminary chant, the ceremonial chief and all the other abbots, in order of rank and seniority, approach the altar to bow before the foot-high bronze statue of the baby Buddha. The statue is decorated with artificial cherry blossoms (Pl. 61), artificial because no one is sure that the flowers will still be in bloom on the day of Buddha's Birthday. Each abbot picks up the long-handled bamboo spoon to dip it in the bronze bowl where the image is placed on a stand and pours sweet tea over it. Instead of a newborn baby, Śākyamuni is always represented as several years old, since the idea of him being without wisdom is inconceivable; yet he has his right arm upraised, as he is said to have had at birth, to announce his coming into the world. The abbots end the ceremony with their compressed circumambulation around the hall described in the "Dawn Ceremony."

At eight the caretaker of the Hombō moves the stand with the Buddha's image to the west entrance of the Buddha Hall for the public to make their spring salutations. This is the only festival, besides the Jizō Matsuri on August 23, when the public is expected, and the only one of the entire year when an ordinary person takes some part in the ritual, even though only after the abbots have left the hall.

Young and old walk up the steps of the stone podium to pick up the bamboo spoon and pour sweet tea over the bronze statue; children, especially, are welcome. After respects have been paid, they are invited for a cup of the same tea sweetened with licorice.

Obon (July 15 and August 15)

In the middle of July each year a wooden plank altar about four feet high and twelve feet long is temporarily erected on the top step of the Abbot's Hall's broad veranda. The altar overlooks the famous garden of raked gravel with its symbolized waterfall and islands represented by small rocks in the northeast corner.

July and August are the hottest months of the year in Kyoto, and during the Shutō ceremonies all the walls of *fusuma* are pushed open to entice a welcome breeze. Even at seven in the morning the abbots' faces are wet with perspiration. The ceremony proceeds exactly the same way as the other Shutō ceremonies except that the walking-chant is omitted. Instead, the ceremonial chief approaches the altar, decorated with offerings of rice crackers, vegetables and flowers of summer, picks up a long wooden stick which he dips in a bowl of water and sprinkles the offerings with water. He repeats this procedure three times, from left to right, and after a short chant, waits for six other senior abbots to do the same. The seven abbots represent the seven Buddhas, since Indian Buddhism recognizes Gautama as the last or seventh Buddha, and the three sprinklings represent solace for all living beings who have died and whose spirits return to earth during Obon.

In such a manner does the official Zen temple salute the three-day Buddhist festival to honor the dead, but

Daitoku-ji also observes the lunar calendar which celebrates the same festival on August 15. Thus the individual subtemples wait until August to prepare the Buddha Shelves (*Butsudan*) and the graveyards for the August Obon. This means cutting down fresh bamboo from the temples' gardens and making short vases to place in front of the graves in the subtemple cemeteries. Even though the grave is centuries old and there are no descendants, every identifiable grave must have fresh bamboo vases and offerings of flowers and leaves.

In addition, like the New Year ceremonies, Obon in August is a most intensive cleaning-up period in the Zen temples. Visitors come to bow before the graves or to visit the inhabitants of the temple. The Buddha Shelves in all the subtemples (some of them have as many as six) are scrubbed and their spirit tablets washed before special sutras are chanted. This is done in front of each shelf in all the subtemples to wish the spirits of the dead a pleasant journey to earth and a pleasant one back. This ritual is performed on August 13 and 16, after which the offerings of buckwheat noodles, tangerines and flowers are removed.

On the last evening the whole of Kyoto participates in the ceremony to wish the departing spirits a safe journey home by lighting five large bonfires on the hillsides. The most important one is the ideograph "*Dai*" of Daitoku-ji, formed by using blazing firepots placed a few feet apart. "*Dai*" also refers to the first syllable in Sanskrit of a Buddhist sutra, the *Saddharmapuṇḍarīka* or "The True Essence of the Lotus." The other famous bonfire is the representation of "*Myō-hō*," which also refers to the same sutra. Other bonfires include the reverse reflection of "*Dai*," supposedly as mirrored in front of the pond of the Imperial Palace, and a sailboat to carry traveling souls to the Nether World (*Meidō*) of the dead.

Everyone at Daitoku-ji breathes a sigh of relief when Obon is over. The intense heat of summer begins to wane and there are only a few other festivals remaining before the year's close.

Jizō Matsuri (August 26)

Just a week after Obon comes the festival of Jizō, a popular or folk festival. It does not form an intrinsic part of Daitoku-ji's history, but it is a concession to the public and the abbots only attend if they feel inclined to. It is also the only time of the year when the abbots wear their full regalia and chant outdoors, and thus it is a rare chance for photography.

Jizō is the bodhisattva who protects children and is regarded as a fertility deity, and the strength of popular belief has forced Daitoku-ji to recognize its importance. Probably Indian in origin, Jizō symbolizes the Earth-Matrix who visits the underworld to spread hope and benevolence among the little children who are consigned there, and thus it is not accidental that this festival follows immediately after Obon.

According to folk Buddhism, children who die go to the beach of a "River of Souls," known as Sai-no-kawara, where they perform penance for their sins and the sins of their parents by piling up stones. But whenever they assemble a pile, a demon appears and knocks it over. This is why passers-by will always add stones to a Jizō statue and women attach a bib underneath the head. Since Jizō is also supposed to protect travelers, these stone statues of the god are found along mountain paths, on forest walks and even in crowded streets, with some offerings set in front of them. Daitoku-ji possesses an area opposite the Mountain Gate where about five hundred Jizō statues are arranged in rows (Pl. 63). On August 26, the altar at the center is piled with offerings of fresh fruit.

At six in the evening the abbots (usually about eighteen) appear in their splendid robes led by the ceremonial chief dressed in purple (Pl. 62). He bows before the altar and then lights candles and incense while the abbots begin to chant. This is followed by a walking-chant, attended also by the monks from the Training Hall, while the elderly employees of the temple gardens look on.

The abbots gather for another prayer at six in the evening before the granite statues of Jizō to mark the end of the ceremony. Half an hour later about thirty children, grandchildren of the abbots and temple servants, will gather in a special canvas tent erected on the premises the day before. They form a large circle to pass the forty-five-foot-long rosary around (Pl. 64). An old woman from the temple beats out the time with a small gong while the children pass the beads, each the size of an egg, from hand to hand, chanting "*namu Amida butsu*," a prayer to console the children on the banks of the "River of Souls." The children are then rewarded with candy and they go to bed.

Founder's Day (November 22)

In a ritual sense, the climactic moment of the year occurs on November 22, Founder's Day. Long, three-foot-wide banners of white, red, yellow, green and blue (Pl. 59) hang from the sixty-foot-high rafters of the Doctrine Hall, Daitoku-ji's tallest building and the center of its universe. This is the only occasion in the year that it is opened. The second part of the ritual is held in the Abbot's Hall, and this, too, is festooned with brightly colored silk banners.

A little before ten in the morning a dull insistent boom starts, signaling the beginning of the ceremony. Fifty priests in all take part in the chanting and the walking-chant, priests who include not only the abbots of all Daitoku-ji's subtemples but those from its branch temples as well. In the hall the wooden effigy of the founder, Daitō Kokushi, sits with lifelike realism on a throne (Pl. 58), illuminated by six two-foot-high candles, in whose flickering light the huge dragon on the ceiling, painted in *sumi* ink amidst lightning and clouds by Kanō Tanyū in the early seventeenth century, seems to come to life. Through the grills of the bell-shaped windows on the south, sunlight enters to outline the forest of *keyaki* (zelkova) pillars in the hall. The purple, gold, mauve, green and brown silks of the abbots' ceremonial capes add further color to the scene.

To preside over this occasion, Daitoku-ji's chief abbot, Hōtani Kōmei (Tōgen Shitsu is his elegant Buddhist name), flies in from Fukuoka city, where he is abbot of Sōfuku-ji and where he lives. His imperial purple robes are held by two youthful pageboys (Pl. XX), who are grandchildren of present subtemple abbots. Normally in the regular dawn ceremonies, the ceremonial chief prostrates himself three times before the altar. On Founder's Day the chief abbot kneels and lies down full length on the floor no less than eighteen times to honor the wooden effigy of the founder. This is the highest honor, which neither the gilded Buddha statue nor the emperors' ancestral tablets in the Buddha Hall ever receive.

The peak of the two-hour-long pageant comes at the end, when the wooden statue of Daitō is offered a bowl of whipped green tea. In the past, this tea was whipped by the chief abbot, as it is in the Holy Room ceremonies. However, since the six hundredth anniversary in 1935, as a sort of popular concession or perhaps as recognition of the tea ceremony as a *upaya* ("skillful means") to teach people something about Zen, it was decided to ask the masters of the three leading tea schools (the schools descended from Rikyū's step-grandson, Sōtan) to serve and whip the tea in turn. Thus the honor is rotated in a three-year cycle. This has resulted in the eager but uninvited attendance at the ceremony of tea enthusiasts.

After being prepared, the bowl of tea is then taken by a future abbot who advances majestically to the steps leading to Daitō's altar. There, mounting them in his Chinese-style shoes, he presents the tea before Daitō's effigy, whose crystal eyes gleam in the dancing light of the candles.

7

DAITOKU-JI
TODAY AND
TOMORROW

The function of Zen is to lead an individual to one-pointedness and then back to many-pointedness.

Kobori Nanrei (1918–)
Abbot of Ryōkō-in

Between half a million and a million visitors tread the famous cobblestone paths of Daitoku-ji each year, but most of them only look upon this temple as a relic of the country's cultural past. They do not stop to think that it is also the home of over a hundred people, who feel the same present-day conflicts as the rest of Kyoto's population and are faced with the same dilemmas as their fellow countrymen. The overriding question that concerns each of these people is how far they should move toward modernization, and how quickly. For those who live in the temple compound, trained as they are in a medieval lifestyle, the problem of adjusting to twentieth-century survival is especially difficult.

The twenty-three abbots in Daitoku-ji are absolute rulers in their own subtemples and therefore free to decide on the future of their individual domains. The courtesy name of each abbot is the same as the name of his subtemple, an indication that the temple is identified with the abbot and his temple must follow him whether he decides to entrench himself in tradition or to move toward the present age.

A few abbots find their solution in leading ordinary family lives. Their subtemples, apart from the large Buddha altar rooms and the extreme tidiness, are no different from average homes, and life in these temples, apart from the special ceremonies and sutra chantings, is the same as for the average individual. But others are caught up in the internal struggle of how to maintain their Zen spirit and also be in touch with contemporary society. How much monasticism is valuable and how secular should they become? Should they start admitting the public into their temples and use the admission fees to pay for utilities, food and clothing? Is color television in keeping with Zen silence? How frugally should they live in Japan's affluent seventies?

Every abbot has undergone a minimum of six years' training in a Zen Sōdō Training Hall, where they acquire a taste for hard physical labor and simple food. In the Sōdō they are trained to discard their intellect and to operate on an intuitive level. Yet when they leave the rigid discipline of the training halls, due to the shortage these days of Zen priests, they are immediately put in charge of a country temple or a subtemple in Daitoku-ji and they find themselves faced with the everyday headaches of administration. After the period in the Sōdō there is little time for *zazen* or for studying *kōan*, and the pressure to make them forget all else but Zen self-discipline is gone.

Running a subtemple is like running a small business. Apart from attending to the daily necessities like food, drink and utilities, custom tailors must be hired to make the priestly robes, gardeners to prune and espalier pine trees, silk merchants to remount ancient scroll paintings. No matter how spiritually inclined an abbot may be, he had better also be able to operate an adding machine.

The young abbot, accustomed to the daily diet of a gruel of rice and barley or wheat in the Sōdō, of soybean soup with vegetables, of buckwheat noodles, must decide how long he will continue with this. Should his health receive the benefit of modern knowledge of a balanced diet, with proteins and vitamins? Should he eat fish, a taste that was missing in his Sōdō diet? Perhaps his stomach is unaccustomed to rich foods such as meat, or perhaps he does not want to get used to them. In every aspect of their life the abbots are faced with the large gap between their former life and the demands of the contemporary world.

A great deal of flexibility is needed to accommodate all the various adjustments. Each abbot, in his own mind perhaps, believes that he has found the best solution to the situation. There is one abbot, for example, who runs his subtemple in the traditional fashion as far as chanting, religious routine and food are concerned, yet he is widely traveled, and when he finds a product more durable than *tatami* matting, he has it laid on the temple floors—everywhere except in the Meditation Hall, the center of his religion, and the tearoom, the heart of his aesthetics.

Is this labeled compromise, or is it indeed a clever blending of East and West? He himself says that all cultures borrow from each other and Zen itself is the result of such a process, so there is no need to be insular. The best answer to the conflicts between twentieth-century survival and Zen essence, he claims, is found in a sort of "existential plasticity."

Other abbots who have not found this kind of solution are like shuttlecocks, knocked back and forth between the two worlds, confused in their own thinking. A rather young abbot found tremendous pleasure one summer in touring with a group of American college students, even acting like a gleeful child in a playground on top of Mount Hiei. But the following summer he declared with a grunt that no American can ever understand Zen simply because he is not Japanese. So the historical origins of Zen, which has traveled to several countries, were apparently ignored.

Certain abbots feel tremendous tensions within themselves in trying to balance their own convictions with their natural skills, in deciding which direction they should move in and how far they should proceed. They are enlightened and know that the depths of Zen Buddhism cannot be communicated through words, yet nature has endowed them with talents for written or oral expression. Maintaining a strict code of silence does not bring in income, nor does it help others on the path toward enlightenment. On the other hand, writing and lecturing can inspire many people to lead more useful lives.

To the casual visitor each subtemple seems fairly similar from the outside. Architecturally they follow one general pattern and most of them have a Hondō

for sutra recitations to the founder or Zen saint whose memorial temple it is; each of them has a *kuri*, or living quarters, all have gardens and some smaller buildings scattered around. But in Zen there is great stress on the individual and once a man is selected as abbot, he has theoretically complete authority inside his tiny kingdom. He may have a retired abbot seated at his table, urging him not to forget the subtemple's traditions; he may also have a council of "elders" associated with his subtemple, keeping an eye on him for a few years; but if he is lucky, he is his own boss from the moment he assumes his title, usually around thirty years or a little older. His formal obligations to the compound are fulfilled if he attends the Shutō ceremonies and the other special ceremonies, and apart from these occasions, he may not see his fellow abbots, or even enter their subtemples during his whole lifetime.

There are certain groups of temples who have closer contact, for example, those associated with the tea master Kobori Enshū, but in general the abbots meet only during the special ceremonies. They may exchange a few casual words over a cup of tea after the ceremony, but beyond this they may know what is going on in the other temples only through kitchen gossip.

Because of his absolute authority in his own subtemple, which he rules over for the rest of his life (an abbot can only be removed from office for breaking the law or committing some heinous offence), there is a hardening of character over the years. The extroverts become more forward and the retiring more aloof.

The Daitoku-ji abbots are grouped into twelve ranks, based on seniority, although money is of some importance, since if an abbot is to qualify to serve as the ceremonial chief at the dawn ceremonies, he must be able to afford the purple robe. All the abbots are presided over by the chief abbot, who at Daitoku-ji is not numbered from the founder, as at other temples, but from the first chief abbot. The earlier chief abbots held the office for a lengthy period of time, but by the late fifteenth century the awarding of this title had become a source of wealth to the impoverished emperor, and consequently the terms the chief abbots held office became increasingly shorter until, by the sixteenth century, they served as little as three months. For in return for the bestowal of the purple robe of office, the chief abbot was expected to make the emperor a very generous gift.

At the present time the chief abbot is elected by and from among the abbots of the three hundred sub- and branch temples in the country. The term is for four years and an abbot can be elected to the position for more than one successive term. At present, the chief abbot (the five hundred and twelfth) is the abbot of Sōfuku-ji in Kyushu, residing there and only coming to Daitoku-ji for important ceremonies. Theoretically all the abbots are eligible for the position, but in fact the chief abbot must, by tradition, be celibate; moreover, the abbot of Ikkyū's memorial temple, Shinju-an, disqualifies himself in honor of Ikkyū's dislike of ceremonial affairs.

The temple business is administered by a board of five abbots, elected every three years with the term renewable. Since these abbots must spend every day working as superclerks in the Headquarters Temple, the posts are usually rotated. For expediency's sake, however, four of the five usually come from Kyoto, for if the elected abbot is from a branch temple in, say, Tokyo, he must live temporarily at Daitoku-ji, and thus must provide his own temple with a substitute. For this service to the Headquarters, a nominal pay of about five dollars a day is given to each of them.

Within Rinzai Zen, there is no equivalent of a pope or an archbishop. The abbots are the highest order, followed by the junior abbots who are ex-pected to succeed to an abbotship, and then the lower-ranking priests of the country temples. There are also the *unsui*, the monks living in the Sōdō Training Hall for a period of three to ten years, who are classed as ordinary priests and may perform a number of religious rites.

One of the most important features of the Zen system in the twentieth century has been the near-disappearance of the *kōzō*, or disciple, system, so strong in medieval times. These *kōzō* are apprentices who take up service in a temple at any age between ten and the early twenties, and who take first vows as a priest at around sixteen. They learn their Zen by watching the abbot of the temple and by following the temple routine. In the past this provided the temple with a system of free labor, because the acolytes' training depended mostly on hard physical work (*samu*) to prevent them from being trapped in intellectualization.

In the turbulent period of the fourteenth through sixteenth centuries the Zen system of meditation and hard work produced men who were strong in mind and body. With the coming of the Tokugawa period, society became more formalized and Zen with it. The Meiji Restoration brought a slight relaxation of feudal rigidity, but through the anti-Buddhist policies of the government, the economic base of the temples was simultaneously destroyed. Zen masters capable of training their own disciples declined in number to such an extent that the Sōdō system was begun, in which many disciples studied under a master (*rōshi*) enlightened enough to help others along the path to enlightenment. The compulsory education laws had also become an added complication in the *kōzō* system, and as the tendency for abbots to marry and have children increased, so did their desire to have their sons inherit their temple, after a suitable period of training in the Sōdō and perhaps after some time spent as abbot of a less important temple.

Now the *kōzō* system has almost disappeared, not only at Daitoku-ji but at other Rinzai temples. Of Daitoku-ji's twenty-three subtemples, only four have attracted such disciples. In addition to the constant hard physical work these *kōzō* must undertake (for they have to do all the cooking, cleaning and other chores, both inside and outside the temple) the conditions in which they live are purposely kept totally lacking in comfort. In summer they have no fans in their rooms, in winter no heaters. Moreover, they must cope with the more religious side of their duties and with their studies at school, even though scholastic brilliance is not regarded as an advantage in achieving *satori*.

This life is hardly likely to attract many in the days of affluent, comfort-crazy Japan, not even the country boys, who are now aware of the luxuries that the twentieth century can offer. Even if a present-day *kōzō* endures the ten-odd years between entering the temple at twelve and finishing college at twenty-two, he must still undergo three to ten more years of rigorous training in the Sōdō, a life in which he must arise at three in the morning and must maintain silence most of the time. It is not surprising that the system that has provided the subtemples with so much free labor and so many enlightened men has become weakened by the alternative attractions of city life.

One subtemple abbot has trained nine *kōzō* in all. Two are already abbots of important Daitoku-ji subtemples; two were lost in the war with China; the remaining five will emerge to become future leaders of Zen. But his is an unusual record. The three other abbots who retain this system have fewer disciples, and with the passing of these four men, the tradition could die out at Daitoku-ji. Not enough Zen leaders have the strength to attract and hold *kōzō* for their period of servitude. It is a feudal custom that is basically unsuited to the twentieth century.

The Sōdō, which has replaced the *kōzō* system, has had a mixed success. The disciples' religious instructor there, the *rōshi*, teaches them that Zen's true temple lies within each individual, buried in his innate intuitive nature, and that it must be uncovered by removing all extraneous thoughts and emotions as one plucks petals from a rose to find the center. But even among those who undergo the Sōdō training, with eighteen hours devoted to *zazen* and to begging and other *samu*, few achieve this Zen ideal of a breakthrough to their original nature. University education, with its stress on logical thinking, has become more widespread; society, with its inflexible demands and constant barrage from the media, soon permeates the individual; social and intellectual conditioning has become so strong that the breakthrough is now all the harder.

Due to this, Zen is going through hard times in Japan and must use what human resources are available. Enlightened or not, any Sōdō graduate who has learned the proper postures, the traditional chants and the ceremonial gestures will be rewarded with a position; the less able ones will be invited to the country parishes, the more capable to the city temples and the very best to major temples like Daitoku-ji. If they are the son or adopted son of an already established Daitoku-ji abbot, the road is shorter and easier.

Once an abbot, the path of even the most enlightened becomes difficult. Trained to scorn the value of money, the new abbot must pay bills and find income to pay them with. Taught to concentrate on his intuitive self, he must concern himself with the other people who live and work in his temple. Imbued with a respect for the past, he must learn to live with the present. Each abbot must decide how he and his temple can and should survive, and thus, since Daitoku-ji has twenty-three subtemples, there are that many variations on the solution to these problems.

Only one abbot now maintains almost total denial of the world, an attitude that is, however, traditional in his temple and is consistent with past abbots who have lived there. In the Meiji period, when Buddhism was suffering through the antagonistic policies of the government and all the Daitoku-ji subtemples were consequently experiencing financial difficulties, this subtemple's twenty-third abbot refused to sell his treasures or teach school, and only obeyed the government's strictures to the extent that he avoided jail. He withdrew from society, shut the gates and welcomed no visitors, and when he retired, he made this acre and a half his "Taoist" retreat and never again went outside the walls.

People heard of his self-imposed confinement and lowered presents of food and *sake* by rope over the closed wooden gates, but the abbot had selected a beautiful prison and he was quite content to let the outside world suffer the political and economic turmoil of the Meiji period. In his retirement, this abbot ordered his wooden coffin to be made ahead of time and had it set up in the pine-shaded cemetery of his temple. Every evening, as the shadows lengthened, the old abbot would totter out to his wooden coffin and he would lie in it, to get the feel of it. In the Zen "nowness" of the moment, he would sit hunched up in his coffin, drinking the *sake* his disciples had brought and tasting the sweetness of death; his heart knew peace before his body met its end.

The succeeding abbot was equally "Taoist" in his lifestyle, though he was more scholarly inclined and retreated from the world into his books. Delicate in health he often sickened in the bitter cold of the Kyoto winter and was forced to go to hospital, the only occasions he left the grounds. For, after governmental neglect lasting for several decades, there suddenly came the realization that the temples were an irreplaceable part of Japan's cultural heritage, and with it the reluctance to allow any modifications to the temple buildings. Even now, while the government's Cultural Properties Commission sits in its Tokyo offices that are air-conditioned in the summer and centrally heated in the winter, it forbids the abbots to change as much as a wall and thus ameliorate their living conditions. In the harsh Kyoto climate, characterized by extremes of temperature and humidity in winter and summer, most of the present abbots who are over fifty suffer from the weather.

The present abbot of this Taoist-inclined temple lives in accordance with his tradition. He seldom leaves his temple compound. He sees few people except museum officials who are concerned with the temple's priceless treasures. He retains the tradition of celibacy and rejects as far as possible the encroachments of everyday life. Money is a daily necessity, but an unwelcome evil, so he lets secular hands deal with the finances and keeps his own conscience clean—or almost clean. He is, however, aware of money's importance, and now more telephone calls are answered positively, for the temple relies solely on the produce of its vegetable garden and on *kifu*, the donations people see fit to give when they visit the temple to view its art treasures.

There is no possible way to shut out the twentieth century entirely. His elderly servant demands the luxury of a color television set; he uses it to listen to weather forecasts to see how his vegetable garden and his *fusuma* paintings might be affected. Through it, almost accidentally, he catches glimpses of the outside world. He was trained to deny the world and yet inside there is a normally curious mind, which, on its brief exposures, takes an innocent delight in what lies beyond his temple's walls. Those who manage to meet him feel that he has a truly spiritual character, but his tradition prevents him from sharing his Zen enlightenment with the world. It would be a waste of breath to tell him about the bodhisattva vow of Mahayana Buddhism—to use one's own enlightenment to assist others toward enlightenment. His overwhelming desire is to preserve the acre and a half of his subtemple in pristine condition until his death. The modernists among the abbots think that he is hopelessly old-fashioned and even the traditionalists feel he may be carrying things a bit far. But the temple's tradition is "Taoist" and he lives content within that tradition.

Other abbots, through their personalities, education, and abilities, lead lives that, while being no less Zen, are far less secluded and more in touch with modern life. One abbot in particular epitomizes this category and a study of his solutions is significant. His subtemple is one of the richer ones, for it has the greatest income from property it owns outside the temple compound.

This abbot comes from a family in which Zen runs in the blood, so to speak, for his father and both his brothers became abbots. His life is remarkable for the amount of activity he manages to cram into it. Beyond the time and energy devoted to *zazen* each day, he finds time to participate in many cultural activities that are in themselves expressions of his religious attitude. His temple is one of Japan's treasure-houses of tea ceremony ceramics and this may have originally fired his own enthusiasm for potting. He is skilled at this and each week, in the workroom he has in his subtemple, he throws or hand-molds several dozen teabowls. He has assembled his own outstanding collection of ink stones, a collection that he is all the more appreciative of because he is adept himself at calligraphy. He likes to spend at least one afternoon a week on this and more than that in the rainy season or in the winter. He is also a devoted and accomplished painter and about ten years ago, when his temple needed money for repairs, he gave donors excellent copies of the famous Sung-dynasty painting that is preserved in his temple.

The synthesis of his achievements and his Zen can be seen when he performs the tea ceremony. Many schools of tea have made a formalized ritual out of the tea ceremony, but this abbot lives up to his temple's rich tea heritage. Familiar with the minutiae of the ceremony since childhood, he has penetrated into the heart of its meaning. Each ceremony that he gives is different because his approach is totally free and unhampered by rules, and thus it becomes a medium to express his individual enlightenment.

As a young man he studied with Suzuki Daisetsu at Ōtani University, and from him absorbed the conviction that it is worth trying to communicate Zen to non-Japanese. He is aided in carrying out this conviction by his ability, rare in Japan, to speak English. On Mondays, Wednesdays and Fridays each week, the Founder's Hall of his subtemple is used as a Zen Meditation Hall (Pl. 5) where thirty or more Western Zen students come and meditate for two hours. Similarly, on the first Sunday morning of each month, some thirty Westerners and Japanese crowd into his *tatami*-matted Reception Room to hear an hour-and-a-half lecture in English on some Zen theme. He is also building a branch temple in the foothills near Kyoto where Western students may live with Japanese Zen students.

Perhaps he is particularly lucky to live in a temple that is financially untroubled and thus is not forced to adopt compromises for purely financial purposes. Those temples which have no property and thus no income must find other means of survival, for apart from the everyday expenses of running the temple, other financial demands must be met. The city administration insists that a modern sewerage system be installed; the Cultural Properties Commission requires that he put in a costly fire alarm system, all at the temple's own expense. Termites threaten his wooden buildings, and replacing the wood is both essential and extremely expensive.

In Japan, marriages are the exclusive province of

Shinto, while Buddhism is allowed monopoly of the funeral rites. Thus the temples that have enough spare land have developed cemeteries, where small plots of land are sold for the erection of memorial stones. Naturally the more prestigious the temple, the higher the fees are. In two average temple graveyards at Daitoku-ji, the smallest of plots costs five thousand dollars and the larger ones perhaps ten times that amount. This, however, is a temporary expedient for the financial survival of a temple; though it provides a nice income now, there will be no land for future generations to sell.

One abbot has gone to extremes in opening his temple to the public. Arrangements are made with sightseeing companies and schedules arranged so that up to a thousand visitors a day can be guided around. In addition the abbot has written paperbacks, and sells his own calligraphy and tea at his temple, all of which places him in the top income bracket among the abbots, though whether this can be achieved without loss of Zen spirit is doubtful.

One general area of Zen life that has changed radically within the last two generations, and has reflected the evolution of modern society, is the attitude toward marriage. A low opinion of women was common to all Japan, but Zen, which did not permit, or at least recognize, wives until the end of the last century was especially feudal in this regard. As one ancient Zen writer remarked, "Woman is not worthy even of being forgotten." During his years in the Sōdō, the priest learns that women are dangerous creatures because their feminine weaknesses are contagious and thus contact with them should be avoided if a man wishes to cultivate his Zen strength. Even today there is hesitation before marrying, although wives have proved so useful as head servants that few Sōdō graduates wait longer than a year or two before taking a wife.

Given this traditional antipathy toward women, it seems incredible that a woman, and an American at that, should have become abbot of one of Daitoku-ji's subtemples. This woman, Ruth Fuller Sasaki, or "Ruth-san" as most of the abbots referred to her, had become a Buddhist when she was twenty-five. At that time she was ill and her eyes had fallen on the line in a book, "In Buddhism there is only one sin, and this is ignorance." She was an intellectual with a cosmopolitan background and she decided to read the Buddhist texts in the original, so she enrolled in the Sanskrit course at the University of Chicago. She and her husband (she was then Mrs. Ruth Everitt) traveled to Japan where she met Suzuki Daisetsu and through him was admitted to Nanzen-ji to practice zazen. (Daitoku-ji refused permission!) When she returned to the States she studied under America's first permanent rōshi, Sasaki Sōkei-an, and on December 10, 1938, she was admitted to the priesthood and given the Buddhist name Enryū, meaning "Dragon's Wisdom." She eventually became the wife of the rōshi Sasaki, whose own master had given the first Zen lectures in the United States in 1905–6, with Suzuki Daisetsu as interpreter.

In 1947, after rōshi Sasaki's death, she came to live at Daitoku-ji, and was granted a small house on the grounds of a subtemple that had fallen into ruins during the Meiji suppression of Buddhism. Over the next ten years she expanded her small house, adding a Meditation Hall and a library, and helped the increasing number of Westerners wanting to study Zen; she acquired a staff of translators, publishing a total of six English translations of major works on Zen. In May 1958, she was installed as the abbot of this subtemple, Ryōsen-an—Rinzai Zen's first woman abbot in over twelve hundred years!

On October 31, 1967, Ruth Sasaki died, and half her ashes now rest at her subtemple of Ryōsen-an, half beside those of rōshi Sasaki in New York. It seems appropriate that her ashes should be divided in this way, for she served Zen in both the West and in Japan. By Hakuin's definition, an abbot must leave behind at least one disciple to be successful. In this sense Ruth Sasaki failed. Her thousand-book library is now closed; her Zen Meditation Hall is under an abbot from Tokyo who speaks no English and seems to dislike foreigners. But her earnestness inspired many people throughout the world, and by transcending the boundaries of race and sex, she may well be symbolic of the future of Zen Buddhism.

In the same manner that Zen died out in China as a vital force at about the time it was imported into Japan, so it seems as though at the present time, when Zen has ceased to be all-important in the life of Japan, it is being transported to America. Modern Japanese youth is caught up in that country's syndrome of materialistic expectations, while American youth, having enjoyed prosperity and plenitude for some time, has become more open to what Zen might mean to them. The number of young people in training in Zen monasteries in the United States is greater than in Japan today, and two of the monks in training at the Daitoku-ji Sōdō are Americans. Though the conservative abbots believe that unless Americans can read the literature first, they are not able to discard the "written words" of Japanese and Chinese Zen, others feel that American Zen will find its own paths, will discover solutions that suit its own culture, and that Zen, as it passes to the West, will experience a revival in purity.

The present book has said very little about "sitting Zen," or *zazen*, since this is the earliest stage and one that is rather obvious and thus has been overemphasized in most books written in English on Zen. Of primary importance to an enlightened Zen master is what may be described as "moving Zen," those physical activities, performed with one-pointedness. Of secondary importance is the ritual chanting of sutras. Ranking third is *zazen*, which is practiced as the easi-

est method of achieving *satori*. It remains to be seen whether or not Americans can take China's Taoist sense of intuitive unity with all life force, weld it to India's metaphysics of the "negative," and achieve the aesthetic results of Japanese Zen, in living and in art. If they can, a new future will unfold for America, too!

APPENDICES

Daitoku-ji and Its Mural Paintings

TEMPLE'S NAME	FOUNDER-ABBOT	DATE	SPONSOR	DECORATION
1. Daitoku-ji	Daitō Kokushi (Myōchō)	1319	Emp. Go-Daigo Ex-Emp. Hanazono Akamatsu Norimura	Kanō Tanyū (1636): 85 *fusuma* for Headquarters
2. Ryōshō-ji	Daiō Kokushi (Nampo Jōmyō)	1303	Emp. Gouda Princess Yanagi	No traces left
3. Tokuzen-ji	Daien Kokushi (Tettō Gikō)	1334 (or 1335?)	Prince Chikuei; rebuilt by Ōwa Sōrin, c. 1479	Kanō Tanyū (1636?): *fusuma*, *sumi-e*
4. Nyoi-an	Gongai	c. 1337	Rebuilt by Ōwa Sōrin in 1480; rebuilt in 1973 by Tachibana Daiki	Kanō Motonobu: *sumi-e*
5. Daiyū-an	Kasō Sōdon	1438	Rebuilt by Ōwa Sōrin, c. 1481	
6. Shōgen-in	Shumpo	1491	Ōwa Sōrin	Kanō Motonobu: color paintings Oguri Sōtan: *sumi-e*
7. Shinju-an	Ikkyū Sōjun	1491	Ōwa Sōrin	Soga Jasoku II (1491) Hasegawa Tōhaku (1601)
8. Yōtoku-in	Jitsuden Sōshin	1464?	Princess Donge-in and Ashikaga Mitsuaki	Oguri Sōtan: *sumi-e* Ri Shūbun: *sumi-e*
9. Ryōgen-in	Tōkei Sōboku	1504?	Hatakeyama, Sasaki, Ōtomo	Oguri Sōritsu: color paintings Hasegawa Tōshun: *sumi-e*
10. Daisen-in	Kogaku Sōkō	1509–13	Rokkaku (daimyo)	Sōami: *sumi-e* Motonobu: color paintings Yukinobu: color paintings
11. Kōrin-in	Shōkei Jōfu	1533	Hatakeyama Yoshitsune	Kanō Motonobu: *sumi-e* landscape Kanō Motonobu: color, birds and flowers
12. Zuihō-in	Tesshū Sōkyū	1541	Ōtomo Sōrin	Kanō Shōei: color paintings Tosa Mitsunobu: color paintings
13. Ōbai-in	Shunrin Sōshuku	1588	Kobayakawa Takakage (Mōri's younger brother)	Unkoku Tōgan: Seven Sages, landscapes in *sumi-e*
14. Jukō-in	Shōrei Sōkin	1565	Miyoshi Chōkei	Kanō Eitoku: *sumi-e* Kanō Kōi: tints
15. Sōken-in (for Nobunaga's mortuary temple)	Kokei Sōchin	1582	Toyotomi Hideyoshi	Tōhaku: landscape, birds and flowers, monkeys, all in *sumi-e*

16.	Tenzui-ji (for Hideyoshi's mother)	Gyokuchū Sōshū	1589	Toyotomi Hideyoshi	Kanō Eitoku: 3 rooms of landscapes, bamboo, pines, chrysanthemums, all in color with gold; two rooms with Mt. Fuji and the "Three Laughers" in *sumi-e*
17.	Sangen-in	Shun'oku Sōen	1588	Ishida Mitsunari, Asa no Yukinaga, Mōri	Hasegawa Tōhaku: *sumi-e*
18.	Shōju-in	Seigan Sōi	1550?	Seki, Hachiya	Kanō Kōi: *sumi-e* Kanō Shōkei: *sumi-e*
19.	Daikō-in	Kokei Sōchin	1591?	Toyotomi Hidenaga (Hideyoshi's younger brother)	Harunobu: *sumi-e*
20.	Kinryū-in (united with Ryōgen-in)	Densō Jōin	1591	Kanamori Nagachika	Hasegawa Tōhaku: landscape, pines, grass in *sumi-e*
21.	Shōrin-in	Sempo Sōken	1590?	Gamou Ujisato	Kanō Yasunobu: *sumi-e* and color paintings
22.	Ryōsen-an	Yōhō Sōshō	1491–99?	Taga, Ieyasu's daughter; rebuilt by Ruth Sasaki in 1948–58	Kanō Kōi: *sumi-e* and color paintings
23.	Unrin-in	Unshuku	1531–53?	Fuyuki	No traces left (South of Kita-ōji Street)
24.	Shinjō-ken	Meishuku	1592–95?		No traces left
25.	Rinryu-ken	Shinkei	1595–1614?		No traces left
26.	Heki Gyoku-an	Rankei	1571–90?		No traces left
27.	Seisen-ji	Shumpo Sōki	Rebuilt about 1600		No traces left (except cemetery)
28.	Daiji-in	Tenshuku Sōgen	1603	Murakami and Yamaguchi	Hasegawa Tōhaku: *fusuma*
29.	Kōtō-in	Gyokuho Jōsō	1603	Hosokawa Tadaoki	Hasegawa Tōhaku: *sumi-e* birds and flowers, landscapes, people
30.	Gyokurin-in	Gekkin Sōin	1598	Manase, Arima, Yamanaka	Kanō Tanyū: *sumi-e* landscape
31.	Ryōkō-in	Kōgetsu Sōgan	1606	Kuroda Nagamasa	Unkoku Tōgan: "Golden Mountain Temple" Hasegawa Tōhaku: landscapes, pines, people in *sumi-e*
32.	Hōshun-in	Gyokushitsu Sōhaku	1608	Maeda Matsuko	Kanō Tanyū: color paintings
33.	Kenshō-an	Banko Sōtei	1600–15?	Masuda Keishō	Unkoku Tōeki: *sumi-e* landscapes, people

34. Kohō-an	Kōun Sōryu	1621	Kobori Enshū	Kanō Tanyū: *sumi-e* landscapes
35. Zuigen-in	Anshitsu Sōkan	1630		Unkoku Tōeki: *sumi-e*; no traces left
36. Kōrin-in	Gyoku Shū	1620–40?	Katagiri Katsumoto	Kanō Yasunobu and Kanō Tanyū: *sumi-e*
37. Teigyoku-ken	Matsurin Jōto (Bokusai)	1491–92	Ōwa Sōrin	(Within Shinju-an) No traces left: name later used for tearoom
38. Tōun-an	Bokushitsu	1491	Ōwa Sōrin	(Within Shinju-an) Momoyama-period painting
39. Tekitō-ken	Saigaku	1491?	Ōwa Sōrin; rebuilt in 1972 by Yamada Sōbin	(Within Shinju-an)
40. Tsūsen-in	Empress Ōgimachi	1583	Nakarai Zuisoku	(Within Shinju-an) Sōami: *sumi-e*
41. Jōraku-an	Kokei Sōchin	1588–90?	Hosokawa Tadaoki	Kanō Einō: landscapes; moved within Kōtō-in, then to Gyokurin-in; no traces left
42. Jiki Nyūken	Kobori Enshū	1630–45?		Within Kohō-an; no traces left

Postscript: The authors are aware of certain discrepancies in these dates. Sometimes a temple's year of erection and its decoration are different. There are some gaps, and a few minor subtemples have been omitted, since no traces remain today except names in the official record. The above is based on a translation of a Daitoku-ji hand-written record made about a century ago.

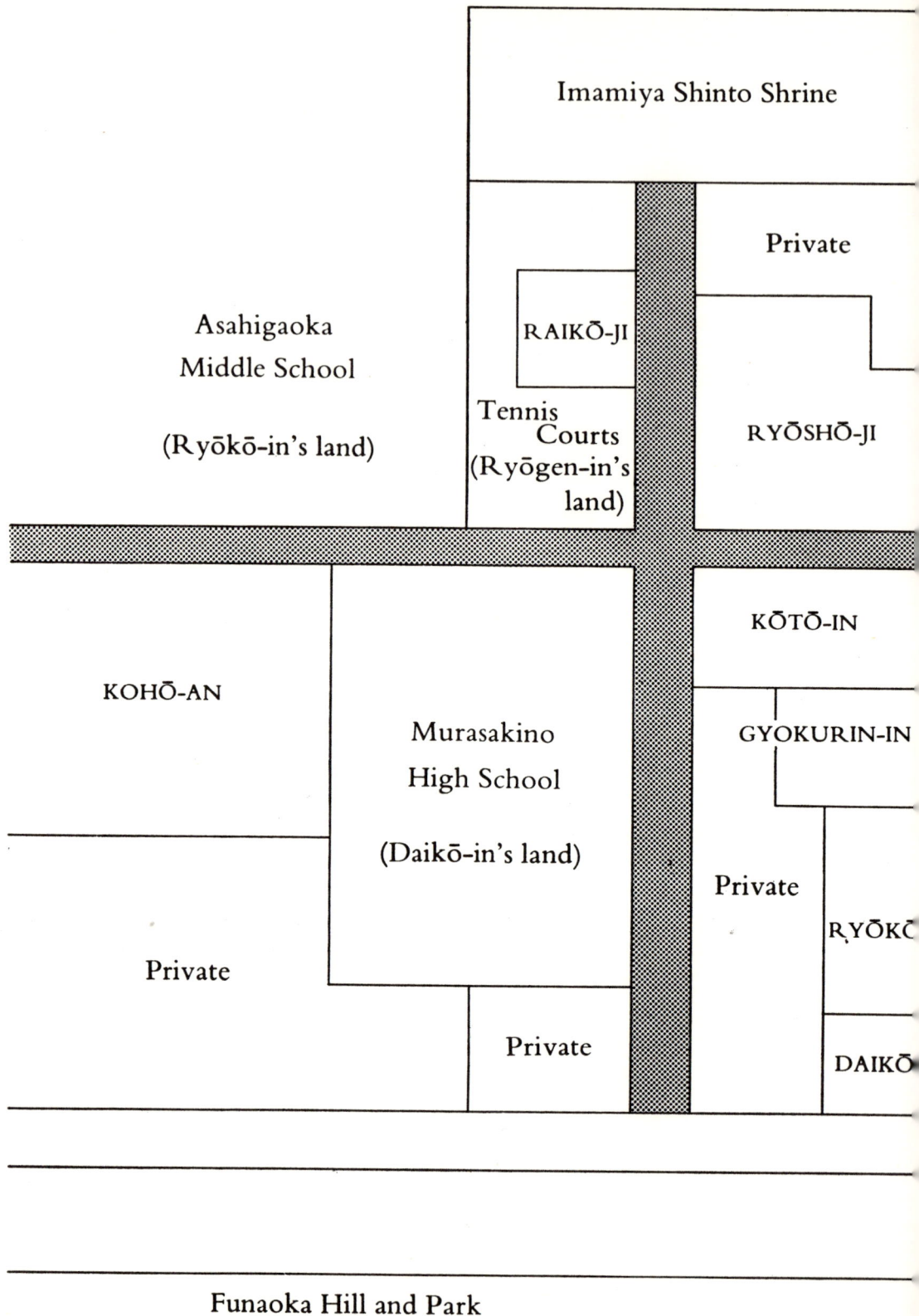

Imamiya Shinto Shrine

Private

RAIKŌ-JI

Asahigaoka
Middle School

(Ryōkō-in's land)

Tennis
Courts
(Ryōgen-in's
land)

RYŌSHŌ-JI

KŌTŌ-IN

KOHŌ-AN

GYOKURIN-IN

Murasakino
High School

(Daikō-in's land)

Private

RYŌKŌ

Private

Private

DAIKŌ

Funaoka Hill and Park

Private

RYŌSEN-AN

NYOI-AN

HŌSHUN-IN

PARKING

DAISEN-IN

SHINJU-AN

ŌKEN-IN

JUKŌ-IN

HEADQUARTERS TEMPLE

DOCTRINE
HALL

Belltower

UIUN-KEN

SANGEN-IN

BUDDHA HALL

Bath

SHŌJU-IN

Jizō
Statues

MOUNTAIN GATE

MESSENGER GATE

Private

KŌRIN-IN

ZUIHŌ-IN

DAIII-IN

RYŌGEN-IN

ŌBAI-IN

Private

TOKUZEN-JI

YŌTOKU-IN

EAST
GATE

PARKING

POLICE

FIRE
DEPT.

Private housing

N

Sidewalk

SOUTH GATE

KITA-ŌJI STREET

Streetcar and Bus Stop

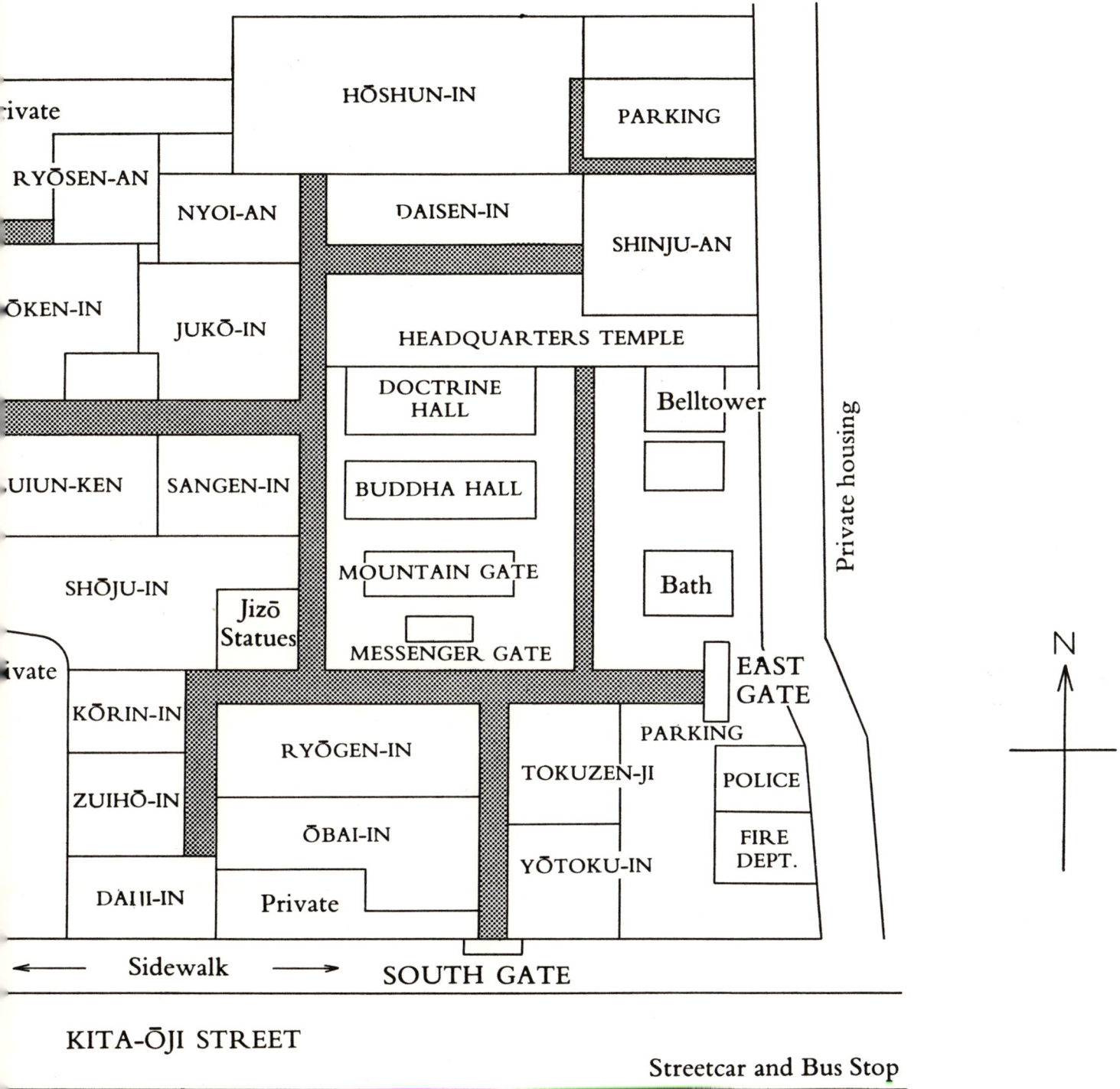

PLAN OF DAITOKU-JI

ZEN STUDY ROOM

Kanō Motonobu "Sages"

Altar

Kanō Motonobu

Sōami

Kanō Motonobu "Bird and Flowers"

Sōami "Eight Views of the Hsiao and Hsiang Rivers"

RECEPTION ROOM

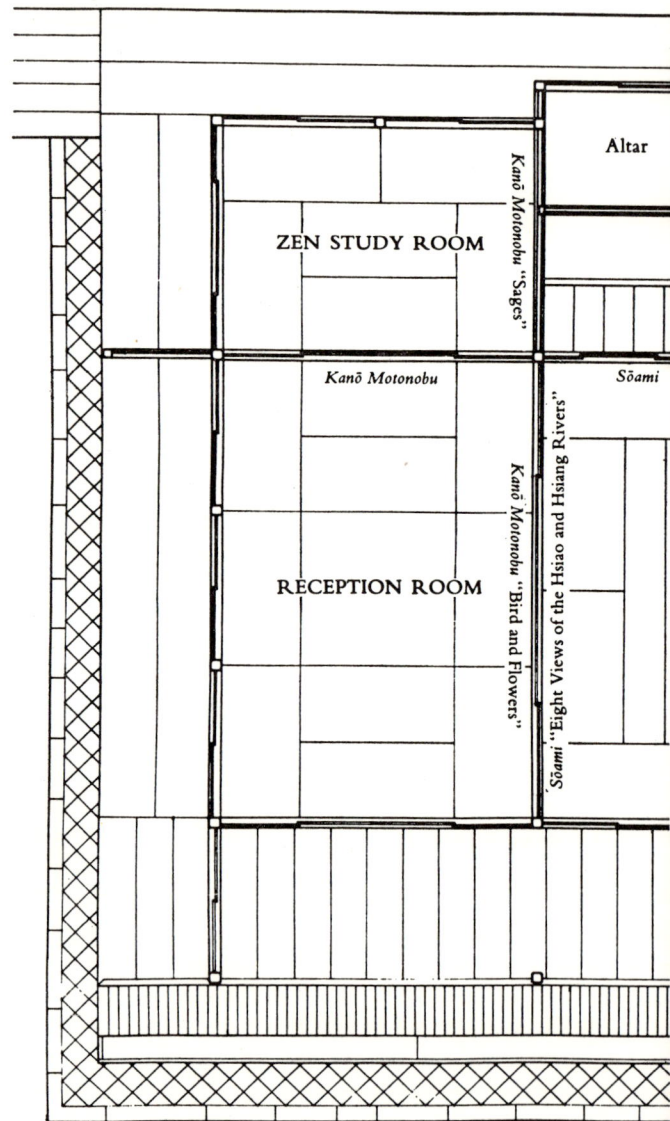

(1 meter = app. 3ft. 3ins.)

0   1   2   3   4   5ᴹ

PLAN OF DAISEN-IN

Living Quarters

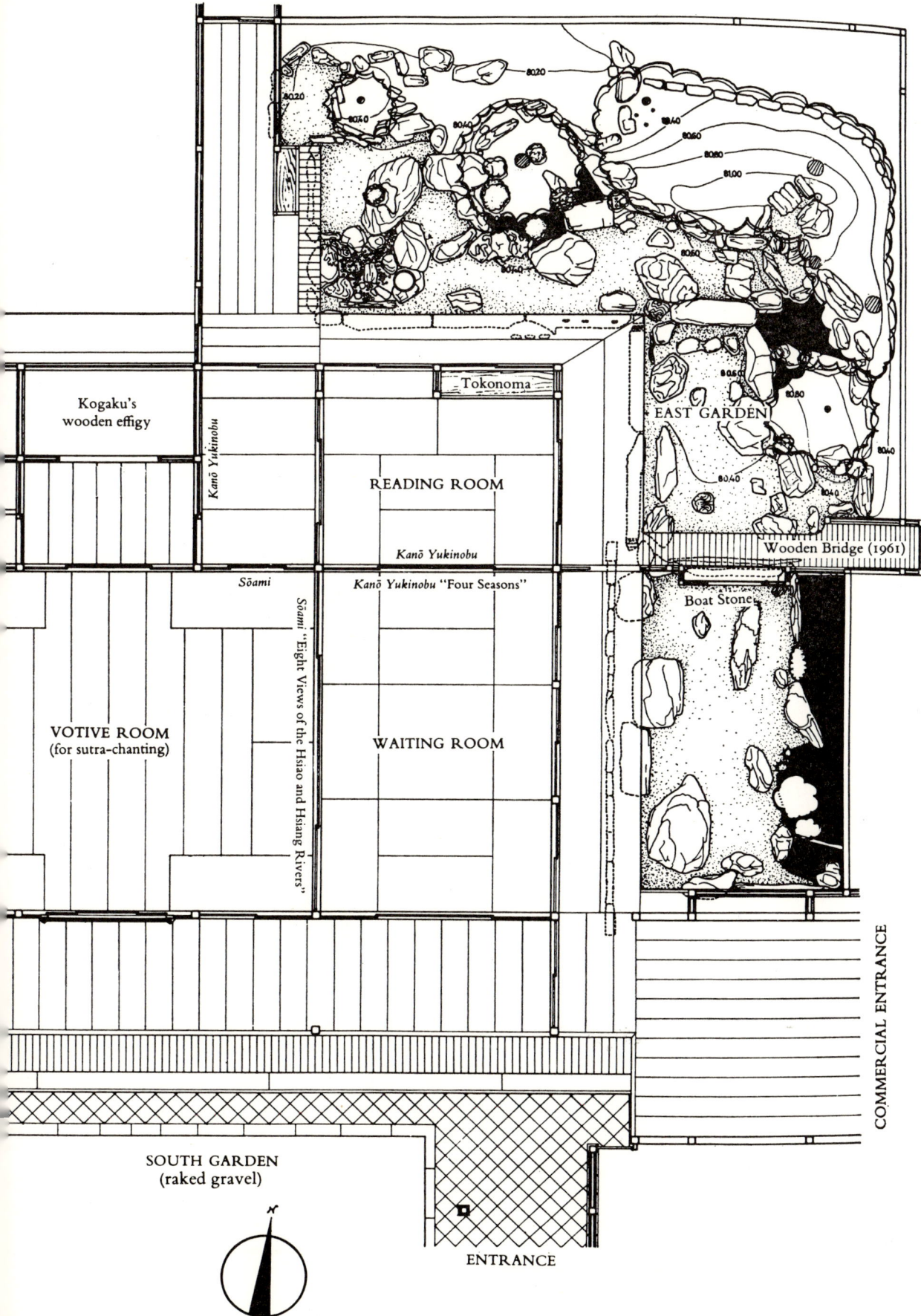

Kogaku's
wooden effigy

Kanō Yukinobu

Tokonoma

EAST GARDEN

READING ROOM

Kanō Yukinobu

Sōami

Kanō Yukinobu "Four Seasons"

Wooden Bridge (1961)

Boat Stone

VOTIVE ROOM
(for sutra-chanting)

Sōami "Eight Views of the Hsiao and Hsiang Rivers"

WAITING ROOM

COMMERCIAL ENTRANCE

SOUTH GARDEN
(raked gravel)

N

ENTRANCE

to vegetable garden

N

Bamboo Grove

Storeroom

Sleeping Room

Kitchen

Back Garden Gate

Room for *miso*-making

Tea Room

TŌUN-AN
(for retired abbots)

Storeroom
(for paintings)

W.C.

Living Room

Study

Covered Walkway

Flower garden

Gate

Tea Garden

DAISEN-IN

Adobe Wall

Sewing Room

Library

Storeroom
(for ceramics)

Flower Garden

Rear Courtyard

Abbot's Study

Rear Courtyard Garden

Bath

LIVING QUARTERS

Sleeping Room

Eating Room

Closet

Abbot's Sleeping Room

Abbot's Reception Room

Store

Stove

Kitchen

Disciple's Sleeping Room

Clothes' Drying Yard

Kitchen

Guests' Entrance

Passageway

Kitchen Yard

Fireplace

Vestibule

Tea Reception Room

Disciple's Sleeping Room

Disciples' W.C.

Outer Entrance Garden

Inner Entrance Garden

Stepping Stones

MAIN GATE

Adobe Wall

(1 meter—app. 3 ft 3 ins.)

0 1 2 3 4 5   10 m.

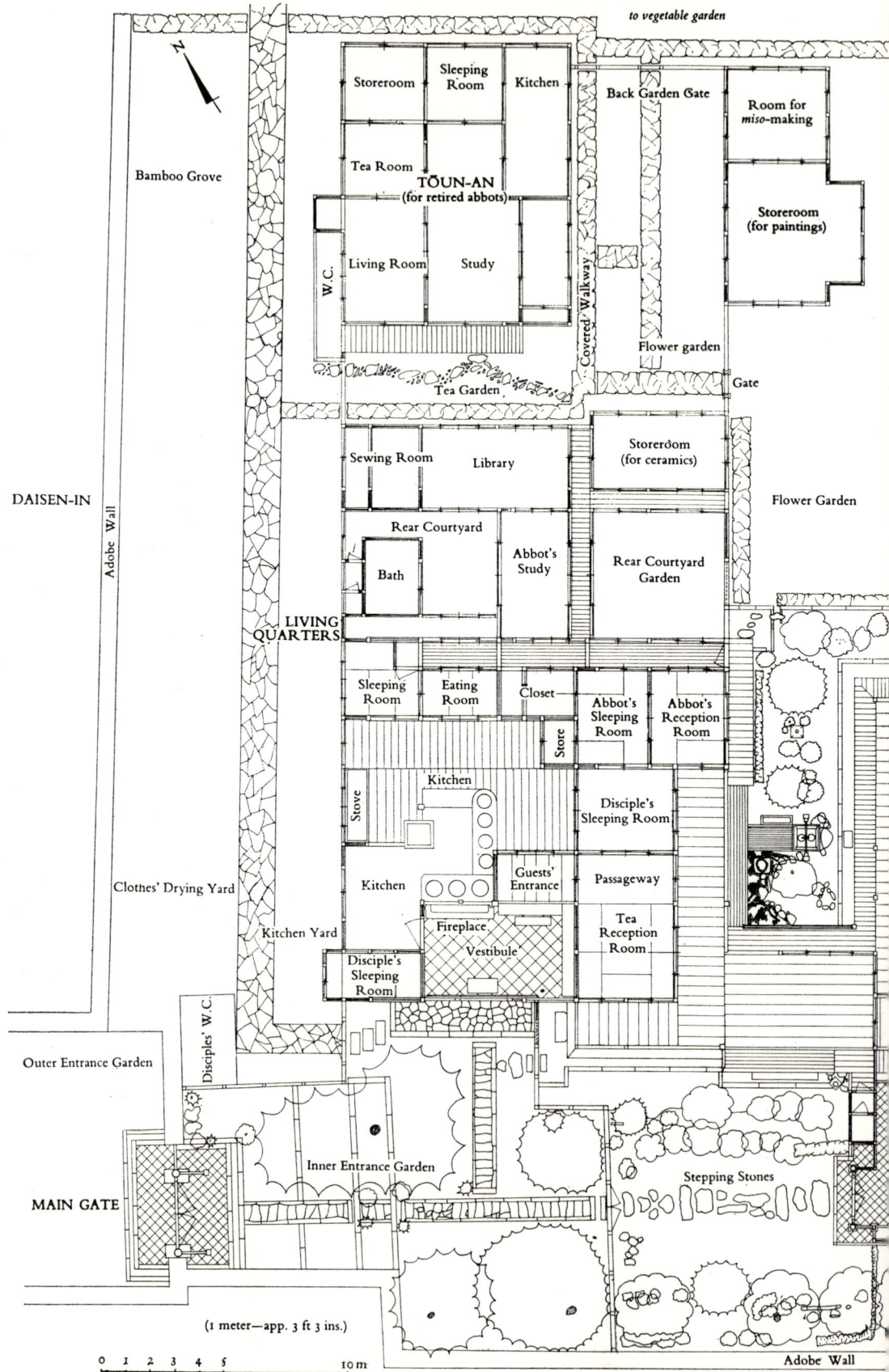

Note: Artists' names in italics are placed where their works can be seen.

to cemetery

Tea Garden

Teigyoku-ken
Tearoom

Kanō Masanobu
Kanō Masanobu

Altar

Bokusai

TSŪSEN-IN
(Dr. Nakurai's present of six
rooms from the 1570 Imperial
Palace)

Guest's
Sleeping
Room

Tosa Mitsuoki

Sōami

Sōami

Hand-washing Basin

Well

Wooden effigy
of Ikkyū

"flinging Landscape"

Altar

Altar

Kanō Kōi

**ZEN
ROOM**

**INCENSE
ROOM**

Jasoku II "Ink-

Jasoku II

Tōhaku "Sages"

Jasoku II "Birds
and Flowers"

Jasoku II

Tōhaku "Pines"

Jasoku II "Landscape"

**GUEST'S
RECEPTION
ROOM**

Jasoku II "Birds
and Flowers"

**VOTIVE
ROOM**

Tōhaku "Sages"

**WAITING
ROOM**

MAIN RELIGIOUS HALL

EAST GARDEN

Adobe Wall

Formal
Vestibule

SOUTH GARDEN

HEADQUARTERS TEMPLE

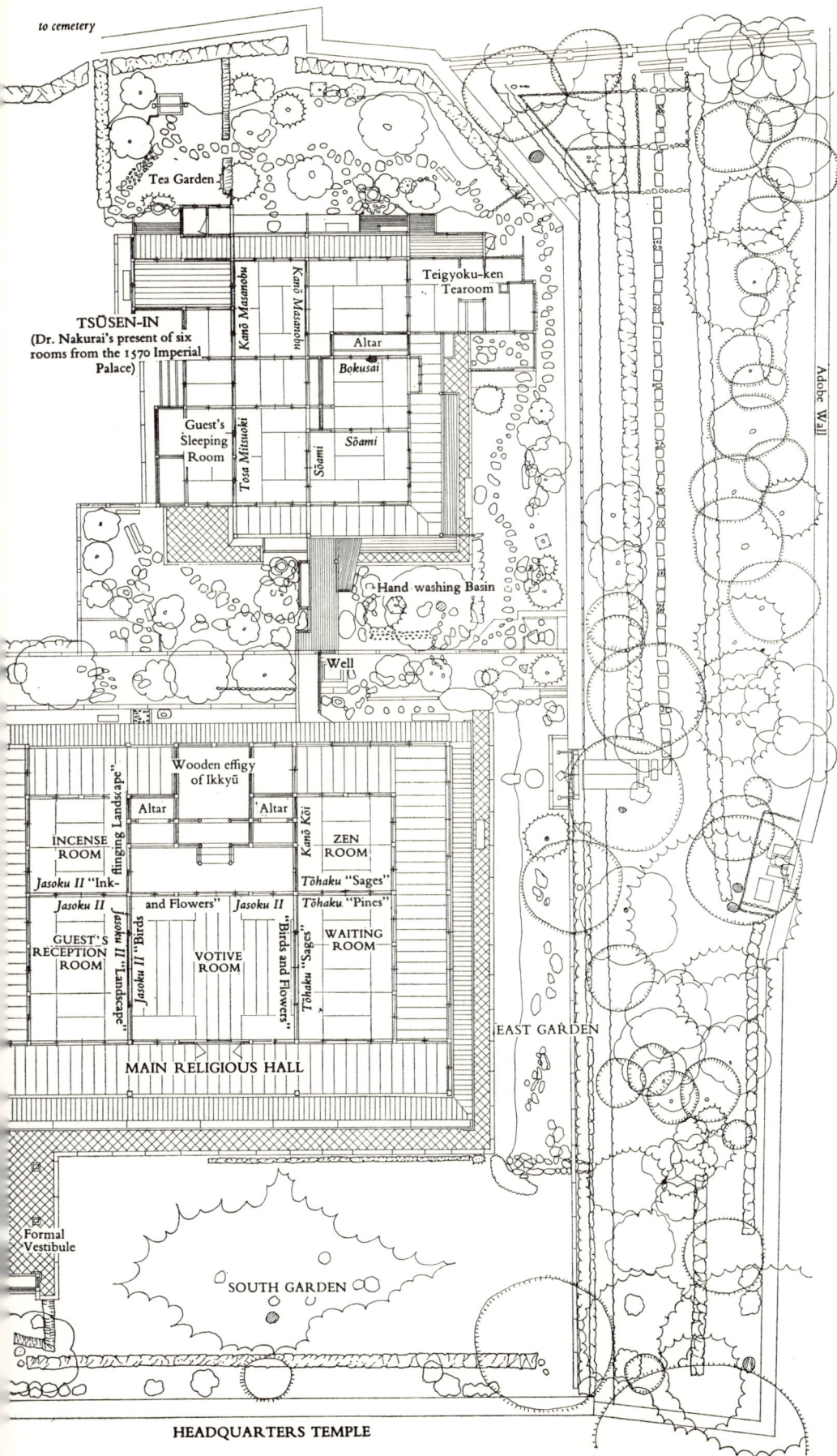

PLAN
OF
SHINJU-AN

Index